GENESIS AND TRACE

Cultural Memory
in
the
Present

Mieke Bal and Hent de Vries, Editors

GENESIS AND TRACE

Derrida Reading Husserl and Heidegger

Paola Marrati

STANFORD UNIVERSITY PRESS

STANFORD, CALIFORNIA 2005

Stanford University Press
Stanford, California

Printed in the United States of America
on acid-free, archival-quality paper

Library of Congress Cataloging-in-Publication Data
Marrati, Paola.
    [La genèse et la trace. English]
    Genesis and trace : Derrida reading Husserl and Heidegger / Paola Marrati ;
translated by Simon Sparks.
        p.   cm. — (Cultural memory in the present)
    Includes bibliographical references.
    ISBN 0-8047-3915-3 (cloth : alk. paper)
    ISBN 0-8047-3916-1 (pbk. : alk. paper)
    1. Derrida, Jacques.   2. Husserl, Edmund, 1859–1938.
3. Heidegger, Martin, 1889–1976.   4. Phenomenology.
I. Title.   II. Series.
B2430.D484M3514   2004
194—DC22

                                                              2004014091

Original Printing 2005

Last figure below indicates year of this printing:
14   13   12   11   10   09   08   07   06   05

For Denis and Léo

Contents

Acknowledgments

This book, published in French in 1998, was written during the years I spent in the department of philosophy of the Marc Bloch University in Strasbourg. The open-mindedness and intellectual rigor that have distinguished the atmosphere of the department have played a very important role in the writing of this book; I would like to thank its directors, Philippe Lacoue-Labarthe and Jean-Luc Nancy.

This book is deeply indebted to Denis Guénoun, Eric Michaud, and Claire Nancy, whose conversation has been a constant in my intellectual and personal life.

I would like to thank my colleagues at the Humanities Center at The Johns Hopkins University: Michael Fried, Neil Hertz, Ruth Leys, Richard Macksey, Hent de Vries, and our students. I am grateful for their intellectual engagement and friendly presence.

I would also like to express my gratitude to Alisa Hartz for her invaluable assistance in the long process of correcting the English translation of this book. The University of Chicago Press graciously provided us with an advance copy of the new English translation of Derrida's *Problem of Genesis in Husserl's Philosophy*, which was of great help.

I wish to pay homage to the extraordinary intellectual and human generosity of Jacques Derrida. Everything he has given us to think has been, and will remain, invaluable, not least in our quest for hope and our "pursuit of happiness."

Finally, thanks to my parents for their warmth and affection; and to Hent, for all that we have shared for so long now.

Translator's Note

Throughout, I have tried not merely to translate Paola Maratti's own words, but to render the fluidity of her style and the specificity of her idiom. In addition, I have preferred in almost all cases to follow what I take to be the best Anglo-American renditions of the Husserlian or Heideggerian lexicon rather than merely transposing the French. Equally, however, I have attempted to reflect those instances when the author chooses to deviate in a determined manner from the translations of Elie, Ricoeur, Lévinas, Beaufret, Fédier, Vezin, et al.

My thanks to Paola Maratti and to Helen Tartar. To the former for having written *Genesis and Trace*, to the latter for her editorial guidance. And to both for their extraordinary patience.

SIMON SPARKS

Introduction

The conviction that underpins this study is that Derrida's work confronts us with a theoretical thinking: a philosophy. If a certain proliferation of texts, themes and styles of writing make Derrida difficult reading, this difficulty stems from a theoretical overdetermination and *not* from the supposedly "literary" character of his work (at least if by "literary" one understands a sort of pure freedom in the play of writing, its being beholden or responsible to nothing other than itself—a conception, it should be said, that scarcely does justice to the idea of "literature"). There are very good reasons why reading Derrida is difficult, reasons that are specific to his body of work; this difficulty of reading, however, is essentially no different from that proper to any philosophical reading. If, as Derrida sometimes likes to put it, the sense [*sens*] of a text is never unveiled by a hermeneutic that takes the infinite as the temporal horizon of its task, for the simple reason that there is no such thing as the sense—in the singular—of a text, then this is something that his own texts can be said to share; which does not, of course, exempt us from attempting the most faithful interpretation possible.

The legitimacy of such a theoretical approach to Derrida's thinking does not strike me as something that could be contested, therefore, either in the name of a poorly understood conception of deconstruction—according to which the absence of a transcendental signified would allow us to dispense with all exegetical rigor—or in the name of an attitude that would seek to deny this thinking any force whatsoever, trusting all too quickly in its explosive appearance and dispensing accordingly with the work of reading.

There are clearly many ways into Derrida's oeuvre. So far as the present study is concerned, it is his relation to Husserl's phenomenology on the one hand and to Heidegger's phenomenology on the other that provides the point of entry and raises the following questions: What is it in Derrida's interpretation of Husserl that runs throughout the trajectory of his subsequent work, particularly through his confrontation with Heidegger? What is it that gives his first texts, which remain almost wholly "classical" in style, such a singular status? How, and why, is Husserl not simply the first "object," subsequently abandoned, of deconstruction, the first philosopher that Derrida would have subjected to his strategy of deconstructive reading? The reasons for the singular role played by Husserl in Derrida's thinking are neither purely "chronological" nor simply "historical." My hypothesis here is that the unique position occupied by Husserl in Derrida's work cannot be explained—at least not fully—by his status as the first paradigm or exemplar of deconstruction. It seems to me that it is only through the singular interpretation that he gives of Husserl's work that Derrida is able to find the formulation for his *own* questions, for those questions that he will continually repeat—and so, one might say, continually *alter* (repetition always involving alteration; such is the status of *ideality*, as thought by Derrida). Equally, if it is through an interpretation of Husserl that Derrida formulates his own questions, then, over and above all historical or biographical reasons one might cite, he does so because there is something in Husserl's work that lends itself or gives rise to just such an elaboration. It is this "something" that I want to try to discover here. Let me say from the outset, then, that this "something" can be seen in the way Husserl raises—and profoundly renews—the question of the transcendental. It is the question of the *genesis* of the transcendental and of its failure that leads Derrida to think the irreducible "contamination" that lies at the very heart of his work. What contamination? The contamination of the empirical and the transcendental that, certain appearances to the contrary, is never an empty, formal structure but always the expression of a double demand—and a double fidelity—for which we will have to account, a demand—and a fidelity—that we will have to *think*. Yet the fact that this double demand ceaselessly guides Derrida's confrontation with Heidegger implies that, between the two equally "deconstructive" readings, there is nonetheless a dissymmetry. Although Derrida undertakes to show, in Heidegger as in Husserl, the point at which the axiomatic of a discourse is called into question from within, the point at which the rigor of distinctions, which should be pure and untouchable, begins to founder, the gesture is not the same—not quite the same.

　　Through Derrida's double confrontation with Husserl and Heidegger, I want to try to follow the trajectory of a *thought of contamination* of the finite and the infinite that no longer has any place either in a phenomenology—of the visible or of the invisible, it scarcely matters which—or in a thought of ontological difference; a thought of contamination that finds in writing its exemplary paradigm and is driven by an ethical urgency that becomes more and more legible.

PART ONE

DERRIDA, READER OF HUSSERL

Genesis and the Transcendental
Sense of Death

Eidos and Time

In any account of the place given to Husserlian phenomenology in Derrida's thinking, a careful reading of *The Problem of Genesis in Husserl's Philosophy*[1] proves unavoidable. Not merely for reasons of chronology and inclusiveness but, first and foremost, because this text, written in 1953–4 while Derrida was still a student at the École Normale, contains the germ of his later interpretation of Husserl, setting in place a problematic that will remain central to his work. Our interest here in *The Problem of Genesis* is thus far more than the simple scholarly curiosity habitually afforded an author's "juvenilia." In it, one already finds many of Derrida's most enduring preoccupations and concerns, despite their being formulated in a language of ontology and dialectic that he will subsequently abandon. *The Problem of Genesis* confirms the centrality of Husserl's phenomenology to Derrida's thinking, and it is only through the questions posed *by* and *to* phenomenology that Derrida will come to encounter those that are more properly his own.[2] The young Derrida already credits Husserl with having most rigorously elaborated an entire system of distinctions that would allow for the restoration of the philosophical project in the purity of its originary sense [*sens originaire*]. It is the extreme rigor of those analyses that means that the difficulties raised by phenomenology cannot be considered contingent limits that could somehow be resolved by broadening the program of research or by a readjustment of method. With the limits of phenomenology one touches, according to Derrida, on the limits of the philosophical project itself.[3]

But what are these limits? In the most formally abstract of terms, they concern the impossibility of phenomenology ever founding itself upon itself. Already in *The Problem of Genesis*, phenomenology is seen as wracked from within, caught in the crossfire between the purity of its project of self-foundation and the analyses that, engendered by that project, contest its very legitimacy.[4] In order to demonstrate this, Derrida takes as his guiding thread *the problem of genesis*. As I shall want to show, it is around the theme of genesis that some of Derrida's most insistent preoccupations will come to be gathered: the question of the contamination of the empirical and the transcendental, the question of the temporality of sense, the questions of origin and history. Granted, the question of writing is absent. And yet, once seen from the perspective of these analyses, that question takes on a dimension which, without being entirely new, reveals it in a quite different light. In *The Problem of Genesis*, one finds an attempt to develop a non-Heideggerian thought of finitude and of history. This attempt stems from Derrida's conviction, already clearly formulated in this early text, that Heidegger's thought of finitude is, in a certain sense, insufficiently radical.[5] What renders insufficient the notion of finitude elaborated by Heidegger is the recourse to a dimension of the originary that excludes every genetic problematic, the concept of genesis carrying with it a tension between the idea of *origin* and that of *becoming*, which is precisely what interests Derrida. The concern here will be to think the paradoxical unity of the possibility of an absolute emergence that does not erase its inscription in the past, that does not forget the fact that every emergence is produced by something other than itself.[6] Already in *The Problem of Genesis*, one of the emblematic sites of this insufficiency as regards the Heideggerian conception of finitude is the problem of death, a problem from which, as we shall see in due course, the question of genesis is not entirely removed.[7] In Derrida's work, the confrontation with Husserl and Heidegger, with a thought of the transcendental and an ontology of temporality,[8] takes the form of an irreducible *contamination*, a contamination, first of all, of finitude and the infinite, of life and death. In this double confrontation, moreover, the empirical will be deployed by Derrida as what disturbs not only Husserlian phenomenology, of course, but also any ontology that attempts to be absolved of it.[9]

One last remark before embarking upon our reading of *The Problem of Genesis*: I shall want to follow this text quite closely in order to bring out the stakes of Derrida's thought as they come to be formulated in terms of the question of genesis that he chooses as the guiding thread for a reading of what was, at the time, all of Husserl's available texts. This choice appears to me decisive for all Derrida's subsequent work, and it is this hypothesis that I will try to argue and to defend. As far as Husserl's own work is concerned, moreover, it ought to be borne in mind that the situation forty years after *The Problem of Genesis* was published is clearly rather different as regards both the critical literature and the publication of the manuscripts. Still, this does not stop Derrida's text from being of continuing interest for readers of Husserl today.

1. The Problem of Genesis: Time and Truth

What does the young Derrida identify as the problem of genesis? And why does he choose this problem as the guiding thread for his reading of Husserl's work? He does so because the concept of genesis introduces a tension between *origin* and *becoming*, which is the very question of the relation of time to truth. Genesis always refers to the absolute emergence of an originary sense, insofar as it is irreducible to anything that precedes it, but a sense that is *also* carried along by a past, produced by something other than itself. How is one to think the autonomy of sense and truth *and* their birth in time? How is one to think both "the radicalness of sense and the radicalness of becoming"?[10] Such would be the challenge set for thinking by the concept of genesis: to account for the irreducible connection between sense and time without first reducing the latter to the transparency of a form that would have no effect on truth. To think time as the unfolding of a teleology amounts to effacing its temporal character, to endowing it with a sense independent of it. For Derrida, by contrast, the "originary sense of temporality" always refers to the profundity of an "originary temporality of sense."[11] The question of genesis thus defined, Derrida sees it at work—sometimes overtly, other times in more covert fashion—in one of the insistent preoccupations of Husserl's work: his refusal of the Kantian formalism that implies a divorce between history and the transcendental. Far from being an unexpected turn in Husserl's later work, the question of history is seen by Derrida as in fact inscribed in the genetic problems that open Husserl's reflections as a whole and that will continue to haunt his work, raised again at every stage of his inquiry until, finally, taking the form of the question of transcendental historicity.

Husserl first encounters the problem of genesis as a question concerning the foundation of mathematics and logic. At the end of the nineteenth century and the start of the twentieth, the philosophical debate in Germany, marked by Kant's theory of knowledge on the one hand and the birth of scientific psychology on the other, turned on the relation between logical laws and the laws of thinking. Might not logic be founded upon psychology? Might there not be a psychological genesis of logical laws? Carl Stumpf, in *Psychologie und Erkenntnisstheorie* of 1891, had reproached Kant for having separated psychology from the theory of knowledge. If it is the latter that establishes the *a priori* conditions of possibility for universal knowledge, then these conditions are themselves always dependent upon an historical and real subject for their actualization, a subject that should be the true object of psychology. Psychology would thus be the disavowed point of departure for any critical philosophy. To proceed in this way, however, is clearly to run the risk of devastating the objective value of logic. And it is against such an unacceptable risk that Natorp, in his polemic against Lipps, reaffirms the independence of logical consciousness with respect to all psychological consciousness. For Natorp, either logic is founded upon itself or there is no logic. The objective and universal value of this position precludes the possibility that logic might depend on a subjective experience. The price for thus assuring the truth of logical laws is to remove them from any genesis and to make them dependent upon a logical consciousness that escapes all real time. Posed in these terms, the debate between psychologism and logicism amounts, according to Derrida, to the alternative between "a genesis without objectivity" and an "objectivity without genesis,"[12] as if there were no possible way of reconciling time to truth. For although the first alternative thinks the becoming of science, the genesis that it envisages remains purely empirical, incapable of accounting for the universal validity of science. The second alternative saves objectivity, but only at the cost of rendering it atemporal. The passage between the empirical subject of an always uncertain knowledge and the transcendental subject of an *a priori* knowledge is interrupted.

Now it is precisely the refusal of the interruption of this passage that constitutes, for Derrida, the originality of Husserl's position. Such a refusal is rooted in the Husserlian conception of intentionality and in the demand that one take originary lived experience [*le vécu originaire*] as philosophy's sole legitimate point of departure. This implies, however, a thought of the transcendental disabused of all Kantian formalism. Respect for originary lived experience requires that the transcendental be envisaged as the constituting origin of experience; if not, it becomes logical and formal and "no longer a constituting source but the constituted product of experience."[13] At the origin of this slippage from the transcendental into the formal, there lies the Kantian conception of the ideality of time.[14] As the *a priori* form of sensibility, time is the condition of possibility for both succession and causality, assuring thereby the formal conditions of possibility for every genesis and every becoming. Yet these conditions are not themselves genetic, and Kant draws a distinction between an empirical subject and empirical time on the one hand and an ideal or formal time, a transcendental subject of *a priori* laws on the other. Such a distinction, however, fails to respect the originarity of lived experience. Why? Because the first requirement of such respect is that one take seriously the intentionality of consciousness and not arbitrarily sever it from its objects in order then to ask how a link between the two might be established. Now, if consciousness is always consciousness *of* something, then this implies that the autonomy of scientific significations is valid outside of any real (*real*) correlation with a consciousness. And yet, the very autonomy of truth has no sense other than *for* a consciousness that, while transcendental, does not "duplicate" empirical consciousness, given that its only "real" content is that of the empirical.[15] Empiricism and formalism come together in the reduction of originary lived experience to the solely historical and psychological dimension, the first in order to confine it there, the second in order to redouble it with a world of *a priori* laws. Neither one, however, can complete the task of a transcendental thinking in Husserl's sense of the term: to explain, at the same time, objectivity and its origins for a consciousness.

Now, according to Derrida, the gesture of this double refusal runs throughout the whole of Husserl's theoretical work, the struggle to avoid both empiricism and formalism motivating the various changes in the direction of his thinking: from psychologism to logicism to transcendental idealism, right up to the thinking of history, even if the hidden unity of such displacements is more the unity of Husserl's hesitation. For Derrida, indeed, Husserl will ultimately have lost his bet: by trying to overcome empiricism and formalism, he comes dangerously close sometimes to one, sometimes to the other. As a project of pure and concrete constitution, phenomenology continually finds itself faced with an irreducible passivity. First and foremost with the passive synthesis of time within the egological consciousness that Husserl tries to reinvest with intentional sense through recourse to the idea of an infinite teleology. Yet the teleological idea reintroduces, in another form, the ideality of time that Husserl will always have refused in Kant. According to Derrida, Husserl's failure to have recognized the necessity of founding phenomenology on a temporal ontology means that he will have failed to resolve the difficulties that nonetheless serve as his point of departure. By following a little more closely the details of Derrida's reading of Husserl, we can see the "genesis" of a problematic kernel that will remain operative long after this early text.

The psychologism of *The Philosophy of Arithmetic*[16] (1894) is already motivated by the desire to avoid severing the objectivity of mathematical significations from their origin in and for consciousness. If one considers mathematical significations only as ideal forms, one fails to understand either the progress of mathematics or the concrete possibility of every actual operation, every synthesis, that can only be carried out in an act of consciousness. In order to reconcile the act of the constituting subject and the objectivity of the intended signification, Husserl turns to the concept of intentionality advanced by Brentano, the dedicatee of the work. His analysis is therefore concerned with the concrete origin of mathematical concepts. Husserl takes as his point of departure the concept of plurality on the basis of which he believes himself able to derive the concept of number.[17] The concept of plurality has its genesis in a psychological act of abstraction practiced on the totalities (*Inbegriffe*) of objects. Yet the totality—and herein lies the difference between Husserl's position and that of classical psychologism—is not the product of an act of assembling, but given from the outset to intentional perception. The synthetic unity of the object is *a priori* because the object itself is immediately present to consciousness. This *a priori* synthesis is not produced by a genesis but, on the contrary, renders the genesis of the concept of plurality possible through abstraction. The already constituted totality on the basis of which one abstracts the concept of number is not the product of an empirical subject but is given *a priori* and renders possible the subject's own activity of abstraction.

As Derrida emphasizes, Husserl's analyses here seem to reverse his genetic point of departure, introducing thus an internal tension that already evokes a problem not addressed until much later, to wit, the problem of the time of transcendental constitution.[18] Derrida's line of argument is as follows: because totality is not the product of an empirical subject, it is given as an *a priori* synthesis that supposes a transcendental act that is itself synthetic. But synthesis implies a duration and a genesis, the time of an actualization, and the whole problem thus becomes one of grasping the status of the time of transcendental constitution. Is it a time constituted by an atemporal subject, or is the subject itself temporal? In other words: is the genesis actual or ideal? This alternative intersects with the one that exists between formalism and empiricism. A purely ideal genesis forever separates the originary from lived experience, condemning it to being merely psychological and constituted. Such is, moreover, the charge that Husserl will have ceaselessly leveled at Kant. On the other hand, however, actual genesis depends directly on a real and historical subject: in this case, the "originary" would be lived [*vécu*], but lived experience [*le vécu*] would still not be removed from the domain of the psychological. According to Derrida, this alternative is ultimately unsatisfying because it requires the distinction, subsequently introduced by Husserl, between the psychological and the phenomenological, between worldly reality (*real*) and transcendental reality (*reel*). This distinction should make it possible neither to sever lived experience from the originary nor to reduce it to the level of a worldly reality.

We can begin to divine thus what, for Derrida, precisely is at stake in reading Husserl in this way. If he is to retain the originarity of lived experience, Husserl cannot dispense with the problem of genesis, a problem that will continually lead him back to the question of time. And it is precisely time that resists being mastered by the system of distinctions that underlies phenomenology: "just as there is a reduction of a certain time," writes Derrida, "so there is also a certain time of reduction," a time that will itself remain irreducible.[19] But Derrida is here looking ahead. On the problematic level upon which *The Philosophy of Arithmetic* is situated, genesis is still merely psychological and, despite the originality of Husserl's psychologism, which prefigures much of his later research, it remains a psychologism, open to the criticism that we have already encountered. Husserl himself will take note of this and, primarily in the wake of Frege's harsh response, will abandon his earlier project and turn, with the *Logical Investigations*,[20] toward a certain logicism.

Derrida nonetheless refuses to read the *Logical Investigations* (1900–1901) as a radical turn toward a pure logicism, choosing instead to show a certain continuity of purpose. If the first volume of the *Investigations* holds the objectivity of logical forms to be independent from the psychological act directed toward them, then the second recognizes this independence as being insufficient, Husserl proposing now an analysis of lived experiences in which these logical forms can become accessible. According to Derrida, objectivity is shown thus to be constituted by a subject that is neither logical nor psychological but transcendental, and the way is opened to the later research on the phenomenological reduction. The notice served to psychologism and to historicism, to genesis interpreted as psycho-physiological causality, becomes the overcoming of the very opposition between psychologism and logicism. For Husserl, this opposition holds on the level of the constituted alone; on the level of originary and constituting lived experience, it has lost its whole *raison d'être*.

2. Being has Always Already Begun: Phenomenological, Ontological, and Empirical Geneses

For Derrida, by contrast, the overcoming of this opposition is illusory: the abandonment of genesis and history to a purely worldly destiny is at odds with the temporality of constituting lived experience itself. Originary lived experience is neither logical nor psychological but *transcendental*, and the sense of this transcendentality is progressively revealed in Husserl's inquiries as being originarily temporal. The fact that access to a transcendental temporality is opened in Husserl's work by a reduction, a neutralization of genesis, is a gesture that, for Derrida, is problematic not only in itself but also within Husserlian conceptuality. "How can genesis be merely 'constituted,'" he asks, "if temporality is 'constituting'? How can the origin of time be static and not genetic?"[21] What is at stake here is a tension that explains why the period in which Husserl sees the notion of genesis as a merely empirical and constituted moment is the same period as the one in which the need to elaborate a concept of *transcendental genesis* becomes increasingly clear. This period begins following the publication of the *Logical Investigations* (1901) and continues up to the lecture course of 1919–20 published much later under the title *Experience and Judgment*,[22] in which Husserl works explicitly toward the notion of a genetic logic and the analysis of the prepredicative world, toward, even, the possibility of a *genetic phenomenology*.

The *Lectures on Internal Time-Consciousness*[23] date from the same period, and it is here more than anywhere else that Husserl will try to accommodate an originarily constituting phenomenological temporality.[24]

The reading of the *Lectures* is central to Derrida's interpretation. It is through Husserl's analyses of time that he is able to trace the reasons both for the impossibility of reducing genesis to the status of an empirical and constituted moment and the ensuing necessity of thematizing a transcendental genesis. Equally, however, and above all, it is here that Derrida sees outlined the impossibility of an absolutely rigorous distinction between transcendental genesis on the one hand, and, on the other, ontological genesis and empirical genesis. The movement of temporalization implies a dialectic of the constituting and the constituted that inscribes passivity at the very heart of the originary. As far as Derrida is concerned, this irreducible passivity marks the limit of every pure constitution and the point at which the constituted can no longer be separated from the empirical. Thus the movement of temporalization will no longer be for Derrida what it is for Husserl, namely the transcendental origin of time, but rather the product of the *contamination* of the transcendental and the empirical. The empirical will be just as constituting—and constituted—as the transcendental itself. What the Derrida of this period calls "dialectic without synthesis" is precisely the necessity of this double movement. The stakes are high and the line of argument merits our close attention, all the more so since it allows us to understand why Derrida will never renounce the categories of empirical and transcendental, and to see precisely how this same choice articulates many of the motives underlying the distance he retains in relation to Heidegger's thinking.

In the *Lectures*, Husserl poses the question of the origin of time from a point of view that aspires to be purely phenomenological. It is again a matter of defining the specificity of phenomenology, its particular field, in relation to psychologism and to Kant's theory of knowledge. This time, however, this definition takes place at what is shown to be the most fundamental level: that of temporality. In order to be truly constituting, the transcendental subject as envisaged by Husserl has to be temporal. This temporality, however, is not that of objective time, the time of the world or of the psyche, nor is it time as the empty form of the Kantian subject. These two critical intentions are present within the very project of retracing the *phenomenological origin of time*. One arrives at phenomenological time by setting the existence of the *Weltzeit*, the time of nature and psychic time, out of play. This reduction leaves us confronted by time and duration appearing as such, which, according to Husserl, are absolute data which there is no sense in doubting. What is revealed is the immanent time of

consciousness endowed with absolute evidence.[25] Husserl's point of departure is opposed thus to the psychological approaches that, having failed to
take the precaution of the reduction, work toward the empirical laws of the
consciousness of time without ever taking into account the specificity of
consciousness, which ought not to be thought as one object amongst others within the world. Yet the fact that the question is posed in terms of origin shows that Husserl has retained a certain psychologistic inheritance
and that his approach is profoundly different from the Kantian one. In
Kantian terms, there is no place for questions concerning the transcendental *origin* of time. Husserl is clearly aiming at an *a priori* of time, but this *a
priori* is its very origin, the manner in which the primitive formations of
the temporal are constituted within consciousness.[26]

    After having set the *Weltzeit* to the side, and so after having delimited
the properly phenomenological field of inquiry, Husserl begins his analyses
with the exposition and critique of Brentano's theory of *originary associa-
tions.*[27] That he does so is hardly surprising, if one takes into account the
fact that the problem raised by Brentano is, despite his avowed psychologism, the same as the one raised by Husserl: the problem of explicating the
unity of a conscience that encompasses both the past and the present. Although Husserl does refuse the psychological level upon which Brentano's
inquiries are situated, he recognizes the great merit of its fidelity to the
phenomena of temporal processes. In order for there to be perception of a
temporal object, a melody for example, perception of the simple present is
not enough: it would leave us with either a succession of isolated sounds
incapable of forming a melody or the coexistence of a multiplicity of co-
present sounds that, once again, would in no way resemble the perception
of something like a melody.[28] It is in order to resolve this difficulty that
Brentano introduces the notion of *originary association,* "the genesis of the
immediate presentations of memory which, according to a law that admits
no exceptions, are joined to particular presentations of perception without
mediation."[29] What this "invariable law" states is that a consciousness of
time is possible only if the immediate past is "preserved" by consciousness,
but preserved in modified form. The perception of a melody as the perception of a succession of sounds requires that the passing sounds are not
immediately forgotten, even though their "presence" is not of the same order as that of the sounds currently resonating. Past sounds, as Derrida
writes, should "leave traces."[30]

    Now, although Husserl subscribes to the phenomenological value of this description, he cannot follow Brentano in according to the faculty of imagination this power of modifying sensations by giving them the temporal determination of the "past." The imagination cannot be the origin of representations of time, recourse to this faculty explaining neither the "modification" which, attached to a present, makes it a past, nor the difference between imagination and perception.[31] If the representations of time were the product of the imagination, time would be merely an unreal predicate added to an originally atemporal experience. And it would be quite impossible to mark the difference between perception and imagination if the perception of time was already the association of a present and the imagination. For how could one distinguish a melody that is perceived from a melody that is represented in recollection or simply imagined?[32] For Husserl, moreover, the constitution of time cannot be explained by the imagination, which, as a psychological faculty, is *a priori* temporal.

According to Derrida, however, over and above Brentano's recourse to the imagination, which is indeed rather problematic, Husserl more profoundly refuses the genetic and dialectic character of Brentano's theory.[33] If, at this point in his investigations, Husserl envisages genetic becoming as relevant to the domain of constituted worldliness alone, it follows that every constitution is essentially static. Which, once it becomes a matter of the analysis of temporality, poses particular difficulties for Derrida: the constitution of lived time and of temporal objectivities can be static only if it is limited to an eidetic analysis in which time is seen, in its essence, as noema.[34] Once the *eidos* of time is isolated, however, one is sent back, as with every essence, to a noesis, to the constituting act of a transcendental subject that is itself temporal; one is sent back, in other words, to a temporality even more originary and necessarily genetic:

> The "*eidos*" of lived time is itself temporal, constituted in a temporality. It appears static only if it is uncoupled from the temporality where it is founded. This last is genetic in essence (but here essence has no need of an eidetic reduction in order to appear. It even excludes it *a priori*.).[35]

With these lines, Derrida gives voice to an objection that he will continue to raise against Husserl in all that follows (and well beyond *The Problem of Genesis*, though the framework of the argument will be quite different): from the moment that time is at issue, the distinction between "fact" and "essence" becomes inapplicable, since "the eidetic reduction of lived time separates what, in essence, is not separable." Reducing time to a "sense" will always allow the question of the temporality of "sense" itself to re-emerge. It is on the basis of this point that Derrida tries to demonstrate the irreducibility of genesis. So while he credits Brentano with having proposed a description of simultaneously genetic and dialectic temporality in which time appears as constituting only because it is constituted, he sees in Husserl's claim to have held only to a constituting origin of time a demand that will be contradicted by what actually takes place in the analyses that Husserl himself puts forward, analyses that seem to reintroduce the constituted into the sphere of the constituting originary by way of a necessity that follows from the intentional character of consciousness. Let us follow Derrida's argument.

The reduction of objective temporality opens onto a purely immanent phenomenological temporality. At the very heart of this immanence, however, the intentional character of consciousness implies the constitution of temporal *objects* (*Zeitobjekte*) that are, or that ought to be, rigorously distinguished from transcendent temporal objects. By *Zeitobjekte* Husserl understands "objects which not only are unities in time but also include temporal extension in themselves," a resonant sound, for example.[36] Extension is an originary aspect of temporal consciousness. The sound, to continue with our example, has a duration, and the passage from the present to the past happens in a continuous manner according to a process that Husserl terms modification: the sound, although originating in a source-point, in the *Ur-impression* of the hyletic datum, is continually changing, the present sound changing to retention and an always new present arising.[37] And each new retention, by adding itself to the others, is not restricted to pushing them further and further away, but modifies them in turn, following thus this process of continual modification. The temporal object is formed by a succession of originary impressions, of retentions and protentions: temporal extension renders necessary the retention of the past and the anticipation of the future in order for there to be perception of the sound's present.

Now Derrida's principle interest here, like that of Husserl himself, is with the necessity of retention. Retentional modification is necessary to the very appearing of the sound. From this phenomenological necessity described by Husserl, Derrida wants to draw consequences that are no longer "purely" phenomenological. The necessity of retention shows a "temporal density" at the very heart of originary impression that will complicate, if not contradict, the idea of a source-point.[38] But if primal impression is, for

Derrida, never reducible to the ideal limit of a source-point it is because, more importantly, temporality is never purely constituting or purely phenomenological. Let us see why. In the terms used in *The Problem of Genesis*, the *Urimpression*—the moment of absolute originarity—is already a *synthesis*. Now, this *a priori* synthetic character of primal impression renders problematic its assignation to a purely phenomenological sphere because of the intentionality of consciousness. In Derrida's eyes, it is intentionality that introduces an ineffaceable ambiguity. The *Urimpression* being the impression *of* real sound, Derrida asks whether the noematic synthesis, the phenomenological constitution of the temporal object, does not refer to the worldly reality (*real*) of an already constituted sound. Retention being both constituting and intentional, what is given intuitively to consciousness would refer to an ontological synthesis "more originary" than any noematic lived experience. In order to show this, Derrida relies on the simultaneously productive and receptive—active and passive—character of intentionality, something that seems to exclude anything like a purely active perception.[39] Now, what is at stake here is clearly the status of the hyletic datum of sound. If this is passively received, if it cannot be constituted by the activity of a transcendental subject, then its purely phenomenological status, its non-inclusion in the world, appear thus problematic:

When Husserl recognizes an "*a priori* necessity of the precedence of [. . .] impression over the corresponding retention" and when, on the other hand, he maintains that retention presents originarily a character of intentional evidence, does not he reintroduce, in the form of the hyletic datum passively received, the transcendent object that he claimed to exclude from his analyses?[40]

Intuition ought originally to "receive" the concrete presence of the object that is given to all construction; if perception is perception of time or of space, a primitive passivity seems to constitute the actuality of consciousness.[41] Once this is the case, however, then the hyletic datum of sound, as something passively received, cannot be constituted by the activity of a subject. It is because of this impossibility that Derrida sees the *Lectures* as already announcing the difficulties that will later lead Husserl to make *passive genesis* one of the major themes of phenomenology.[42] The passive synthesis of time announced by the necessity of retention is the point at which, so far as Derrida is concerned, the question of the radical discontinuity between the phenomenological past (past lived experience) and the worldly past is raised:

If it is recognized, as Husserl will, that the originary "now" appears only through a passive synthesis of time with itself and through an immediate retention of the past, that the present is constituting only because, in emerging from the radical newness of an immediately constituted past, it roots itself in it and appears to itself as present only against the background of its passive continuity with the former moment, then one has the right to pose the following question: What radical discontinuity is there between this already constituted past and the objective time that imposes itself on me, constituted without any active intervention on my part?[43]

If phenomenology finds its ownmost resources in the distinction between empirical and transcendental, what would then happen if constituted time were shown to be inseparable from worldly time? Derrida does not deny that, on a literal level, there is a difference between constituted phenomenological time and objective temporal facts. His argument is more subtle, more "internal." If Husserl fails to address the question of this radical discontinuity, if he considers it evident in a way that defies all doubt, this stems, according to Derrida, from the fact that the analyses of the *Lectures* are still situated on the level of a purely noematic temporality.[44] That toward which immanent intentionality is directed is the *noema* of time, its eidetic sense. Thanks to the eidetic reduction, one can move from the order of the constituted to that of the constituting itself.[45] What is thus freed up is the *signification* of time. Such a move, however, always conceals the *time* of signification. In other words, time resists being divided between essence and fact. If the eidetic reduction appears applicable to material facts, Derrida will want to challenge its possibility when it comes to time. Now, in order for the passivity of past lived experience to be radically different from that of the worldly past, it has to be possible to submit it to reduction. Derrida's concern is to show that such a reduction leaves us with an alternative that is unacceptable either way. On the one hand, although one can assimilate "the eidetic character of the region of 'consciousness' to that of the region of 'things,'" this amounts to considering every constituted lived experience as an empirical fact, implying thus the introduction of a "fact" into the intimate consciousness of time since the retention of a constituted moment is necessary to the appearance of phenomenological time. If, on the other hand, according to Derrida, one resolves to distinguish constituting lived experience from the constituted world—and this is Husserl's preferred choice—the eidetic reduction "no longer has any foundation." When it comes to time, essence and existence can no longer be separated in consciousness. The *eidos* of time is itself temporal.[46] The absolute freedom that reduction implies finds itself limited by the *irreducible* passivity of time:

The freedom of the reduction seems then limited *a priori* by the temporal necessity of retention. I cannot not make a temporal act out of an act of my freedom. To the degree that this act lasts, it must negotiate with the determinate temporality that it "retains," with the history that it assumes, in order to know itself as a free act. *Its impurity is originary because it is* a priori *temporal.*[47]

The act of reduction knows itself to be free only by knowing itself to refer back to the past whence it came. The essence of time, which lies in its very existence, cannot be purely active: no transcendental consciousness can retain the constituted past without acceding to an irreducible passivity. An active retention can never make a past as such appear. At best, pure activity leaves one faced with the punctuality of a now or with the protention of a future.[48]

    This *a priori* synthesis—and, for Derrida, synthesis is here synonymous with genesis—reintegrates the constituted into the constituting and marks the impossibility of pure phenomenology. If Husserl presents the *a priori* necessity of synthesis as a *phenomenological* necessity, Derrida tries to show that it is also *ontological* and *empirical*. What this means, however, is that the limit that separates the constituted from the worldly is always already broached. Within its own field phenomenology has to acknowledge that ontology is already in place, that "being has always already begun."[49] In order to be faithful to the radicality of its project, phenomenology has to accept its limits and recognize itself as being founded upon a temporal ontology. The transcendental subject, as temporal subject, encounters the unbroachable limit of its capacity for pure self-constitution. The passive synthesis of time introduces an irreducible "contamination"—the word is already present in *The Problem of Genesis*—and alterity. There can be no pure constitution. And with this, all other distinctions upon which phenomenology rests are eroded:

Temporal dialectics constitutes alterity *a priori* in the absolute identity of the subject with itself. The subject appears to itself originarily as tension of the Same and the Other. The theme of a transcendental intersubjectivity setting up transcendence at the heart of the absolute immanence of the "ego" has already been called for. The last foundation of the objectivity of intentional consciousness is not the intimacy of the "I" to itself but [is] Time or the Other, those two forms of an existence that is irreducible to an essence [and] foreign to the theoretical subject, [two forms] always constituted before it, but at the same time, the only conditions of possibility of a constitution of self and of an appearance of self to self.[50]

This insufficiency of the monadological ego, which Husserl will later thematize as transcendental intersubjectivity and the infinite teleology of history, is also marked by his recourse to the idea of an intuition of the infinite totality of time. The difficulty here is one of bringing together time as form and time as matter, the actual now as a form that persists and the linking of concrete lived experiences, the oscillation between the absolute as the infinite flux of time and the absolute as the pure ego [*moi*] of subjectivity.[51] How can the unity between the now as pure form and the linking of concrete lived experiences be rediscovered while still retaining the phenomenological principle of intuition as the ground of all evidence? For Derrida, it is once again a question of knowing how the transcendental subject can be both the subject of an originary lived experience *and* originally temporal, a transcendental subject that does not fall into Kantian formalism. Husserl's own solution, however, is still very Kantian: it consists in rediscovering the pure unity of the ego and of the temporal form in the idea of an *infinite totality* of the succession of all possible nows. Derrida points out that Husserl seeks a solution to the problematic idea of the *intuition* of an infinite totality by maintaining that that of which there is an actual intuition is not the infinite totality of the succession itself, but its *indefinite character*.[52] And yet, the decision to make an indefinite the content of an intuition rather than the limit of all possible intuition is one dictated by Husserl's idealism. It is precisely because of this idealism that he refuses the "essential finitude" of consciousness, a refusal that marks the point of departure between Husserlian phenomenology and a philosophy of existence:

The intuition of the indefinite is intuition of the possible infinite. It is here that the split is made between Husserlian idealism and a philosophy of existence. This latter, starting at the same time from the possibility or from the existential necessity of death and from the idea of an indefinite possibility of time, leads us to bring together the impossibility of the possible and the possibility of the impossible. The inauthenticity of a supposed intuition of the indefinite in the face of the noncompletion of the present and indetermination of the future is exceed in "anguish" faced with the absolutely indeterminate.[53]

This remark, which might at first glance seem to be a straightforward echo of a theme very much in vogue in post-war French phenomenology and existentialism, takes on its full import if one considers two things. Firstly, in *The Problem of Genesis* Derrida already sees the possibility of an authentic existence that assumes "being-toward-death" in "resolute decision" as being a suspension of the dialectic of originary temporality. It forces one to recommence indefinitely the movement toward the originary, a movement that no "authenticity" can arrest and that constitutes the condition of *the very possibility of history.* The impossible return to the origin, far from being the moment of crisis, is the very chance of historicity. I shall come back to this in due course. Second, one takes the measure of the theoretical stakes only by paying attetion to the role that Derrida allocates to the question of empiricity, not only in *The Problem of Genesis* but in all his later texts as well. If the project of founding phenomenology on a temporal ontology can be read—and this is an entirely legitimate reading—as the development of Heidegger's critique of Husserl by way of the finitude that is played out in the possibility or the existential necessity of death, such a reading ought not, for all that, to neglect the originality and import of Derrida's claim. When he says that the genesis of time is not only a phenomenological genesis but is also an ontological and *empirical*[54] one, this ought not to be seen as a naïve confusion of ontology and empiricism or an unimportant juxtaposition of terms. On the contrary, its implications are crucial. It is not by chance that Derrida plays the question of ontology off against Husserl and, at the same time, holds onto the question of the transcendental and the empirical in order to demonstrate their irreducible contamination instead of following Heidegger and simply allowing this question to drop. Rather, the reference to the empirical will allow him to think the finitude of the subject and of history in relation to the question of being, of course, but also in relation to what this other question leaves in its margins. The limit that time imposes upon the self-constitution of the transcendental subject, as Derrida retraces it in his reading of Husserl, points toward *finite existence.* But Derrida's passage through phenomenology leads him *elsewhere* than the place where Heidegger was ultimately led:

Was this autoconstitution of the subject not going to put into question again the very sense of its phenomenological and theoretic activity? Would it not reduce it to the concrete existence of a *living being* in general?[55]

Derrida is moving here toward the question of a *contamination* of life and death disallowed by Heidegger's notion of Dasein in its "ownmost being-toward-death."[56] These are the themes that will give his reflection a greater part of its specificity, and that I shall want to follow at length throughout this study. For the moment, however, let me emphasize that it is within phenomenology *itself* that Derrida finds the motifs that allow him to contest this. Phenomenology's limit is not an external one; rather, it is phenomenology's *own* project—which is, moreover, the always repeated project of assigning unbroachable limits—that reveals it to be untenable. The conditions of its possibility are at the same time the conditions of its impossibility. It is this "law of contamination" that, in a certain sense, makes Derrida's thinking an extremely faithful one: there can be no question of dispensing with philosophy. And it is for this very reason that his discourse resembles nothing so much as a transcendental one, with the difference that conditions of possibility are at the same time conditions of impossibility—a difference that, *up to a point*, devastates the very idea of the transcendental.[57] I will return to this in due course, but we should keep in mind that the strategy of deconstruction, as Derrida will later elaborate it, is already in place, even if it is not named as such. And not only in the most formal of its "demonstrative principles," but also in its deepest motivations.

In *The Problem of Genesis* Derrida describes the necessity of founding phenomenology on ontology. The "dialectic"[58] of constituting and constituted at the heart of temporal lived experience amounts to an "always-already-thereness of being" that no reduction, whether eidetic or transcendental, can ever reabsorb into the absolute freedom of a purely constituting subject. The "fact" will never be completely mastered by "sense." And what prevents this neutralization is finitude. Husserl refuses to locate the origins of philosophy in an existence whose finitude appears, his transcendental idealism closing off any access to an ontology of temporality, and the temporal dialectic that he describes remaining exclusively phenomenological rather than opening onto the temporality of being.[59] Despite Derrida's continued recourse in this text to dialectic and to ontology, a recourse that is displaced, moreover, by the preoccupations which we have just mentioned, what he says here is not so very different from his subsequent observation that *infinite différance* is *finite*.[60] It is already a matter of what binds time, alterity and history in a thought that, no longer being merely a thought of *pure* finitude, diverges from the Heideggerian project in certain essential questions. In saying this, I do not want to suggest that the analyses of *Speech and Phenomena* add nothing to those of *The Problem of Genesis*. Quite the contrary. Abandoning the language of dialectic and ontology is not simply a matter of terminology. Moreover, the demonstration of the effacing of the pure distinction between the empirical and the tran-

scendental, passes, in *Speech and Phenomena*, through the problem of signification, which will have more than one consequence. All the same, the
essential intuitions of that later work can already be found in *The Problem
of Genesis*, and the attention to the trajectory that these insights will follow
and the modifications that they will undergo are not only of historical but
theoretical interest, if one can still trust in such distinctions. Such, at least,
is what I want to try to show.

3. Transcendental Teleology and its
Empirical Crisis: The *Eidos* of Europe

We have already seen that, for Derrida, the question of transcendental historicity does not mark an unexpected shift in Husserl's thinking. On
the contrary, from the perspective of that thinking itself, it is entirely necessary. Finding the point of departure for his reflection in the psychological
genesis of number, Husserl appears to distance himself from every genetic
question from the moment that he elaborates the properly phenomenological themes of his thinking. But genesis again takes its revenge: a non-ge-
netic temporality can only reduce time to its eidetic signification and
Husserl is thus thrown back onto the actual temporality of the pure subject
in which the genetic dimension of the reduction itself appears. It is on this
level that the question of the passive synthesis of the temporal *hylè* appears
to render problematic the distinction between phenomenological and
worldly time. The inseparability of the essence and existence of time seems
to call into question the possibility of isolating a purely phenomenological
lived experience and thus the very validity of the eidetic transcendental reductions.[61] Or at least it does so according to Derrida, who founds not only
his reading of Husserl but also his entire philosophical undertaking on precisely this gesture of calling into question. Husserl himself, however, has to
thematize transcendental genesis if he is to provide a new foundation for the
distinction between the empirical and the transcendental.

It is at this point that history returns to Husserl's thought, this time
in a transcendental dimension. We have seen that the only subject for
which phenomenology is possible is a temporal one; and we have seen, too,
that the auto-constitution of time cannot be purely active. A merely active
retention would imply a consciousness without past, yet the monadological ego is insufficient to reinvest the passivity of time with intentional

sense. It is because of this insufficiency that Husserl introduces into the *Cartesian Meditations*[62] the idea of an infinite teleology. Through this idea, he hopes to be able to found phenomenology's pretension to absolute science, the foundation of all possible science, of all science that exists in history and that is constituted in a culture. The first moment of constitution is thus no longer the pure I, but the teleological idea (*Zweckidee*): the infinite totality of an oriented becoming. The transcendental ego merges with the pure life of this teleology. According to Derrida, however, Husserl remains faithful to a profoundly idealist and rationalist intention: even though he continually encounters the idea of becoming he can think it only as reduced to an *eidos* or to a *telos*, which amounts to the same thing. From which it follows that history is encountered only to the extent that it is oriented by a sense. So it is hardly a coincidence that history, for Husserl, is first the history of science as pretension to the universal and to an absolute foundation. What Husserl privileges above all in the sciences is not their factical existence, but the pure scientific intention that animates them and that remains hidden by "factical history." The phenomenological reduction suspends the real activity and results of science in order to free its pure sense. One could say that what interests Husserl about history is not history *per se* but what it hides: its originary but "buried" sense that needs to be reawakened. Constituted and perverted history exists only as a necessary point of departure for attaining the true sense that, behind all the sedimentations, animates it. Facticity is inescapable and it is only by way of it that one can ask in return the question of origin. It is this necessity that interests Derrida above all: once the *essential delay of thought* has been recognized, its measure must be taken. To interpret it as methodological and provisional, as Husserl tends to do, is not enough: it has to be interrogated in its sense and its necessity and then another dimension of history will be sketched out accordingly.[63] Once again, Derrida addresses the question in terms of genesis:

> Is it not precisely the problem of genesis to know how what is *a priori* present in history cannot be revealed except at the end of historical synthesis and how history can be the creator of what appears as "already there"?[64]

The difficulty of thinking history is the same as the difficulty of thinking genesis: what has to be thought is the tension between sense and time, between sense's pretension to truth and its temporal production. By eliminating this tension, by choosing truth over time or vice versa, the specificity of history is thereby lost. A truth without time, an essence that is fully an essence, would have no need of a genesis and, were it ever to have had one, it would be only a secondary appearance, one devoid of all necessity. If, on the contrary, a truth is produced in and by a genesis, how is its absolute value to be thought? How can one account for the fact that it is able to impose itself as something irreducible to any and all contingency? Now although Husserl was indeed confronted with the depths of a transcendental historicity and with the question of the origin of sense and truth, Derrida still thinks that he does so in a way that leaves him unable to sustain the necessary tension. When the themes of passive genesis and intersubjectivity reintroduce the constituted world into the transcendental sphere, Husserl's response, which passes through teleology and the *ego* as the infinite task of philosophy, fails both to resolve the aporia of genesis and to safeguard phenomenological purity. Why? Derrida gives several reasons.

First, it fails because of the status of a teleological idea within phenomenology. The idea of a teleology, prior to all active constitution and excluded from intuitive evidence, seems to him to reintroduce an *a priori* idea that certainly saves the autonomy of the transcendental but at the cost of falling back into a Kantian type of formalism; we have already seen this schema at work. Second, the very idea of a *crisis* of history seems problematic to Derrida: how can there be crises of a transcendental idea? The teleological idea, the transcendental opening of history, ought to be able to withstand the threat of any empirical event, at least if the relation of the empirical to the transcendental is one of constituted to constituting. And yet, empirical events "cover up" or "veil" the constituting origin, concealing it to the point of allowing it to be forgotten.[65] Such is the peculiar destiny that Husserl describes in *The Crisis of the European Sciences*.[66] Hence Derrida's remark that the very idea of crisis ought to oblige us to "make the idea of philosophy come down into a 'worldly' history and lend a constituting role to the empirical event itself."[67] Husserl seems unprepared to do this. He seeks a mediation between the transcendental *ego* and the "empirical incarnation" of the teleological idea: this is Europe as the spiritual birthplace of philosophy. And it is around this spiritual figure of Europe that Derrida's questions are going to concentrate.

At the very moment that Husserl gives *a time* and *a place* to the birth of the infinite idea of philosophy—and it is in the Greek nation of the seventh and sixth centuries B.C. that such an idea appeared "in a nation or in individual men and human groups of this nation"[68]—he withdraws from this place every signification that is not purely spiritual. The *eidos* of Europe is not a territory, a geographical place, but a place of spirit. Yet it is not as if Greece could be replaced by some other nation or by some other people. Its *eidos* resists all imaginary variation. The idea of philosophy comes to coincide with the finite existence of a people. Husserl wants to give a spiritual sense to an empirical event without renouncing the radical distinction between empirical and transcendental. As Derrida shows with the example of the *eidos* of Europe, however, this leads to the most acute form of the aporia that we have repeatedly encountered. If the infinite idea of philosophy, as absolute idea, is buried, hidden, but *also* present in the empirical history that precedes its happening, one would have to say that its "birth," at a particular time and place, is a pure accident. It could have appeared elsewhere, at another time, and, in the most extreme case, not appeared at all. Europe has no right to be such a privileged place. And this will be the case even if the birth of philosophy is empirical and worldly. In which case, too, the spiritual meaning of Europe would be unjustified; there should be no way of distinguishing it from all other empirical places. For Derrida, the effort of separating at any cost empirical meaning from transcendental meaning results in a paradox: since a purely spiritual genesis is no longer a genesis, the teleological idea is transformed into an empirical finality and the *eidos* of Europe takes on thus the figure of an accident.[69]

Derrida sees Husserl, years later, almost at the end of his philosophical journey, as once again obliged to confront time and truth, to choose between genesis as the unveiling of a truth which was already there and genesis as the creation of the truth, between a birth that is not in fact a birth and a truth that is not in fact a truth. The opposition between formalism and empiricism, which should have long been overcome, is still very much in place. In order to think the specificity of Greece, it would be necessary, according to Derrida, to think an existence in which "the transcendental and the empirical [are] originarily implied," "an existence that would still be opened to the truth of being, while still being 'in-the-world.'"[70] And this is why Husserl, remaining faithful to the eidetic point of view, cannot truly account for the genesis of a transcendental idea. Genesis implies that, on the level of originary temporal existence, fact and essence, the empirical and the transcendental, are inseparable and dialectically interdependent. The tension evoked above must not be eliminated, and it is for this very reason that Derrida calls for a dialectic without synthesis. To think this inseparability is the task of a "new ontology," but an ontology that is merely the deepening of the phenomenology of temporality. For the Derrida of *The Problem of Genesis*, it is phenomenology itself that evokes its own overcoming.

In order to understand the birth of the idea of philosophy and its crises, history has to be thought otherwise. The teleological idea, which coincides with the idea of philosophy, cannot do without history. It is only the infinite development of theory, a development in which is played out not only the objective progress of science but, above all, the recognition of transcendental consciousness as the absolute source of all spiritual activity. As infinite task, the teleological idea is transcendental constitution itself rather than its product. *But what conception of history is needed for an infinite teleology?* There is but one idea of philosophy, one that coincides with what Husserl understands by phenomenology; yet, even if the true sense of the philosophical project has always been one and the same, it was not something that flourished from the moment of its inception. It had to go through a long history before it was able to recognize itself in the purity of its own essence. Far from being a point of no return, however, this moment of recognition is fragile and always under threat. "Knowledge" of the activity of transcendental consciousness is less a theoretical knowledge than an ethical responsibility.[71] Husserl's incessant call for an assumption of responsibility, the whole pathos of *Verantwortung* and *Bestimmung*, graphically illustrates the point. The movement of the philosophical idea is not that of a continuous development, therefore. Rather than progressively flourishing from the moment of its inception, it "suffers an internal dissolution."[72] At every stage in its evolution, philosophy has failed to recognize its authentic source; having arrived at the threshold of a recognition, it immediately turns back. The "interruption" or the "corruption"[73] of the philosophical idea always takes the same form: by taking a merely constituted product as absolute, originary and constituting, transcendental activity disowns itself. Captivated by its own production, it loses its way. The perpetual danger is one of objectification and it is hardly a coincidence, therefore, that a call for the full assumption of philosophical responsibility—on which, to Husserl's mind, the fundamental importance of phenomenology rests—comes at the very moment that the threat of scientific objectification reaches its peak. The moment of crisis signals not a pause in theoretical production but, on the contrary, a moment of frenzied activity in which its sense and its source run the risk of being forgotten. The crisis of philosophy is the "forgetting" or the "covering over" [*recouvrement*] of the transcendental subjectivity that was born with it and has run alongside its entire history. Husserl sees this quite clearly although he does not, according to Derrida, address himself to the sense and possibility of this ever-present threat. *Although the teleological idea is transcendental, its crisis is empirical*: such is, for Husserl, an evidence that cannot be gainsaid, a founding distinction beyond question.

For Derrida, however, it is precisely this distinction that prevents Husserl from thinking the very sense of crisis and hence another dimension of history. Crisis is the very possibility for a transcendental subject to be "forgotten" or "covered over." For Husserl, this forgetting sometimes takes the figure of a simple accident, at other times the figure of an ethical failure.[74] But how can an accidental forgetting or a subjective failure affect a transcendental idea? How can the empirical be seen as threatening the transcendental, which ought to constitute it? If such a threat exists, and Husserl clearly thinks that it does,[75] it would have to be questioned in its conditions of possibility. If there can be and if there is indeed a crisis in philosophical sense, it has to be asked what, within this sense itself, renders such a crisis possible.[76] Contrary to what Husserl says, Derrida undertakes to show how crisis is "*an internal necessity of history*,"[77] an undertaking that will leave intact neither the sense of the concept of crisis nor that of the concept of history. Insofar as every intention that is directed toward a constituted product is, in itself, "a critical instant in which subjectivity not only runs the risk of losing itself but ought necessarily to lose itself," this necessity is one that depends on the transcendental constitution of significations. The "naively natural" objectivist attitude for which Husserl reproaches philosophy, is inseparable, according to Derrida, from the essentially synthetic character of intentionality, which is always a consciousness *of* something. This synthesis is nothing other than the *passive genesis* of time that introduces into the very originality of the Living Present (*lebendige Gegenwart*) the retention of a constituted past. The movement of temporalization itself implies the sedimentation of sense. In what Husserl calls "crisis," Derrida espies the work of a time that can be originally constituting only because it is passively constituted.[78] It is within transcendental consciousness itself that the empirical and the transcendental can no longer be rigorously distinguished, the passive synthesis of time assuring, to the contrary, the continuity between the worldly and the transcendental. Confronted by history, Husserl retains only its teleological sense; faced with the alteration or decomposition of this sense in "empirical" history, all he leaves us with is astonishment. An idealist astonishment, according to Derrida, from which the sense of crisis, temporality and history escape. What has to be rethought, to the contrary, is the necessity of this alteration, since it is only "from the point of view of the philosopher's subjectivity, or of philosophy as already constituted, that the constituted, the alienation, the 'outside,' and so forth appear as simply possible."[79]

In rethinking the Husserlian project of a purely phenomenological temporality, Derrida, guided by the problem of genesis, concludes that phenomenology, in order to be faithful to the radicalness of its own project, has to recognize its limits and accept that it is founded upon a temporal ontology. For the Derrida of 1953–4, the irreducible contamination of the empirical and the transcendental calls for a "new ontology." *Already,* however, the "temporal ontology" in question cannot be identified with Heideggerian ontology. Although Derrida recognizes Heidegger as the first to start on the path toward an ontology of temporality, it remains the case that temporality is thought by Heidegger as authentic. The possibility of taking on being-toward-death in a "resolute decision," a possibility on which the authenticity of existence is founded, for Derrida, "suspends the dialectic of originary temporality."[80] Derrida interprets the resolute decision as an act that is in some way definitive, an act that renders possible an existence henceforth free from all inauthenticity, whereas originary temporality itself renders impossible a definitely authentic existence. What Derrida here calls "dialectic" is the movement of temporal constitution that, as we have already seen, can never be pure. One has infinitely to begin the movement toward the originary and toward the authentic yet again, a movement that every constitution both conceals and reveals in one and the same gesture. Whether or not this interpretation of the resolute decision is correct is relatively unimportant at this point.[81] What is important, however, is the link that Derrida establishes as early as *The Problem of Genesis* between the "dialectic without synthesis" of the movement of temporalization and a certain empiricity, a link that takes the form of a contamination of the originary that will guide all his subsequent reflections. This contamination, however, is also a contamination of finitude and the infinite, of life and death, and leads Derrida toward a thinking of writing irreducible to the Heideggerian question of being. The phenomenology of temporality and the Husserlian question of genesis give Derrida the elements of reflection, the theoretical instruments that, through the fundamental transformations to which he will subject them, are going to help him develop such a thinking.[82] From *The Problem of Genesis* onward, Derrida touches on a group of questions—the contamination of the empirical and the transcendental, the complication of the origin, the temporality of sense, the necessity of thinking historicity otherwise—that he will continue to develop in his subsequent work. Let us follow this problematic and the modifications it undergoes as it confronts other preoccupations.[83]

The Absolute is Passage

If, for Husserl, philosophy is essentially and unequivocally a thought of the transcendental, the transcendental itself is not immune from equivocation. Understood as a world of *a priori* laws severed from consciousness, it immediately fails to accomplish its task and runs, on the contrary, the risk of an aberration of thinking. Only if the transcendental is recognized as the constituting source of experience can the philosophical demand to begin from originary lived experience be respected. Without this rootedness in lived experience, there can be no possible legitimacy for philosophy. The most fundamental vocation of Husserl's thinking thus obliges him to confront the problem of genesis: if genesis is not thought in terms of the profundity of the transcendental, then the transcendental is itself destined to remain purely formal, to be merely the specular accomplice of empiricism. Whence, for Derrida, the reason why Husserl is forced to take on the theme of passive genesis and, with it, the difficulty or, indeed, the impossibility of simultaneously respecting both the phenomenological data of the analyses of temporality and the demand of a pure constitution, a constitution without passivity. If, for the monadological *ego*, constituted history is always already there, Husserl is obliged to follow the path toward a transcendental historicity so as to overtake the delay of thought on being. He has to show that all constituted history stems from a transcendental historicity, from an infinite teleology that is itself nothing but pure constitution and that, as such, is preceded by nothing whatsoever. The delay of thought that questions the sense of what is already there would thus be merely methodological. The necessity of beginning with constituted sense in order to get back to the constituting origin of this sense, is a matter of fact, not of right. It is a matter of being confronted by a methodological demand that draws nothing from the juridical hierarchy between constituting and constituted. If *de facto* one is obliged to begin with the constituted, the constitutive moment always precedes it *de jure*. According to Derrida, however, what needs to be called into question is precisely this distinction between fact and right, a distinction whose relevance becomes increasingly uncertain from the moment that the necessity of the delay of the thought on being is questioned. This opens onto a dimension that exceeds all purely methodological considerations, in introducing the properly Derridean question of the link between ideality and writing.

1. Reactivating the Origin: Return Inquiry

It is not particularly surprising that Derrida, continuing his research into Husserl's work, should be interested in a text like *The Origin of Geometry*.[1] On the contrary, his choice of this text marks a continuity with the sort of questions elaborated in *The Problem of Genesis*. Indeed, he takes *The Origin of Geometry* as being the sole text in which Husserl concerns himself with the task of *reactivating the origin*. Unlike the usual method of iterative reduction, the concern of *The Origin of Geometry* is not to arrive at the sense of an already constituted object, but to retrace sense's dependence on the inaugural and foundational act by which it is created. What is in question is not the reactivation of sense but the reactivation of the *origin* of sense. *The Origin of Geometry* situates itself thus on the level of the transcendental historicity that, according to Derrida, has become the fundamental issue of Husserl's thinking.

If we can begin now to understand why the question of history is posed by Husserl in terms of a question of origin, it is perhaps harder to determine the reason why he chooses science as a paradigm for historicity, and why among all the sciences, it is geometry that is accorded such a privileged status. As far as the first question is concerned, let us note that the concepts of science and history are only apparently opposed; in truth, they are fundamentally interdependent. One can speak of history in the proper sense of the term only once something like an infinite becoming, oriented by a *telos*, appears as a spiritual form. Such a possibility arises in Greece with philosophy, that is, with "universal science, science of the universe, of the all-encompassing unity of all that is," according to a translation of the term *philosophy* that Husserl himself deems particularly relevant and faithful to its original sense.[2] And it is only on the basis of this theoretical attitude that "interest in the All" separates out into "the general forms and regions of being"[3] and that philosophy, the one true science, branches out into a multiplicity of subordinate sciences. Now this theoretical attitude would not be what it is without the idea of an infinite development and transmission of knowledge:

For the developed theoretical interest each goal acquires in advance the sense of a merely relative goal; it becomes the pathway to ever newer, ever higher goals within an infinity marked off as a universal field of work, as the "domain" of science. Science, then, signifies the idea of an infinity of tasks, of which at any time a finite number have been disposed of and are retained as persisting validities.[4]

For Husserl, the horizon of history is the infinite horizon of the accumulation of knowledge. Hence science is not only the highest form of history but itself what reveals the very possibility of a universal history in general. Without science, there would be no concept of (universal) history. As to the second question, the one concerning the privilege extended to geometry, it stems from another of the fundamental traits of Husserl's thinking. If history is determined in advance as the history of sense, then sense itself has a prior determination: the "sense of sense" is thought as *object*. Between the "form" consciousness and the "form" object there is a fundamental interdependence: "the object in general is the final category of everything that can *appear*, i.e., that can *be* for a pure consciousness in general."[5] One can understand thus the privilege accorded by Husserl to the geometrical object. Yes, it is an object but, as an object absolutely independent as regards all empiricity, as the theoretical object *par excellence*, it constitutes the paradigm of the *ideal object*. Now, Derrida grants a key value to Husserl's notion of ideality; on it the whole of Husserl's transcendental project will rest. All the aberrations of philosophy, including objectivism, the gravest threat, stem from one and the same root: blindness as regards ideality's authentic mode of being. Ideal objects are only ideal insofar as they are indefinitely repeatable while preserving the identity of their sense; as such, they *are* only to the extent that they do not *exist*, only to the extent that they are not *real* (*real*) but unreal. And yet, this non-worldly character of ideal objects ought not to be seen as referring in some way to another worldliness, as a form of existence in a *topos ouranios*, as conventional Platonism would have it.[6] The origin of ideality is nothing other than the always new possibility of repeating a productive act. What guarantees this absolute repetition is the presence of the present: the Living Present as *the form* of ideality.[7] From this point of view, the ontological reduplication of the Platonic perspective is not merely philosophically naïve, but dangerously so in that it covers over the productive activity of transcendental consciousness.

The question of the origin of geometry becomes thus a question of the *genesis of ideality*. How can an ideal sense be born? And how can it be transmitted if transmission, the *tradition* of knowing, forms part of the sense of being of every science? In order to pose such questions properly, however, the whole of factical history needs first to be neutralized. In order to respect the sense of geometry, its pretension to truth, one has to consider as inessential all the empirical circumstances of its origin. It is not a matter of conducting a historico-philological inquiry into first theorems or the first geometers, into some more or less imaginary Thales. On the contrary, every empirical knowledge supposes the prior determination of the sense of what one calls geometry *per se*, that is, of its original sense. There can be only one such sense: without the presupposition of the unity of the sense of geometry, the Husserlian approach would have no foundation. One can inquire into the history of geometry only if one grants that geometry has *a* history; it is only on the basis of a unitary sense that the shifts and revolutions within the history of geometry can be sketched out.[8] Unless one knows what geometry actually is, one cannot even know what empirical facts concern it. The question of phenomenological origin has thus an absolute juridical priority. In order for the normative independence of the ideal object to be respected and discovered, factical history has to be reduced. Only then is it possible to thematize the *transcendental* historicity of the ideal object, by avoiding all historicist or logicist confusion.

For Husserl, to inquire into the origin of geometry means to extricate its *a priori*. We know, according to an *a priori* necessity, that geometry was born at a particular time and place. Whatever the circumstances of this birth, whether they are known or not, we know that geometry *had an origin*. And it is the necessity of this origin that concerns transcendental historicity; ideal objects, inhabiting no *topos ouranios*, necessarily made a first appearance, their very ideality imposing thus the necessity of an origin. From this first *a priori*, this essence-of-the-first-time (*Erstmaligkeit*),[9] there follows a second: if geometry has an origin, it has to have arisen from a pre-geometrical experience; if geometry was indeed born, it did not always exist and another relation to the world and to experience had to have preceded it. Equally, however, we know, according to a third *a priori* necessity, that geometry originally had *the same sense* that it has today. Empirical and factual circumstances can in no way change the evidence of this identity of sense. And if this is indeed the case, it is because the *reactivating reduction*, which allows one to return to the constituting origin of sense, presupposes the *iterative reduction* that reveals the "phenomenon" of geometry. One has to begin with the sense of geometry today in order to be able to question its origin; once again, therefore, we are dealing with the essential delay of thought already at the center of Derrida's attention in *The Problem of Genesis*. The need for the reactivating reduction to be always preceded by the iterative reduction refers not to the independence of sense as regards its origin, however transcendental that may be, but to the necessity of a *fact* or an event that should not be too quickly interpreted as purely empirical or simply transcendental. If "the sense of the constituting act can only be deciphered in the web of the constituted object,"[10] the concern is not, as we have already begun to see with our reading of *The Problem of Genesis*, with a fatality that is both accidental to and outside of the sense of history, but with an inescapable necessity that announces a dimension of history as irreducible to the notion of empirical history as it is to that of transcendental historicity.

The juridical priority of a phenomenological questioning of the origin emerges only "after the fact" (*après-coup*): such is, for Derrida, the stake of the Husserlian theme of the *Rückfrage*. And it will be thus a matter of extending the signification of such an "after the fact," of questioning phenomenology's capacity to explain what it itself brings to light, that is, to explain that the path toward the transparency of sense is produced both thanks to and despite the sedimentations that conceal it. It is as if the evidence of sense could never do without the density of facts. In the *Introduction* to *The Origin of Geometry*, Derrida translates *Rückfrage* as *question en retour*, return inquiry, thereby giving notice of the importance that this notion is going to play.[11] His concern is to give a more pointed sense to a notion that, in the end, is rather common. Like *Rückfrage*, *question en retour*, the notion of return inquiry, is marked by a "postal" resonance, pointing as it does toward the distance necessary to all communication:

Like *Rückfrage*, return inquiry is asked on the basis of a first posting. From a received and *already* readable *document*, the possibility is offered me of asking again, and *in return*, about the primordial and final intention of what has been given me by tradition. The latter, which is only mediacy itself and openness to a telecommunication in general, is then, as Husserl says, "open . . . to continued inquiry."[12]

Now, it is easy enough to hear in these remarks echoes of themes whose importance is going to be central to Derrida's work up to *The Post Card*[13] and beyond, themes of sending, of the postal service, of communication at a distance, etc. Moreover, it seems to me that such themes are not readily comprehensible, at least not in their philosophical import, unless we are prepared to relate them to the work on historicity and temporality that Derrida has produced through his readings of Husserl.[14] I shall come back to this in due course. Again, however, I want to underline the extent to which Derrida's thinking forges its own path by way of an interpretation (although the word is not entirely appropriate here) of Husserl.

In *The Origin of Geometry* Husserl is engaged thus in what Derrida, following Husserl's own remarks in the *Crisis*, calls a "zigzag" way of proceeding: in order to understand the beginnings of science we have to begin with science as it is actually given to us. Conversely, however, the becoming of science as the becoming of sense remains inaccessible unless we have an understanding of its beginnings. Return inquiry shows that the origin is accessible only through the *Wechselspiel* between *archè* and *telos*: originary sense is intelligible only on the basis of the horizon of its teleological sense. All of which explains the increasing importance that Husserl will ascribe to the teleological idea, even if, as the idea of an infinite horizon, it seems to contradict one of the most fundamental principles of phenomenology, the principle of the fulfillment of intuition.

If we reach the origin only by moving back, if we never begin with the origin, it might well follow that origin, as a simple and punctual beginning, is little more than a philosophical myth, always already an effect of a non-origin, according to the celebrated formulation of *Of Grammatology*.[15] This is not what Husserl says, of course, for whom the way back to the origin will never efface the origin as a pure and absolute point of departure, but it is the point at which Derrida wants to arrive with his reading of Husserl. The shadow of genesis, in which continuity with the past always accompanies absolute emergence, continues to weigh heavily on its diaphanous sister, the origin.

2. Truth Lives Only by Surviving

The need to proceed in a zigzag, theorized by Husserl in the *Crisis*,[16] is marked clearly in the detours he is forced to take in *The Origin of Geometry*. As Derrida points out, once Husserl has freed up the various *a priori* of history, themselves nothing more than the conditions of possibility for the appearance of history itself,[17] he does not describe, as one might have expected, the origin of geometrical sense in the first time of its emergence. Rather, he considers it to be already established and confines himself to recalling the general form of all evidence, the intuitive character of which has to conform with phenomenology's "principle of principles."[18] The originary sense of geometry is no exception to this rule; it, too, has to be given "in person." For the moment, however, Husserl says nothing as to the particular contents of geometrical evidence, which he considers to be already established, and addresses himself to the genesis of objectivity in general. His question bears on the passage from the subjective experience of sense to its objective value, a passage that can only be accomplished by way of intersubjectivity. The point is to understand how sense, once it has appeared to a consciousness, becomes ideal, that is, universally valid and intelligible to everyone. Put differently, Husserl questions the conditions of possibility for ideality itself: namely, *language* and *writing*.

Considering the number of texts in which Husserl asserts the priority and independence of sense in relation to its linguistic expression and, *a fortiori*, to its consignment to writing, this move might seem surprising.[19] For Derrida, however, the logic at work here is the same as the one that governs the relation between empirical history and transcendental historicity. Just as the ideal object is independent as regards all factical history but dependent on the very *possibility* of history, so the ideal object is independent as regards all factical language, and *a fortiori* all writing, but dependent on the *possibility* of language and writing. Given that ideal objects inhabit no *topos ouranios*, their ideality is assured only by the pure possibility of their being repeated such that their sense is identical. In order for meaning to become ideal it needs, once it has arisen within an egological consciousness, to be intelligible to everyone and indefinitely enduring: "to constitute an ideal object is to put it at the permanent disposition of a pure gaze" writes Derrida.[20] So far as this function is concerned, language is not only the place of an external consignment but what, by conserving the ideal object, makes of it a common object, one henceforth available to everyone.

Now what is at stake in this consignment of sense to language is truth: there would be no truth without the accumulation and transmission of sense; language is not limited to recording truth, but it renders truth possible as a project of truth, as infinite task. It is because durability belongs essentially to truth that Derrida can write that "the conditions for its survival are included in those of its life."[21] What this means, however, is that language is necessary to a truth that, in order to live, needs to survive. No tradition will be possible without a language that can assure the memory and future of sense beyond any individual finitude.[22] What makes an object ideal is its identity and its permanence. From which it follows, however, that ideality as such will only be the always open possibility of the repetition of this identity. And the necessity of this repetition does not only concern other subjects, but is already at work within the egological consciousness itself:

Thus before being the ideality of an identical object for other subjects, sense is this ideality for *other* moments of the same subject. In a certain way, then, intersubjectivity is first the non-empirical relation of Ego to Ego, of my present present to other presents as such, i.e., as others and as presents (as past presents). Intersubjectivity is the relation of an absolute origin to other absolute origins, despite their radical alterity.[23]

This remark, made in the course of the analyses of his *Introduction* to *The Origin of Geometry*, could well pass unobserved. It takes on its full depth, however, once one reflects on the consequences that the link, already clearly established in *The Problem of Genesis*, between subjectivity, temporality and alterity will have in the developments of *Voice and Phenomena*. Phenomenological fidelity to what gives itself as the originary lived experience of temporality contests the phenomenological project on the level of its most intimate intentions. For Derrida, time will no longer be a matter of what, in Kantian terms, is called "internal sense." Exteriority and alterity work on it from within, from an inside originarily exposed to an outside, such that the clear distinction between inside and outside becomes unsustainable. This exteriority first makes its appearance in the *Introduction* to *The Origin of Geometry* through the figure of writing, and is one of the most recognizable themes of Derrida's thinking, certain stages of which I shall want to follow. For the moment, however, let me address only the form that it takes in the *Introduction* to *The Origin of Geometry*, a form that foreshadows, moreover, many of the problematics of the later work.

Now, although the possibility of language is indeed constituting of ideality, it is not sufficient. The permanence of sense cannot be confined to language alone. Language assures the circulation of sense within a given community: by relieving it of its dependence on an empirical subject, it frees the ideal object from individual subjectivity while leaving it tied to the synchrony of exchange within the community from which it arises. Although the ideal object ought to be free as regards any given community, it has to depend on only a transcendental subjectivity that can assure its universal transmission. And the only possibility for the fulfillment of this function is writing. Writing alone can emancipate sense from its present evidence, transmitting it beyond every empirical community.[24] Husserl sees the decisive function of writing in its capacity to render communication possible *in a virtual mode*.[25] The spatio-temporality of writing does not make truth fall back again into the empirical historicity from which writing has allowed it to escape; on the contrary, it brings into existence a pure, transcendental historicity. Without it, all language would remain bound to the empirical intentionality of a speaking subject or of a community of speaking subjects. Writing alone is able to attain the level of absolute objectivity, to guarantee language the permanence that it demands by freeing dialogue and the possibility of tradition from the synchrony of an empirical community. And it is on the basis of the possibility of such a virtual dialogue that transcendental subjectivity can fully appear. The condition for this to occur is writing.

3. Writing and the Transcendental Sense of Death

But how can Husserl ascribe such a role to writing? Only, according to Derrida, by distinguishing body and soul. If writing renders possible the permanence and hence the absolute objectivity of sense over and above any given community, the transcendental field that it thus freed up continues to refer to a transcendental subjectivity that is all the more apparent with the hypothesis of the absence of any empirical subject, whether singular or collective. Writing is indeed a condition of ideality, but this holds only for the pure relation that it sustains with a conscience, not for its graphic body which, as such, is only a facticity devoid of meaning. It is only through this necessary distinction that Husserl can conceive of the constitutive role of writing. Writing allows every real [*réel*] subject to be dispensed with; its specificity as regards language is its capacity to do without every act of actual reading, thereby freeing up absolute objectivity. But it is only able to do so because it brings to light the juridical possibility of its being intelligible for a transcendental subject. It is the virtual intentionality that inhabits writing that gives it a constituting function; deprived of this virtual intentionality, it is a dead letter, pure materiality belonging only to the world.

Up until this point, Derrida follows Husserl's argument quite closely. Now, however, he takes a further step, tying the absolute of *de jure* intentionality to the ineffaceable possibility of its failure, in which something like a *transcendental sense of death* is revealed:

The originality of the field of writing is its ability to dispense with, *due to its sense*, every present reading in general. But if the text does not announce its own pure dependence on a writer or reader in general (i.e., if it is not haunted by a virtual intentionality), then there is no more in the vacuity of its soul than a chaotic literalness, or the sensible opacity of a defunct designation, a designation deprived of its transcendental function. The silence of prehistoric arcana and buried civilisations, the entombment of lost intentions and guarded secrets, the illegibility of the lapidary inscription disclose *the transcendental sense of death* as what unites these things to the absolute privilege of intentionality in the very instance of its essential juridical failure [*en ce qui l'unit à l'absolu du droit intentionnel dans l'instance même de son échec*].[26]

So while Husserl's analyses aim, through the notion of writing, to separate intentional animation from the graphic sign, Derrida looks to show their inseparability. If Husserl has recourse to the objectifying function of writing, to its ability to constitute an absolute free and permanent ideality, he is able to do so only by distinguishing rigorously between the spiritual corporeality (*geistige Leiblichkeit*) and the empirical body (*Körper*) of writing. The transcendental function of the latter is entirely on the side of the living intentionality that animates it, or which, *de jure*, always can animate it. On the side of its graphic inscription, its sensible body, there is only the silence of insignificance or death, a death that is always and only *empirical*. Husserl does not doubt the legitimacy of this distinction and, because of it, quickly confers on writing the possibility of truth itself, given that the highest stake of ideality is nothing other than truth. This distinction between fact and right, between *Leib* and *Körper* (a distinction made from

the point of view of sense since writing, as Husserl would be the first to ac-
knowledge, has only one body) justifies his indifference to all empirical destruction and allows him to set aside the dangers inherent to writing. Why?
Because the ability to communicate on the virtual level not only renders
ideality possible, but also, and by the same token, renders possible all the
phenomena of forgetting, of empty repetition and of crisis against which
Husserl will continually struggle. The virtuality of writing is somewhat
ambiguous, but Husserl can cut through this ambiguity. The crisis opened
by writing, and by the sign in general,[27] is never radical and irreparable.
The death of sense is impossible. Sense, once it has arisen within egological
consciousness, does not completely disappear; it is preserved under the
form of sedimented habits and can always be reawakened. Sense and truth
are thus sheltered from all empirico-worldly destruction. A worldly catastrophe, the loss of all archives, for example, could never damage their sense
of being, which is not worldly. From which it follows, therefore, that death
has only the figure of an empirical and extrinsic accident:

Forgetfulness of truth itself will thus be nothing but the failure of an act and the abdication of a responsibility, a lapse more than a defeat.[28]

According to Derrida, Husserl takes the historical category of forgetting
back to the status of an intentional modification of the *ego*. The disappearance of intersubjective truth becomes forgetting as a particular phenomenon of the *ego*, one of its intentional modifications. Envisaged as a modification of the pure *ego*, forgetting, no matter how profound it may be, will
never be a radical loss of sense; as a forgetting, it can always be reactivated.
By contrast, all Derrida's efforts are directed toward bringing together the
virtual intentionality that inhabits writing and the ineffaceable possibility
of its failure, as well as establishing a link between historical forgetting and
the forgetting of the *ego*.[29] Therefore, the gesture is the same as the one that
led him, in *The Problem of Genesis*, to maintain that crisis is not an accident
but an internal necessity of history. There the concern was to show that
"crisis" rests on the very movement of temporalization, in which the constituted and passive moment contributes to the originary now of active
constitution, whence the necessity of rethinking in its entirety the concept
of crisis. This time, Derrida is concerned to show that the ineffaceable possibility of the loss of intentional animation in writing is indissociable from
the ideality that writing itself renders possible. The two crises, the crisis of
history and the loss of living animation, are, moreover, one and the same.

It is by deepening the sense of this crisis that Derrida is able to elaborate a concept of historicity that will be as irreducible to Husserl's transcendental historicity as it will be to Heidegger's notion of historicality.

There is still some way to go before this point can be reached, however. On the level at which the analyses of the *Introduction* to *The Origin of Geometry* are situated, the notion of writing shown to be constituting of ideality is still writing in the habitual sense of the term: a technology of memorialization. What those analyses show is that the transcendental, in order to come into effect, has to pass through an exteriority (and I want for the moment to leave this word deliberately indeterminate), an exteriority that will prove to be difficult to reduce. Before being able to demonstrate this rigorously, however, Derrida has to confront the decidedly difficult task of deconstructing the final basis of Husserlian phenomenology: the self-presence of transcendental consciousness in the Living Present. It is the Living Present that allows Husserl, in the last instance, to gloss over the possibility of an empirical destruction of sense and to consider death, like the phenomena of crisis and forgetting, as inessential and external to the trajectory of truth. This trajectory will lead Derrida to elaborate the notion of *arche-writing* through that of writing in the usual sense of the term. He will want to show that everything threatening and dangerous about writing is already present in language and, above all, in the intimacy of transcendental consciousness itself: its Living Present.[30] The logic that wants to situate writing outside of language, which will, in turn, be situated outside the self-presence of consciousness, will have to be deconstructed.[31] Something like a "transcendental sense of death," which we have seen just seen emerging, will need to be read as haunting the "life" of the Living Present. But if that proves to be the case, then the very notions of life and death, like those of transcendental and empirical, will themselves have to be rethought.

The *Introduction* to *The Origin of Geometry* takes up by other means the questions that were already at work in *The Problem of Genesis* and allows Derrida to expand upon them. In the earlier text, it was around the notion of crisis that Derrida gathered everything that was, for him, problematic in Husserl's history of philosophy. The crisis in question is the threat of the forgetting or the covering up (*récouvrement*) of the constituting activity of the transcendental consciousness. What is threatened in history is not the development of knowledge, the progress of the sciences, but the loss of *sense*; we run the risk of employing symbolisms that become empty from the moment that their rootedness, their origin and so their sole source of right and value in transcendental subjectivity is forgotten. The teleological idea that opens history to the horizon of its sense, to the infinite task of reason (which can no longer be identified as practical or theoretical, once *theoria* is envisaged as the *telos* of humanity) is threatened. As regards this crisis, the question that Derrida raises is at once simple and disarming: How is it possible for the empirical to threaten the transcendental if both terms are to retain the sense that the entire philosophical tradition, including Husserl himself, have always ascribed to them? On the basis of this question, he undertakes to bring crisis and history together, although in so doing he can no longer trust the concepts of history or crisis, nor, to an even greater extent, can he trust the whole system of distinctions upon which such concepts are based. As we have already seen, that to which we come back in the last instance is time itself. The crisis is set in motion by time, by the passivity that always inhabits it and that is necessary to the very appearance of the originary movement of active constitution. At this level of analysis, however, not only is passivity irreducible but the very distinction between passivity and activity, like the separation between constituted and worldly, loses its relevance.

4. The Crisis of History: Fact, *Eidos*, and Fault

The theme of crisis is taken up and developed most extensively in the *Introduction* to *The Origin of Geometry*. Precisely why this has to be the case becomes clear once we consider that, in Husserl's eyes, the way in which *The Origin of Geometry* proceeds is paradigmatic of the only possible response to the danger simultaneously threatening history, science and reason. And since, as we have seen, it is only the fundamental unity of these three dimensions that allows us to envisage something like a trajectory of humanity, it is, in each case, the *same* danger calling for the *same* response. There is crisis each time that we do not inquire in return toward the production that originally gives meaning; as such, the only possible response to the crisis is precisely this return inquiry itself. *Rückfrage* is the very gesture of the full assumption of responsibility because the response *has* to be made by way of reason and sense. This is precisely what sets Husserl on the path of the reactivating reduction. And yet, the concept of crisis that he puts in play is not so straightforward. Derrida identifies three different meanings of the term: sometimes it denotes a subjective fault, sometimes an accidental forgetting, and sometimes, although rather less often, an eidetic necessity.[32] The exemplary figure here is Galileo: his goal of an infinite mathematization of nature, which Husserl situates at the origin of the modern spirit that is under threat, rests on a "fateful omission."[33] To what is Husserl referring here? To the fact that Galileo, at the very moment that he opens a new chapter in the history of reason, neglects to question the tradition from which his project draws its sense, to the fact that he fails to inquire in return into the origin of idealising production.

Now although this forgetting to inquire *in return* is a "fateful omission," Husserl himself in turn "forgets," according to Derrida, to question the signification of such an omission, never really interrogating the sense of this forgetting, the threat of which is nonetheless recognized as always present. Depending on context, the omission (*Versäumnis*) of the *Rückfrage* amounts to an empirical necessity that stems from individual or social psychology; it is thus of the order of factical history, its necessity external and contingent as regards the history of reason, leaving its sense untouched. Equally, however, the omission of *Rückfrage* can take the form of a "radical ethico-philosophical fault," referring thus to a culpable abdication of philosophical responsibility, even to a thoroughgoing renunciation of freedom. Finally, though, the omission can assume the figure of an eidetic necessity: the constitution of sense prescribes its accumulation and transmission; without the sedimentations of sense, no history would be possible. This necessity is simultaneously valorized and devalorized by Husserl: it is positive insofar as it allows for the progress of science and the infinite becoming of reason, dangerous because it implies the forgetting of origins. It is, as Derrida puts it, a truly "threatening value."[34] Now it is precisely the unity of these three significations that interests Derrida here. Apparently incompatible, they allow us to divine a common provenance through which history itself is announced:

It is a matter of course that these three significations, apparently irreducible to one another, are conceived by Husserl on the basis of one and the same latent intuition. History itself is what this intuition announces. Even if we managed simultaneously and without contradiction to think the unitary ground on the basis of which these three propositions can be received, it is history itself that would be thought. But then the possibility of a crisis of reason would disappear, the negativity of which ought to be unthinkable in itself.[35]

"History itself" is given to thought insofar as a historicity that rebels against every archeo-teleological horizon appears; that is, a historicity that eludes the domination of the present as a *form* of time. We have already seen that, for Derrida, the *eidos* of time, time as a form, effaces every properly temporal dimension. Now, a history understood within an archeo-teleological horizon is a history that knows only the present: either the actual present or its two modifications of the same form, the past present and the future present. In other words, it is a history that does not know time. Any such history is, therefore, a false history, a fiction of time. By contrast, "history itself," *history as such*, is thus no more than a history that knows time, on the condition that it know neither *archè* nor *telos*.[36] Within the carefully determined context of the *Introduction* to *The Origin of Geometry*, this is precisely what Derrida undertakes to think by way of the essential limit of the Husserlian project of a thoroughgoing reactivation.

The reactivating reduction, to which Husserl entrusts the task of leading us back to the origin of sense, not only always presupposes an iterative reduction—by letting us glimpse in this way that the "fact" is not outside sense—but is itself necessarily finite. Husserl is well aware of the fact that the power of this form of memory, the reactivation, is a finite one. Geometry, like any other science, implies a level of development such that no one can effect the complete reactivation of its sense by moving back through the connections between its theorems to its arche-premises.[37] If such a reactivation *were* possible, moreover, it would render unworkable all geometric progress, drawing its history to a halt. The very structure of geometry, the internal dependency of its theorems, renders all actual reactivation unthinkable. The power of the reactivating reduction cannot go beyond the finitude of the individual or the community.[38] No one can fully take on the origin of sense or, consequently, sense itself. From which Derrida is able to draw the conclusion that the possibility of *a pure history of sense* is a decidedly unlikely one.[39] Now, if Husserl is able to relegate to the background any worries that he may have about this, it is only by appealing to teleology; doing so, however, he neutralizes, according to Derrida, any historicity that might appear. In effect, for Husserl the finitude of the reactivation does not call its value into question: infinite memory, access back to the origins, is a teleological horizon that has a sense as such. In the *Introduction* to *The Origin of Geometry*, just as in *The Problem of Genesis*, Derrida underlines the decisive role that the infinite Idea plays in Husserl's analyses, a role that, in his opinion, is an essentially defensive one. Acknowledging the evidence (*Einsichtigkeit*) of an infinite Idea, despite the *a priori* impossibility of having an adequate intuition of it, transgresses thus phenomenology's "principle of principles"; such is the price Husserl pays in order to defend his idealism.[40] For Derrida, however, the price is too high, since recourse to a teleological Idea is what prevents phenomenology from thinking through the consequences of the "phenomena" that it nonetheless brings to light. Were the necessary and irreducible finitude of the reactivation *not* to be "neutralized" in the name of an infinite idea, it might open onto *another* reflection on history:

> Without that essential concealment of origins and within the hypothesis of an all-powerful reactivation, what would consciousness of historicity be? Also, no doubt, that consciousness be nothing, if it was radically prohibited access to origins. But, so that history may have its proper density, must not then the darkness which engulfs the "original premises" (it can be penetrated but never dissipated) not only hide the fact but also the instituting sense? And must not the "critical" forgetfulness of origins be the faithful shadow in truth's advance rather than an accidental aberration? The distinction between fact and sense (or the de facto and the de jure) would be effaced in the sense-investigation of a primordial finitude.[41]

Although, for Husserl, finitude can appear only by way of the Idea of an infinite history, for Derrida recourse to any such Idea is precisely what prevents a thinking of *either* finitude *or* of history. Moreover, it is less a matter of disagreeing with Husserl than with inflecting his discourse in another direction. The ambiguity of the teleological Idea is the same as the ambiguity of the absolute *Logos*,[42] envisaged by Husserl sometimes as the fullness of an infinite expressed *through* transcendental historicity, sometimes as only the polar *telos* of transcendental historicity *itself*:

> In the first case, the essential and present plenitude of an infinity would be *unfolded* only in an historical discursiveness from which it would let itself be *derived*. In the second case, infinity would be only the indeterminate *openness* to truth and to phenomenality for a subjectivity that is always finite in its factual being.[43]

For Derrida, this alternative ties in with the one that opposes a speculative idealism to an authentic transcendental phenomenology that forges its path through concepts borrowed from metaphysics. As such, it is a matter less of choosing between these two possibilities than of simultaneously thinking both of them on the basis of a more fundamental unity. The *Logos* may seem to *traverse* history, only insofar as history is empirical and constituted, but to the contrary it is only the Pole of transcendental historicity itself. The *Logos* may well be dia-historical or meta-historical in relation to empirical history, but it "is merely the pure movement of its own historicity."[44] It shares thus the identical condition of all ideality: it will never be a real transcendence.

Now, the figure of history that is taking shape is that of a passage, the passage of an originary *Logos* toward a polar *Telos* that exist only in this passage itself, in the indefinite referral of one to the other:

> *If there is any history*, then historicity can be only the passage of Speech [*Parole*], the pure tradition of a primordial *Logos* toward a polar *Telos*. But since there can be nothing outside the pure historicity of that passage, since there is no Being which has sense outside of this historicity or escapes its infinite horizon, since Logos and Telos *are* nothing outside the *interplay* (*Weschselspiel*) of their reciprocal inspiration, this signifies then that the *Absolute is Passage*.[45]

And yet, the absolute of this passage is the absolute of a danger. Consciousness does not travel a pre-existent path but, in a double movement wherein "every venturing is a conversion and every return to the origin a daring strike out toward the horizon," "invents" its own path. Yet if sense dwells nowhere but in the absolute nature of this passage, it is always possible that sense can lose its way. The word that bears it and vouches for it cannot be sheltered from the inauthenticity of a language, nor from a speaking being's renunciation of its ethical responsibility; this, then, is the worry that haunts Husserl. For Derrida, by contrast, the fact that no word can ever take on sense in its entirety is simultaneously the consequence and the very possibility that there is history at all. If history is the absolute of a passage and if this passage is itself the absolute of a danger, then the danger and the crisis have to be thought not only as what threaten history, but also as what render it possible. For once, it is negativity that is "an ambiguous value."

What took, in *The Problem of Genesis*, the form of a complication of origin, is articulated in the *Introduction* to *The Origin of Geometry* in terms of the irreducible *Wechselspiel* between *archè* and *telos*: the delay of thought on being takes the form of tradition (and history) as an inquiry necessarily *in return*. The space (and the time) of a tradition is marked and constituted in relation to an origin from which one never departs, and to an end, a *telos*, that is never reached, an origin and an end that draw their meaning only within a passage constantly referring from one to the other, without ever being truly able to settle on either one.

What needs to be retained above all from the *Introduction* to *The*

Origin of Geometry, however, is the appearance of the theme of ideality in its relation to language and to writing. Husserl's demand that the transcendental be thought as the *constituting* source of a lived experience and not as an empty formalism, is tied in the *Introduction* to *The Origin of Geometry* to ideality's authentic mode of being. If the transcendental is not a world of *a priori* laws outside of time, it can only be the always renewed possibility of repeating an ideal object such that its sense remains identical. The possibility of this absolute repetition that opens ideality is the Living Present, the self-presence of transcendental life. The notions of the transcendental, of ideality, of presence, of "life,"[46] are so interrelated that we cannot touch on any one of them without touching on all. By insisting upon the constituting role of language and writing in relation to ideality, Derrida gives the first impetus to his later strategy. It will be a matter of showing how, within ideality itself, the contrary notions of such a chain— the empirical, absence, death, etc.—are themselves already at work, thereby calling into question the sense of the oppositional structure itself.

There is, however, one more important aspect that needs to be underlined. The notion of ideality will remain central for Derrida, too. With one difference: the paradigm of ideality will no longer be the geometrical object, but *signification*, in the broadest sense of the term. And it is precisely this difference that will allow Derrida to gather under the same heading his analyses of Husserl and his work on writing, on writing as a technique of memorialization, certainly, but also on writing as literary and philosophical writing, that is, fundamentally, as an experience of language.[47] Which has, as we shall see, some significant consequences.

1.3

Forgetting and Memory (of Ideality)

For Derrida, the originality of Husserl's transcendental project lies in the intuition that truth has to have an origin *in* time, even if its value does not depend *on* time. Truth has to be born, otherwise it could not be the product of a subject, however transcendental that subject may be. And yet, this birth can in no way affect the sense of the being of truth. Were it to do so, truth would not be truth. And it is in the tension that exists between these two necessities that the notion of ideality is held. The philosophical project of truth cannot be rescued if its constitutive link to the transcendental activity of consciousness goes undemonstrated. Ideality is the constitution, tradition and reactivation of the origin of sense; if ideality does not exist, either in this world or some other, it is because it depends on a constitutive *activity*. Every ontological reduplication, every objectivism, every conventional Platonism, are the very forms of the straying (*Abweg*) of philosophy, because they conceal the link between truth and the (transcendental) subject. Ideality, *which does not exist*, exposes the link: it is merely the possibility of the infinite repetition of sense by the act of a subject that intends it. For Husserl, the interdependence of repetition and presence is incontestably evident. What is repeated is presence as the face-to-face relation of the object with consciousness in the presence of the now as the form of time. The *origin* of truth in time—its birth—and the becoming of truth—its tradition—are both thought by Husserl from out of the horizon of the present: from the present of the origin of sense, transmitted in the present of the reactivation of sense, toward a future present that is the *telos* of history as accumulation and transmission of knowledge.

This privileging of the present has, however, the effect of limiting the scope of Husserl's intuition as to the connection between truth and time. The present as *form* of time implies that there has and that there will have been only the present. Temporality is reabsorbed into an *eidos*. For Derrida, by contrast, time is what can be said to elude all form whatsoever: *time cannot be present.* The movement of temporalization carries with it the irreducible passivity of the past, and the surprise, equally irreducible and unmasterable, of the future.[1] We are forever caught between "the irreparability of the past" and "the imprevidibility of the future."[2] Were there to be such a thing as an experience of time, such would be it. And the present can only be the (never punctual) moment of the passage between past and future whose respective passivity and surprise are equally irreducible. Only through passivity of the past can there be a future as the opening onto the new. Rather than thinking the past and the future as a modification of the present, the present must be thought on the basis of the irreparability of the past and the imprevidibility of the future. Time, when it is not eternity, is both ineffaceable passivity and surprise. This is the direction indicated by Derrida's affirmation of the temporal character of the *eidos* of time. Husserl, however, while stressing the birth of truth in time in order to tie it to transcendental activity, remains faithful to the form of the present. And although he does undertake to think genesis, he thinks, according to Derrida, only in terms of one of its implications, that of the originary sense of temporality, and not its other, which is nonetheless inseparable from the first: the originary temporality of sense itself. The reduction of time to an *eidos* or to a *telos*, which amounts to much the same thing, makes its most obvious appearance in Husserl's thinking of transcendental historicity.

Transcendental historicity should account for the need for truth to be born, for its having an origin in a time and a place. According to Husserl, however, this inscription of truth in a time and a place in no way affects truth itself. He wants to tie truth to the constitutive possibility of its having appeared at a particular time and place, yet this time and place are in no way to retain their empirical singularity, being only the *pure possibility* of a *pure time* and a *pure place*. The singularity of empirical time and empirical place are there only to be reduced in the operation of the *epochè*. Once truth has been tied to an origin, however, it becomes difficult to estrange it after the fact (*après-coup*) from this empirical and hence unique and irreplaceable time and place from which it actually emerged. Therein lies the whole riddle of the *eidos* of Europe, previously evoked. The *eidos* of Europe is what resists imaginary variation. If the singularity of a date and a place, and hence of every empirical date and place, is effaced in favor of their pure transcendental possibility, then history, even in its transcendental dimension, becomes little more than the contrived scene of the appearance of something that essentially has and always will have been there, of a present that, in order to be absolutely present, absolutely living, hopelessly resembles nothing so much as an eternity without time.

Husserl's difficulties in thinking the originarity of the temporality of sense are highlighted by his hesitation when faced with the crisis of the "European sciences," which is the crisis of history. The infinite becoming of transcendental historicity as the constitution, tradition and reactivation of sense, is under threat and has always been under threat, even in moments of the greatest progress of knowledge, and never more so than today. But whence the danger? True, Husserl himself ties the life of truth to its survival, since there could be no truth that could not be transmitted out beyond its origin into this realm of *survival* that constitutes the infinite tradition of knowledge. But what is it that worries him, if no empirical event, no empirical crisis—not even the destruction of the world—could damage the pure possibility of the tradition of sense? If transcendental historicity, the life of sense, is not threatened even by the hypothetical prospect of world catastrophe, a hypothesis that merely shows all the more clearly the distinction in principle between the empirical and the transcendental, what place can there be for the idea of crisis? The only possible answer is that it is the transcendental itself that is under threat and, since this threat cannot come from the world—which, by definition, is unable to affect it—it has to come from within itself. As such, the form taken by this danger cannot be that of the destruction, however complete it may be, of the worldly archives of knowledge and the whole empirical world that produces and preserves them. The only form it can take is that of the forgetting of sense, *the transcendental forgetting of truth*. And it is against the possibility of just such a transcendental forgetting that Husserl's best efforts will be directed. The forgetting that threatens in the crisis of history is never envisaged as a historical category, but shown to be a modification of the *ego*.[3] With this, then, Husserl sets his mind at rest: sense, once it has arisen, can certainly coincide with sedimentations, can certainly be forgotten, but this forgetting, this covering over, can never be radical. Sense and its origin can always be reactivated and hence always *have* to be so. The crisis of the European sciences stems from an ethical abdication. What has to be awakened is the *responsibility* for sense.

In fact, the problem has simply been displaced. If the being of truth is ultimately immune from being damaged by forgetting, would it be such a serious problem if, at a given moment, one were to forget, since any such forgetting could never be anything more than a momentarily distracted gaze, turned slightly away, that could *always and in principle* be turned back toward the forgotten truth? Indeed one might think that for Husserl what is really threatened is not actually truth *per se*, but the ethical responsibility of subjectivity as regards truth. And even this always possible ethical failure is never irreparable. For Husserl, transcendental forgetting is an impossible category: the form of transcendental life is the Living Present, and no living present can accommodate within itself, within its intimate relation to itself, a true, irreparable forgetting. Such a forgetting makes no sense whatsoever if time is only a succession of presents. For what could one forget, without being able to bring it back to memory at any moment, if one has lived only a succession of present instants? Yet for all that, Husserl's anxiety remains.

We have already seen that, for Derrida, it is the question of the crisis of history that most clearly brings the irreducible contamination of the empirical and the transcendental to the fore. It is the movement of temporalization itself that entails the crisis as the crisis of the contamination of the empirical and the transcendental. This contamination, however, is not a formal structure.[4] It suggests that if sense and truth do have an origin in a time and a place, then this time and this place cannot be erased after the fact (*après-coup*) from this origin; they do not free up an essence with no debt to the time and the place from which it arose. And if the relation of *eidos* to time is not an external and accidental one, this requires us to rethink not only the concept of time but *also* that of *eidos*. If the inscription of truth in a time and a place is necessary to its origin, all the consequences of this have to be thought. Can a truth that is born still be thought as a truth that knows only the present? If it is born, really born, can the possibility of dying, of being forgotten, be entirely estranged from it? Insofar as the life of truth is tied to its survival, does survival have to be thought as the always repeated presence of life or should life *as such* be thought as being already a form of survival? Would this not imply that life is not *in itself* absolutely living, that it experiences a certain work of death?

Now, there is something in ideality itself that makes a sign in this direction, namely the relation that it sustains with language and writing. Language and writing, the moment of the sign, are both necessary to the constitution of ideality but, according to a gesture analogous to the one regarding time, Husserl draws from this necessity only a *pure possibility*. Language and writing, themselves the site of the inscription of truth in a time and a space, ought only to inscribe truth in order to render it immediately free from every (empirical) time and every (empirical) world.[5] What we are again seeing is the strange movement by which truth has to originate in *a* time and *a* place in order to exonerate itself of *every* time and *every* place. It is not a matter of putting into question the possibility that a truth, a sense or an event can clear a path *through time*, be transmitted, leave a heritage or a trace, in short, the possibility that it can *make* sense; but in particular, this possibility has to traverse time, not dispense with it. For Husserl, it is true, supratemporality (*Überzeitlichkeit*) or timelessness (*Zeitlosigkeit*) are defined in their transcendence or their negativity only in relation to worldly temporality and, once this latter has been reduced, appear as omnitemporality (*Allzeitlichkeit*), itself a concrete mode of temporality in general.[6] What is in question, however, is the very possibility and rigor of precisely these sorts of phenomenological distinctions.

Language and writing are the site of the inscription of truth in a time, in a time that can no longer dispense with a world. The question of language and writing that we saw appearing in the *Introduction* to *The Origin of Geometry* and that will be at the heart of *Speech and Phenomena*, is not a different question from that of genesis that constitutes the enduring preoccupation of Derrida's first work on phenomenology; in both cases, it is the same question, just worked differently and displaced. In *The Problem of Genesis* it was the movement of temporalization that carried with it the irreducible contamination of the empirical and transcendental, a contamination most acutely marked by the notion of the crisis of history, which, in order to be thought, had to be shielded from its purely negative dimension and which brought to light the necessary implication of the empirical and the transcendental in an existence that, although *in the world*, could nonetheless open onto truth. In the *Introduction* to *The Origin of Geometry*, the same question is inflected more fundamentally in the direction of transcendental history and ideality, notions that are in fact inseparable: as the constitution, transmission and reactivation of the origin of an *eidos* that exists neither in this world nor in some other, ideality can no longer do without historicity as the possibility of origin. What is again being put into question, therefore, is the separation of the empirical and the transcendental. Language and writing, themselves constitutive of ideality because assuring the pure possibility of repetition and of the tradition of sense beyond its empirical emergence, reveal in their very capacity for idealization something that threatens the purity of the division. If they can secure the repetition of sense beyond its empirical emergence, they do so only because they can function in the absence of the intention that animates them. And yet, this functioning on the virtual level can only achieve ideality by protecting it from the absence and disappearance of every *empirical* world and subject. The only thing that interests Husserl is the possibility of *intentional animation*, the purely spiritual face of language and writing in their relation to consciousness. The factical body of the sign is abandoned to the world, having no function and no signification. According to Derrida, however, *the absolute right of the intentionality of living animation is bound to the ineffaceable possibility of its failure.* And it is the possibility of this failure that allows one to think something like a transcendental sense of death. This transcendental sense of death is only a *figure of time*, of a time removed from the domination of the present. But if everything that *The Problem of Genesis* had sought to gather on the basis of the movement of temporalization is now taken up and pushed in the direction of the question of language and writing, it is because the inscription of truth in time is also an inscription in *space*, in the *space of a world*, in the space of an outside that holds onto its reference to a materiality: one can no longer separate a certain temporality from a certain spatiality. It is, moreover, also because of a certain conception of language that renders the philosophical project of a transcendental thinking possible in the first place. And with that, we arrive at the stakes of the analyses of *Speech and Phenomena*.

1. Difference Dwells in Language Alone

So far as Derrida is concerned, the Husserlian notion of ideality is a *determination of being*. In a gesture that is simultaneously ethical and theoretical, Husserl asserts the *non-reality* and the *non-existence* of ideality in order to underline its irreducibility to any form of empirical existence or reality, placing it thus alongside the Platonic determination of the *ontos on* as *eidos*.[7] Ideality is a determination of being, of being as presence. Yet this presence, existing neither in an empirical world nor in a transcendent one (which could not have the status of the transcendental), is only able to be presence because of an infinite power of repetition. This capacity is not the capacity of an empirical subject: no worldly subject is open to the possibility of infinite repetition. No worldly subject is immortal, all empirical existence being contingent and fated to disappear. As such, there is no empirical subject that could protect the omnitemporal value of truth. And yet, the transcendental subject is not a subject *other* than the empirical I, its more or less spectral double. The gap between the empirical and the transcendental does not exist; rather, their difference is one of a strange "parallelism" that tolerates no ontological redoubling.[8] The difference between transcendental and empirical life is absolute. Yet it is a division that separates *nothing*.

The transcendental is always defined by Husserl as the act of a living. The source of sense is a living act, the act of a living being, *Lebendigkeit*. Such transcendental life, however, only appears once empirical life, and even the region of purely psychical life, has been bracketed. Since empirical life cannot dispense with death, transcendental life appears only at the price of reducing empirical life. And this is precisely why the last instance of phenomenology is not that of the purely psychic. Phenomenological psychology ought to fix the sense of what is usually called the *psyche*, but this eidetic and *a priori* science ought not to be identified with transcendental phenomenology. Even if the domain of pure psychic experience coincides with transcendental experience, the difference still remains. The subject of transcendental experience is not the *psyche*, which remains a worldly region, but the "soulless [*seelenloses*] consciousness."[9] It is precisely this non-substantial difference that allows phenomenology to avoid being transcendental psychologism, to put a distance between them, a distance that must be *nothing*: "if the world needs the *supplement of a soul*, the soul, which is in the world, needs this *supplementary nothing* which is the transcendental and without which no world would appear."[10] And yet, between the *psyche*, which is in the world, and the soulless consciousness, which is not, the covering over is total.

Where then is the difference, what is it that sustains the parallelism that defines the relation? For Derrida, this parallelism is what bears the entire weight of the distance between the eidetic and the phenomenological reductions: without the "invisible distance" that lies between these two acts of *epochè*, the very possibility of transcendental phenomenology would be under threat. It is this distance that allows us to think the transcendental I both as being radically different from my empirical I *and* in no way distinguishable from it. Now, so far as Derrida is concerned, the distance that ought to separate what dwells in the world from what does not—without, for all that, dwelling anywhere else—takes place in language alone: *the difference between the empirical and the transcendental,* he writes, *does not reside in the world,* "but only in language, in the transcendental disquietude of language."[11] Language is singled out thereby as the fundamental condition of possibility of phenomenological difference. All the distinctions through which Husserl will want to construct and protect the possibility and rigor of the phenomenological project take place in language: language alone can assure the difference between fact and right, between worldly life and transcendental life, to say nothing of all the other divisions in which phenomenology finds its *raison d'être.*

And yet, the question of the possibility of a transcendental *Logos,* of an explicit meditation on the essence of language in general, is something that is continually set to one side in Husserl's philosophical reflections.[12] The unity between ordinary language or the language of traditional metaphysics and phenomenological language is never broken nor called into question by Husserl. According to Derrida, phenomenology's concern with language is limited to placing traditional concepts in quotation marks, a strategy unlikely to be enough to force a break with a heritage.[13] Take, for instance, the concept of life. The unity of living runs through all of phenomenology's concepts. After empirical life, even the purely psychic, has been bracketed, Husserl still uncovers a life, the life of the transcendental subject, the Living Present. And it is to this unity, which appears to escape any form of reduction, that Derrida addresses himself. To maintain, as Husserl does, that the concepts of empirical and transcendental life are radically heterogeneous, that they sustain only a metaphoric relation, amounts to little more than a displacement of the question: we are still left with the concept of life as the common root of this metaphor.[14] As Husserl is well aware, if it is language's role to assure the non-substantial distance between the empirical and the transcendental, then "we must stringently assemble and protect in our discourse" its "frivolous, subtle, 'seemingly trivial nuances'" for it is in these that "the right and wrong paths [*Wege und Abwege*] of philosophy" will be most decisively played out.[15] It is only by way of such "trivial" and apparently futile "nuances" that philosophy can reassure itself as to the possibility and rigor of its discourse. But are quotation marks, whether visible or invisible, around a concept enough to guarantee the rigor of a distinction? When, at the end of a patient elaboration of a whole series of distinctions, we find ourselves again before a transcendental life, we cannot but wonder about this concept nor can we content ourselves with maintaining its absolute heterogeneity as regards empirical life. Why, then, the same word? Does the unity of the word, if it is not the unity of a concept, mean anything at all? Can we really be sure about this? Might not the concept of life, instead of being abandoned to pretranscendental naïveté, point toward an ultra-transcendental concept of life?[16]

These are the sorts of questions that Derrida will want to raise. What is already clear, however, is that this notion of the ultra-transcendental is going to be irreducible to the division between the empirical and the transcendental, a division that it overflows while also rendering it possible. This ultra-transcendental must take into account *both* the demand that one tried to respect through a thought of the transcendental, *and* the demand that one tried to respect through a thought of the empirical. Taking both of these demands into account implies that neither can be maintained as they were formulated in the history of philosophy—the best-known theme of Derridean deconstruction. But it implies something else as well. It implies that the "contamination" of the empirical and the transcendental, far from being an empty and formal structure, is in fact an expression of fidelity to a double heritage that is *also* a double demand. If transcendental life is indeed disclosed through the reduction of empirical life, it is because the latter is finite and contingent, a life that knows death, beyond itself, at its end, but first and foremost *through* itself. There is no empirical life that is not worked by death from the outset.[17] By contrast, transcendental life would be a life that knows nothing of death in the sense that it does not have an end, but also and above all in the sense that there would be no death within it, that its life would be subject to no limit: absolutely living, absolutely present, it would know no interval from itself, no absence, no distance, no forgetting. And this is why, for Husserl, the only possible death is empirical death, while the transcendental is the absolute of life.

Derrida's attempt to make a transcendental sense of death appear is an attempt to show that everything that damages empirical life, the death that works it, cannot be reduced to the *philosophical* dimension of the empirical; that is, to the order of a facticity and a contingency that would be outside of what is worthy of being thought, of the determination of a veritable being that is always beyond the empirical, whatever form this beyond might take.[18] In fact, the notion of a transcendental sense of death marks the point at which the division between the empirical and the transcendental is no longer assured, the point at which its limits become blurred, the point of insecurity at which a discourse can no longer "protect itself" by way of "seemingly trivial nuances,"[19] the point at which one can no longer speak of a transcendental life on the one hand and an empirical death on the other (which, if followed through to its logical consequence, would suggest not only that there is no transcendental death, but that there is no empirical life either, or at least no empirical life worthy of the name of life). All of which implies that what has to be thought is a death that is in fact irreducible, as is the case with all empirical death, but one that no longer bears the name death. Why? Because in the history of philosophy this name has always meant that this irreducibility is merely factual, hence contingent, and hence divested of sense and value.[20] Reciprocally, moreover, it implies the need to think a life that can survive itself, a life not condemned to disappear without trace into the singularity of its event, a life that keeps its sense and its promise, but one that should no longer bear the name of *transcendental* life since its sense and its promise run through its death, a death that they cannot dispense with since they are, to a certain extent, possible only through this very mortality. Life—singular life—its sense and its promise, survives itself only through death.[21]

If the question of life and death is tied to the question of language, to the unity of a word ("life") whose inclusion in quotation marks is perhaps not enough to assure it a heterogeneous sense, to guarantee the rigor of a division between its transcendental and its worldly senses, then this link between the question of life and of language will have more than one *raison d'être* and more than one consequence. We have already seen that the non-substantial difference between these two senses of the word "life" is one rooted in language alone. Now although Husserl never actually thematizes the possibility of a transcendental *Logos per se*, although he never actually interrogates the heritage of originary and metaphysical language (his anxiety over the subtle nuances vital to all philosophical discourse notwithstanding), what he does do is develop a reflection on language, and theoretical language. The basic distinctions that he establishes as regards a pure logical grammar in the first of the *Logical Investigations* will guide all his subsequent work. So much so, indeed, that Derrida considers the notion of language elaborated there to be what makes the entire phenomenological reduction possible in the first place. If the link is not made explicit by Husserl himself—which would not have been possible, given that the notion of phenomenological reduction postdates the *Investigations*—the conceptual premises of that work, especially its premises concerning the problem of signification and language in general, reveal "the germinal structure of the whole of Husserl's thought."[22]

The concern, then, is to think a language that can protect the difference between the transcendental and the empirical, that is, a language that can guarantee ideality as the infinite repetition of sense. Now, language is able to protect ideality only if it has no need to pass through the externality of a world. It implies, of course, a certain externality, that of the departure from the self of a noetic act that is directed toward a noematic sense, a departure that should be repeated, reflected, in another departure toward the linguistic expression of sense. But this double departure from the self, first of an act, then of a sense, should remain proximate to itself; it should open a peculiar sort of outside that would be wholly within, an outside that opens onto no exteriority.[23] Derrida will try to show that such a language, which would, in fact, be a purely phenomenological language, a language that completes the phenomenological reduction by allowing consciousness to be present to itself and to the ideal object toward which it is directed, is a language no longer *worthy* of the name. He will try to show that, on the contrary, language exists and that, from the moment that it does, it resists all reduction; and along with language, a certain time and a certain space that can no longer be called empirical, simply empirical, also resist reduction. This way of putting into question the distinctions of Husserl's pure logical grammar opens onto another conception of language and ideality, one that will allow him to think the contamination of life and death and this double fidelity to the transcendental and the empirical which has, as we shall see, thus far been discussed in a rather allusive fashion.

2. Memory and Forgetting of Ideality

The first of the *Logical Investigations* opens with the "essential distinctions" that will guide the later analyses. These distinctions rest in their entirety on Husserl's insistence that the word "sign," *Zeichen*, has a double sense: sign can mean *Ausdruck*, expression, or it can mean *Anzeichen*, indication. These distinctions are meant to be purely phenomenological; they are not supposed to imply any preconstituted knowledge, and this absence of all presupposition ought to assure their validity. Although the point of departure can only be located in the *Faktum* of language, the attention to the contingency of every example will nonetheless allow the results to hold equally for the theory of knowledge, that is, to be independent of the factual existence of languages and the people who speak them. From which it follows that the register of the phenomenological analyses is not that of contingent existence, but that of the imagination and of the mode of possibility. Phenomenological vigilance thus sees itself as devoid of all presuppositions and, above all, of all specifically metaphysical presuppositions. Now, according to Derrida, such vigilance is ultimately insufficient, not because it fails to take all the necessary precautions, but because of its very form. "Phenomenological vigilance" is metaphysical from the outset. This is clear in the avowed intentions of Husserl himself, who wants to restore the originary sense of metaphysics in opposition to the degeneration that has struck it down in the course of its history.[24] The very idea of a theory, and of a theory of knowledge, is a philosophical idea that, far from being sheltered from all presuppositions, is, on the contrary, determined by presuppositions whose legitimacy has never been explicitly questioned. Particularly so with respect to language.

With this, Derrida announces the most general form of his question.[25] Husserl's attempt to redefine the relation between pure grammar and pure logic in order to constitute a pure and meta-empirical morphology of the system of rules that allows a discourse in general to be recognized, to know whether it has a sense, whether it is not struck by falseness or by contradiction (*Widersinnigkeit*), aims not at the entire *a priori* of language, but merely at its logical *a priori*.[26] Husserl wants to elaborate a pure *logical* grammar, but this pure logical grammar not only outlines a region within language itself but designates the normativity of a *telos*; it determines an essence which is the very destination of language in general.[27] This destination of language corresponds, according to Derrida, to a determination of being and of being as presence: and from this point of view, phenomenology is inscribed in the history of metaphysics, in Heidegger's sense of the term.[28]

We have seen that ideality as an always open possibility of repetition of sense in its sameness ought to serve to unveil the constitutive activity of consciousness against all objectivism. But the act of this consciousness is only the constitution of an (ideal) object. Self-consciousness appears only in the relation to an object whose presence it can guard and repeat. The solidarity between consciousness and its (theoretical) object is an evidence that goes unquestioned by Husserl. The privilege of the object as a paradigm of knowledge does not contradict but, on the contrary, fundamentally supports the fact that Husserl's philosophy is a philosophy of consciousness. The philosophical concept of consciousness is constituted in the correlation with the object. It is for this reason that Heidegger can say that, fundamentally, Husserl never really asked what consciousness was, what its own mode of being was. And from the moment that Heidegger poses this question, he calls in doubt the subject-object correlation and renounces the very term "consciousness," judging it inadequate for thinking Dasein's mode of being.[29]

Derrida is keen to underline that the interdependence of consciousness and object is determined by Husserl as a relation of presence: the presence of sense as the object's being-before, its availability to the gaze, and as proximity to self in interiority.[30] And he questions the specifically phenomenological form of this relation. If ideality is indeed "the salvation and mastery of presence," it is the salvation and mastery of the presence of *nothing* that exists in the world. If this is indeed the case, what would the "outside" of the object be? Its being "before" certainly implies an outside, but if this outside is not an outside in the sense of a world, there will need to be something that opens the possibility of a purely internal outside. We have already seen that the relation of the object to consciousness implies a twofold departure from the self: first that of the act that aims at sense, second that of sense toward its linguistic expression, the latter being necessary if sense is to attain any sort of universal and intersubjective value. As such, the relation of the object to consciousness cannot dispense with language. Phenomenology needs language in order to sustain an entirely internal proximity; it needs a language that is not a language. Derrida's line of argument here is intended to show that phenomenological language has to respond to a twofold demand: it has to be both necessary *and* superfluous. Necessary because it has to produce the element of conceptuality, superfluous because it ought never be anything other than the mirror in which the pre-expressive and originally silent stratum of sense is reflected. On the one hand, therefore, language ought to be productive—ought to produce the conceptual form—but it ought to do no more than reproduce that to which it is added: pre-expressive sense. What we have here is the paradox of a productivity that produces nothing.[31]

Now, this paradox is made possible by the prior determination of language as theoretical language, and by the determination of the theoretical itself: the determination of knowledge as knowledge of objects. It is easy to see in this Husserl's fidelity to an entire philosophical tradition: language truly speaks only when it speaks of objects, and thus only when it does not speak. For only when faced with full intuition, with the restoration of the object in intuition, can language efface itself, or *seem* to do so. Language speaks in order to speak the truth, and truth is merely the finally restored presence of the object.[32] In his fidelity to this tradition, Husserl encounters the difficulty of thinking a language that, while necessary to the production of the object, does not threaten its absolute proximity to consciousness. His solution to this difficulty commits him to an even more profound fidelity: voice alone can respect this dream of proximity. But if, according to Derrida, the privilege of the *phonè* is implied in the entire history of metaphysics,[33] Husserl, thanks to the resources of phenomenology, is able to give it a profoundly new form. He withdraws voice from the world in order to give it the ability to hear itself in the absence of the world:

> It is not in sonorous substance or in the physical voice, in the body of speech in the world, that [Husserl] will recognize an original affinity with logos in general, but in the voice phenomenologically taken, speech in its transcendental flesh, in the breath, the intentional animation that transforms the body of the word into flesh, makes of the *Körper* a *Leib*, a *geistige Leiblichkeit*. The phenomenological voice would be this spiritual flesh that continues to speak and to be present to itself— *to hear itself*—in the absence of the world.[34]

The phenomenological voice has the power to suspend in its phenomenon all reference to the world: it implies no relation to the externality of the world and guards thus the pure intimacy of consciousness. The same cannot be said of visible signifiers, the graphic signifier, for example (although, as we shall see, it is far more than an example). Writing, too, of course, has its ideal aspect, but as a phenomena it cannot suspend the relation to the world. Only voice allows something like a pure and universal auto-affection. If voice does not fracture proximity, it is because it sustains the strictest links with presence: in the very instant that it is proffered, the *phonè* would seem to complete the wholly internal passage between consciousness and the object that it intends. The absence of any detour is the essence of the Living Present as the punctual form of time. The notion of ideality, the privilege of presence and the phenomenological voice are interdependent; neither one can be thought unless in the coherence of their reciprocal connection. The essential complicity between a particular conception of time, a conception of being and a conception of language is thus revealed. One cannot be altered without simultaneously calling each of the others into question.

Before turning his attention to the manner in which those essential distinctions established by Husserl at the outset of the first *Logical Investigation* should allow him to extract a conception of language that, founded on the phenomenological voice, is alone capable of carrying out the *epochè*, Derrida announces, in the most general terms, precisely what it is that troubles the systematic coherence between being as presence and ideality as repetition. The common root of these two determinations is clearly shown in the formulation of phenomenology's *principle of principles*. If the source of all sense and all evidence ought to be sought in the originary giving of a presence to intuition, this implies that the form of all experience is the present: I know with absolute certainty that "the universal form of all experience (*Erlebnis*), and therefore of all life, has always been and will always be the *present*."[35] Being is only presence or a modification of presence. This determination of being necessarily implies a movement of transgression as regards everything that is of the order of empirical existence: the transgression of all contingency, all factuality, all worldliness. Yet ideality, as the authentic form of this determination of being as presence, implies another, subsequent transgression. It is not as if what lies beyond the contingent and the empirical is another *form* of existence. Ideality, as we have seen time and again, *does not exist*. Its irreducibility to the empirical is also an irreducibility to existence. And it is here that the question of repetition, of the *possibility* of repetition, becomes essential. Except for the fact that this possibility, opened by the movement of the transgression of the empirical, finds itself irreducibly tied to the very thing that it transgresses:

> To think of presence as the universal form of transcendental life is to open myself to the knowledge that in my absence, beyond my empirical existence, before my birth and after my death, *the present is*.[36]

Transcendental life, while not the ontological double of empirical life, is nonetheless what remains of "life" in the absolute self-certainty once the freedom of the transcendental *epochè*, the freedom to go beyond any singular empirical life and so beyond any *possible* empirical life, has been granted. The certainty of the universal form of presence is the "strange certitude" that even if I empty it of all empirical content, its presence remains unaffected. And it is in this radically new sort of freedom that the transcendental is disclosed as such. Such unprecedented freedom, however, is rooted in the relation to death, to disappearance in general, and first and foremost, to *my own* disappearance. The freedom of transgression toward the transcendental is opened through the relation to this indelible contingency that is, first and foremost, that of my empirical existence:

> If the possibility of my disappearance in general must somehow be experienced in order for a relationship with presence in general to be instituted, we can no longer say that the experience of the possibility of my absolute disappearance (my death) affects me, occurs to an *I am*, and modifies a subject. The *I am*, being experienced only as an *I am present*, itself presupposes the relationship with presence in general, with being as presence. The appearing of the *I* to itself in the *I am* is thus originally a relation with its own possible disappearance. Therefore, *I am* originally means *I am mortal. I am immortal* is an impossible proposition.[37]

The determination of being as presence, the opening of ideality as the possibility of infinite repetition, is thus rendered possible by the relation to death as a relation to disappearance in general and by a relation to a death that is determined as *mine* and as *empirical*.[38] Something of the contingent, of the factual, of the worldly, is inscribed in the very opening of ideality such that it can no longer be effaced. Yet in this relation to death, itself still the opening of ideality, this is precisely what is concealed in the determination of being as presence. Now, according to Derrida, there is a privileged site where this relation both is concealed *and* can be read: the site of signification. While the relation to death of which we have been speaking constitutes the very possibility of the sign, the metaphysical determination of the sign, which intends its effacement, will be the dissimulation of this relation.[39]

As we have already seen, it is language alone that can sustain the difference between the empirical and the transcendental. In its purely intentional aspect, language allows for the repetition of the ideal object, and opens the transgression of the empirical time and place whence sense emerges and renders it thus free for an absolute transmission, one in which all trace of the contingency of its origin should be lost. This is what is meant by the determination of repetition on the basis of presence: every contingency, every worldliness has to be effaced and, with it, temporality, too, this radically temporal dimension of the origin of sense. The pure repetition of sense in its identity with itself, of truth in its identity with itself, implies the effacement of the *singularity* of the event of sense and of truth. Were one able to think an ideality severed from any value of presence, one would be able thereby to think the singular event of the emergence of a sense that, in order to be sense, in order to have the possibility of making sense,[40] would actually have to traverse time, to go beyond its empirical origin. For sense reduced to this origin would be consumed in itself and disappear into its pure singularity, thus having no possibility of making sense, or leaving a trace or a heritage—no possibility of surviving itself. Such a path through time, however, can only truly be *through time* if it is also a path *through the world*. Why? Because it is only the world and world-time, the anchorage in *a* time and *a* place and not in a pure possibility of time and place, that can inscribe contingency as that which points toward a singularity that there should be no question of reducing.

Ideality severed from any value of presence would be one way of thinking the possibility of something singular (whether this be a matter of a being, a poem, an event, or anything whatsoever) being repeated and transmitted, of course, but in a repetition where something of this singularity has to be lost in order for *its* memory to remain. An ideality severed from presence would no longer be, if ever it was, an absolute memory, but the place where a certain memory and a certain (non-psychical) forgetting intersect, and are each the condition for the other. Such is, moreover, the only way of thinking the origin, in the world and in time, of something that is singular and contingent, radically contingent, but that ought not to be termed empirical, since its singularity and its contingency can *make* sense, can seek a path through time, can aspire to eternity as well, can be worth remembering.[41] Such a memory, however, in order to be the memory of a singularity, is not only *exposed* to forgetting but *destined* to a *certain* forgetting. Ideality, if it is to be the memory of a singularity, ought no longer to be the infinite repetition of the same, but an ideality that bears forgetting in its memory, an ideality that is the memory of forgetting itself, the truth of forgetting.[42]

This is the double fidelity about which we have been speaking: fidelity to the transcendental as the possibility of sense or truth, and fidelity to the empirical as the ineffaceability of the contingency of the singular.[43] It goes without saying that each of the terms being used here would have to be reworked, since the intersection of sense and singularity is precisely that which has never been intended by words such as sense, truth and empiricity in our history (or, at any rate, in its current and conventional interpretation). And language is far from a neutral field as regards this question. We have only begun to see the extent to which the difference between the two conceptions of ideality is played out within language, between a language from which one can—and above all should—retain only the purely intentional aspect, the spirituality of its body, and a language in which body and soul can no longer be distinguished. The possibility of a purely phenomenological language, of a language that can submit the world to *epochè*, is the very possibility of distinguishing body from soul *within* language itself. There is no absolute life, no absolutely living life, unless the soul does not need the body.

3. *Epochè* and Solitary Discourse of the Soul

We saw earlier on that the word "sign" has a double sense (*Doppelsinn*). The same word encompasses two heterogeneous concepts: that of expression (*Ausdruck*) and that of indication (*Anzeichen*). Every sign is a sign *of* something, but not every sign has a *Bedeutung*, a sense (*Sinn*) that is expressed with the sign.[44] Derrida points out that translating *Bedeutung* as "signification" generates a certain confusion. Although in English, as in German, one can legitimately speak of signs being meaningless or senseless, *bedeutungslos* or *sinnlos*, the same cannot be said of French; one cannot speak of *signes* without *signification*, of signifiers without signifieds. Signs in the indicative sense—such as distinctive signs, marks, etc.—are, for Husserl, signs that *express nothing*. Signs replete with *Bedeutung*, however, are signs that are marked by a will to express, and it is in order to take this distinction into account that Derrida proposes to translate *Bedeutung* and *bedeuten* by *vouloir-dire*, "meaning."[45] All discourse, therefore, and every part of discourse, is an expression that *means* something, and it is in the name of this will to express that Husserl excludes from the ambit of expressive signs facial expressions and the various gestures that accompany speech, etc. All such expressions (*Äusserungen*) are devoid of *Bedeutung* since they lack the *intention* of making any thoughts whatsoever explicitly manifest, whether for others or for oneself.[46] At least to begin with, therefore, the distinction between expression and indication appears straightforward enough: *Ausdruck* refers to linguistic signs that have an expressive value insofar as they *mean*, whereas indication, *Anzeichen*, refers to signs that express nothing, to signs that are limited to indicating beyond any expressive intention. Yet Husserl immediately complicates the distinction, noting that the difference is *not* a substantial one, but functional: the same phenomenon can be apprehended as either expression or as indication. Linguistic signs themselves, from the moment that they are caught within a communicative discourse, have an indicative function. And it is the indicative *function* alone that renders the sign an indication, Husserl defining this function as the possibility of one thing serving a thinking being as an indication of something else. In indicative functions, he writes,

we discover as a common circumstance the fact that certain objects or states of affairs, *of whose reality [Bestand] someone has actual knowledge*, indicate [*anzeigen*] to him *the reality of certain other objects or states of affairs* in the sense that *his belief in the reality of the one is experienced* (though not at all evidently) *as motivating a belief or surmise in the reality of the other.*[47]

From this, we can see why linguistic signs, expressions, function as indications from the moment they take on a communicative value. For Husserl, the articulated phonetic complex becomes a spoken word, communicative discourse in general, only when the one who is speaking produces it with the intention of expressing something; only when, through certain psychical acts, he confers on it a sense that he wants to communicate to someone else.[48] Now, the one who is listening to what is thus expressed has no direct access to the psychical lived experiences of the speaker and can understand his intentions only through the mediation of the physical aspect of discourse. But if it is oral discourse alone that can by rights be described as expressive, and if all oral discourse, from the moment that it becomes communicative, functions in an indicative fashion, what happens to the distinction between expression and indication? Where might one find an expressive function in its pure state, an expressive function severed from any intertwining with indicative function?

Husserl answers that this can occur in psychical life in which, in the absence of any communicative relation, expressions play a central role. The question that needs to be addressed, therefore, is whether there can be *a word that communicates nothing*. For Husserl, the absence of communicative value does not affect the essence of expression but, on the contrary, reveals what is proper to it. In psychical life, expressions do not cease to have *Bedeutung*, words do not cease to be words; from which it follows that the function of manifestation, of indication, is not essential to them. In solitary mental discourse, words are still words, still signs; their designatory function, however, is not equivalent to the function of the act of indicating (*Anzeigen*) that characterizes indications and that makes it possible for even words to be indications when used in a communicative discourse. This stems from the fact that *Anzeigen* is an act of designation that implies *existence*:[49] It denotes a passage from an *existing* sign to the presumed *existence* of what is indicated *by* the sign. Now, it is precisely this relation to existence that is suspended in solitary mental life; here, writes Husserl, "we are in general content with imagined rather than with actual words. . . . The word's non-existence neither disturbs nor interests us."[50] This suspension of any relation to existence is central in determining expressive function as pure expression. When one speaks to oneself, as it were, one is not speaking in the proper sense of the term, speaking in the sense of communicating. One has nothing to communicate to oneself; one merely represents oneself as a speaking and communicating subject. And why does one communicate nothing? Because such a communication would, as Husserl remarks, be wholly pointless (*ganz zwecklos*); in monologue, words do not function as indications since the acts in question are lived experience at the very moment of their communication.[51]

Authentic expressiveness can take place *only* once any and all relation to existence has been suspended. And yet, this relation to existence is also the relation to the externality of the world. Only the bracketing of the world, therefore, opens this other outside, the purely internal space in which the pure expressiveness of *Bedeutung*, the intending of an ideal object, can come face to face with meaning-intention, *Bedeutungsintention*. This is the strange paradox of which we have already spoken, the paradox according to which the true inside, the internality of consciousness, is constituted only as a relation to the strange outside of the ideal object, an outside that, in order to avoid any reference to a world, has to suspend all spacing [*espacement*]. And it comes as no surprise, therefore, to see that such a gapless outside can be thought only as time, as the time of the instant in which presence is opened, but opened in absolute proximity. According to Derrida, however, what might well seem to be a mere paradox is, in fact, the very essence of the phenomenological project itself:

Beyond the opposition of "idealism" and "realism," of "subjectivism" and "objectivism," etc., transcendental phenomenological idealism answers to the necessity of describing the *ob*jectivity of the *ob*ject (*Gegenstand*) and the *pre*sence of the present (*Gegenwart*)—and to objectivity in presence—from the standpoint of an "interiority" or, rather, from a self-proximity, an *ownness* (*Eigenheit*), which is not a simple *inside* but the intimate possibility of a relation to an outside in general. This is why the essence of intentional consciousness will only be revealed . . . in the reduction of the totality of the existing world in general.[52]

With this, we can see a little more clearly why the possibility of phenomenology rests on the possibility of a purely expressive language. Such a language would accomplish the bracketing of any existence and would secure self-presence as the wholly internal relation of consciousness to its object. This is because the separation between expression and indication is not, in the last instance, a separation between linguistic and non-linguistic signs; it is, rather, a separation between signs that do not allow for the immediate self-presence of the living present, on the one hand, and signs that respect this proximity without gap, on the other (but would a sign produced in the effacement of any gap still be a sign?). This is because the necessity of a detour lies at the root of all indication. Indication comes into play each time an animating intention, the living spirituality of meaning, is not fully present. All non-presence sets a limit on the life of animation, a limit that is encountered by communicative discourse in three very different forms. First, in the form of the body of the sign; then in the form of what is indicated, which is something that exists in the world; and finally in the form of the other who is never present to me in an originary and full intuition, in the other whose lived experience is never there for me "in person," so to speak.[53] In solitary mental life, however, there are no limits to living animation. There is no need for the body of the sign, since the ideal and identical form of this body, wholly animated by meaning, is indifferent to all existence; the transgression of expression toward sense, of the signifier toward the signified has no need of any detour; and finally, my relation to myself does not pass through the other:

While in real communication existing signs *indicate* other existences which are only probable and mediately invoked, in monologue, when expression is *full*, non-existent signs *show* significations (*Bedeutungen*) that are ideal (and thus non-existent) and certain (for they are presented to intuition). The certitude of inner existence, Husserl thinks, has no need to be signified. It is immediately present to itself. It is living consciousness.[54]

The reduction to solitary mental discourse, to purely expressive discourse, is a bracketing of all worldly and empirical existence, the most radical form of *epochè*.[55] But this can only be the case if purely expressive discourse is possible.

4. Originary Intuition and Signification

In order for a language as pure expressivity—a language without signs[56]—to be possible within solitary mental discourse, Husserl has to show two things: on the one hand, he has to show that in its monologue the subject communicates nothing, that it only pretends to communicate something, that it, in fact, *represents itself* as a speaking and communicating subject (which implies, moreover, that one can distinguish an actual from a represented communication); on the other hand, he has to show that the subject is only able to represent itself in the act of a communication because an actual communication would have no finality. The subject has direct access to its own psychical lived experiences and has, accordingly, no need to signify them to itself, no need for the detour through a sign since the proximity of consciousness to its object is assured by the Living Present as a punctual form of the instant. Pure expression is the transparency of the signifier—the phenomenological voice—close enough to signified sense and to the consciousness that intends it to mean that its function is no longer one of indication.

Husserl's two arguments here come down to the same point: if the subject has no need to communicate anything whatsoever to itself, it is because, in a present without rift, in the *Augenblick*, consciousness is immediately close to itself through the absolute proximity of the object. Despite this unity, however, Derrida is careful to consider both of Husserl's lines of argument: first, the question of the possibility of distinguishing between an actual and a merely represented language; second, the question of the punctuality of the instant. Husserl's argument to prove that there is such a thing as a purely expressive act, an expression without any indication, is based on the premise that in solitary discourse one does not speak in the strict sense of the term, in the sense of communication, but one only represents oneself (*man stellt sich vor*) as speaking and communicating. Why? Because the indicative function of the existence (*Dasein*) of psychical acts can have no purpose (*ganz zwecklos wäre*) given that such acts are experiences we live in the instant itself (*im selben Augenblick*). That solitary discourse is *represented* discourse is fundamental to Husserl's line of argument: in the intimacy of consciousness, there is no need for real words:

In imagination, a spoken or printed word floats before us, though in reality it has no existence. We should not, however, confuse imaginative presentations, and the image-contents they rest on, with their imagined objects. The imagined verbal sound, or the imagined printed word, does not exist, only its imaginative presentation does so. The difference is the difference between imagined centaurs and the imagination of such beings. The word's non-existence neither disturbs nor interests us, since it leaves the word's expressive function unaffected.[57]

Husserl cannot be content with merely distinguishing between the existing word, the perceived word and the "being-perceived of the word," its phenomenon, since the phenomenon of perception carries with it a reference to the existence of the word. The sense of "existence" necessarily belongs to its phenomenon. Imagination, by contrast, does not imply existence, not even as intentional sense. As such, imagination allows for a phenomenological reduction that isolates subjective lived experience as the sphere of certainty and absolute existence. Now, and as Derrida underlines, this absolute existence appears only at the cost of reducing the relative existence of the transcendent world.[58] The link between ideality, representation and imagination is thus intimate. In fact, representation as *Vor-stellung* plays a fundamental role in Husserl's phenomenology: it is the site of ideality as the neutralization of factical existence. Now, it is to expression alone and *not* to language in general that Husserl wants to accord the status of representation as *Vor-stellung*. According to Derrida, however, not only does representation as *Vorstellung* traverse language *as a whole* and not merely expressive language, but the representational structure of language itself is not limited to *Vorstellung*.

Language does denote representation in the sense of *Vorstellung*; however, it *also* denotes representation in the sense of *Vergegenwärtigung*, a reproduction or repetition that modifies presentation (*Präsentation* or *Gegenwärtigung*) and in the sense of a representative taking the place of or standing in for another *Vorstellung* (*Repräsentation, Repräsentant, Stellvertreter*). According to Husserl himself, the structure of discourse can be described in terms of ideality alone: first, in terms of the ideality of the sensible form of the signifier that has to remain the same and can do so only insofar as it is ideal; then, in terms of the ideality of the signified (of the *Bedeutung*) or of the sense that is being intended, which ought not to be confused either with the act of intending nor with the object, neither of which is necessarily ideal; finally, in certain cases, in terms of the ideality of the object itself, which can then assure the ideal transparency and perfect univocity of language. No matter what a sign may be, it is caught from the outset in a structure of repetition whose element cannot but be representative. A phoneme or a grapheme is necessarily different each time that it is employed, but it can function as a specific sign and as language in general only if its formal identity can be reproduced and recognized. This identity is necessarily ideal and thus implies representation: representation as *Vorstellung*, the place of all ideality, as *Vergegenwärtigung*, the possibility of reproductive repetition, and as *Repräsentation*, insofar as each signifying event is a substitute (for the signified as well as the ideal form of the signifier). If language can only function as ideal, in all the various senses that we have seen, the distinction between "actual" language and merely "represented" language, a distinction that Husserl evokes in order to demonstrate, as he must, the existence of a site of pure expressiveness, becomes problematic. According to Husserl, it is first and foremost as imaginative representation (*Phantasievorstellung*) that language attains the level of pure expressiveness. In the sphere of interiority thus opened up, Husserl terms fictitious the communicative discourse that a subject might ultimately address to itself, implying thereby that a purely expressive, non-communicative discourse can *actually* take place. And he stresses thus the possibility of a rigorous distinction between fictive and actual communication, at precisely that point where, for Derrida, the ideal structure of the word will prevent the distinction between fictitious and actual, ideal and real, from ever taking place. Actuality cannot befall an expression "like an empirical and exterior cloak to expression, like a body to a soul."[59] But then, Husserl's further supposition as to the possibility of distinguishing in solitary mental life actually representative discourse from fictitious discourse is even less assured. If one grants that, given the complex and differentiated structure that I have outlined here, all signs in general are originally constituted by repetition and representation, then there is no essential difference between the actual and the fictitious use of a sign. According to Derrida, there are thus no criteria for distinguishing between an external and an internal language nor, if the hypothesis of an internal language is conceded, between an actual and a fictitious one.[60]

What, in the last instance, underpins Husserl's argument, made in order to isolate a sphere of pure expressiveness, is the possibility of a pure *presentation* that does not require mediation by the sign, of a presentation that thus has no fundamental need for language. This should clarify the sense of the claim, above, that phenomenology depends on a language that is not a language. Each one of the distinctions evoked here implies another, more fundamental distinction: the distinction between presentation and representation. They imply the possibility of a prior presentation to which representation can be added. And it is for precisely this reason that Derrida reads phenomenology's principle of principles—which, remember, assigns to originary intuition the character of an absolute evidence—as *a principle of non-signification*. The thing that is thus given in the flesh is, for Husserl, "a sign of itself,"[61] and being a sign of itself amounts to not being a sign at all. The sign, therefore, would be foreign to the self-presence of the Living Present that constitutes the ground of all presence. It is because lived experience is immediately self-present on the level of certainty and absolute necessity that communicative discourse in mental monologue is merely represented discourse. Communicative discourse is impossible because superfluous, without cause or reason; without, if you like, a *principle of reason.* The subject does not indicate anything to itself—it cannot. And it cannot because it does not need to.[62] The whole of Derrida's analysis of the wholly representative character of language is thus directed at phenomenology's very principle of principles: the evidence and possibility of an originary intuition.

5. Duration of the *Augenblick*: The World in Time

Between *perception* on the one hand and, on the other, *the presentation of a symbol in the form of an image or meaning* there is an unbridgeable and essential difference.[63]

Originary intuition is thought by Husserl as the experience of the absence and of the uselessness of the sign. According to Derrida, this absence and this uselessness are only justified by way of a certain idea of the form of time: that of the punctuality of the instant. If it is true, as Heidegger thought, that the Husserl of the *Lectures* was the first to complicate—if not to attempt an outright break with—a concept of time inherited from Aristotle's *Physics* and thought on the basis of notions of the "now," the "point," the "circle" and the "limit," this break still maintains a tension.[64] This tension, which Derrida identifies as early as *The Problem of Genesis,* is between fidelity to the description of phenomena themselves and another sort of fidelity, one sworn to an irreversible philosophical decision expressed in phenomenology's principle of principles. In the *Lectures,* Husserl grants that any particular now can only be isolated as a purely punctual instant, that punctuality is only an ideal limit. The intuitive consciousness of time is transformed through constant modifications; the essence of lived experiences is to spread in such a way that a purely punctual phase can never be isolated.[65] And yet, temporal extension is always thought on the basis of a source point that, according to Derrida, functions as the guarantee of the

self-identity of the now. Any originary donative intuition, any absolute beginning, has its origin in a now defined as a source *point*:

> To begin with, we emphasize that modes of running-off of an immanent temporal
> Object have a beginning, that is to say, a source-point. This is the mode of running-
> off with which the immanent Object begins to be. It is characterized as now.[66]

If time is defined by a duration, if there is a continuity of modes of running-off, this continuity is indeed that of each *point* of the duration. This
is why the diagram given by Husserl in order to describe the concrete continuity of the running-off of instants originates from a point:[67]

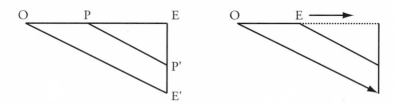

OE—Series of now points
OE'—Sinking-down [*Herabsinken*]
EE'—Continuum of phases (now-point with horizon of the past)
E→—Series of nows which possibly will be filled with other Objects.

Despite its complexity, the structure of time has a "living core," a
now that is and remains necessarily punctual and to which the other phases
are attached as a sort of "comet's tail" of retentions.[68] So far as Derrida is
concerned, what is at stake with the punctuality of the instant is nothing
other than the *self-identity* not merely of the instant, but also of the present
and of consciousness. Indeed, one might go so far as to say that what is at
stake here is *identity as such*, at least in its philosophical definition (which
raises the question of whether there could be any other sort of definition).[69]
Derrida's concern will be to show that the whole array of distinctions proposed by Husserl depend, sometimes overtly, sometimes covertly, on the
punctuality of the instant as the arche-form (*Urform*) of consciousness and
he will wager accordingly that the present is never *simple*, that it is always
an *originary and irreducible synthesis*.[70] With this, then, he takes up again a
question that has been his own since *The Problem of Genesis*; this time,
however, he supplements this question with that of the sign. Certainly,
originary synthesis was effectively described by Husserl himself; what

Husserl failed to do, however, was to recognize it as such, still less to recognize its consequences—consequences that he will, on the contrary, always have denied—principally at the point where it becomes a matter of separating perception from non-perception. The *Lectures* are shot through by a series of analogous distinctions: between presentative perception (*Gegenwärtigen, Präsentiren*) and representation (*Vergegenwärtigung, Repräsentation*), between secondary and primary memory, between imagination and originary impression, etc. Most assured amongst these distinctions, however, the one that guides each of the others, is that between perception and non-perception; and it is precisely this distinction, moreover, that Derrida finds most problematic. We have already seen that the originary now can only appear in its very present thanks to a retention and a protention. Or, retention and protention, themselves indispensable to the constitution of the actually perceived now, are neither perceptions nor presents. According to Derrida, this is something simultaneously recognized and denied by Husserl when he confirms that retention is a perception, albeit the unique case of a perception whose perceived element is not a present but a past as a modification of the present:

> . . . if we call perception the act in which all "origination" lies, which constitutes originarily, then primary remembrance is perception. For only in primary remembrance do we see what is past; only in it is the past constituted, i.e., not in a representative but in a presentative way.[71]

In this passage from the *Lectures*, cited by Derrida, Husserl confirms the necessity of retention to perception, its necessity to the origin, and so confirms also that retention has to be *presentative*. But what is seen in retention is a non-present, an inactual past. Nonetheless, if Husserl does choose to term this perception, it is because he has to safeguard the difference between perception and non-perception, which itself implies that a radical distinction separates retention from reproduction and not perception from retention. There should be no "continuous reconciliation" between perception and its contrary, without which the origin and non-origin would resemble each other to a dangerous extent. Rather than originating in the concrete character of the analyses, however, this necessity is dictated by what Derrida calls an "ethico-philosophical decision" that is itself contradicted by those analyses. And Derrida cites in support of this another passage from the *Lectures* in which Husserl describes the continual slippage of perception into non-perception:

If we now relate what has been said about perception to the *differences of the given-ness* with which temporal Objects make their appearance, then the *antithesis of perception* is *primary remembrance*, which appears here, and *primary expectation* (retention and protention), whereby *perception and non-perception* continually pass over into one another. . . . In an ideal sense, then, perception (impression) would be the phase of consciousness which constitutes the pure now, and memory every other phase of the continuity. But this is just an ideal limit, something abstract which can be nothing for itself. Moreover, it is also true that even this ideal now is not something *toto caelo* different from the not-now but continually accommodates itself thereto. The continual transition from perception to primary remembrance conforms to this accommodation.[72]

The temporality that Husserl is describing here is actually non-punctual; however, the necessity of the point source as the necessity of the origin is also ceaselessly reconfirmed. Derrida plays the concrete character of the analyses, their fidelity to phenomena, off against the philosophical decision that forces Husserl to posit nonetheless the necessity of an origin, a punctual origin. If one grants, as Husserl himself clearly does, that there is a continuity between the now and the not-now, between perception and non-perception in the sphere of *primordial* impression, if the *Augenblick*, the blink of the instant, *does* have a duration, then the difference between retention and reproduction, between primary and secondary memory, is no longer the insurmountable difference between perception and non-perception, but "*the difference between two modifications of non-perception.*"[73] The duration of the *Augenblick* introduces alterity as the condition for presence and presentation *prior to* all the dissociations analyzed by Husserl. Of course, Derrida does not want to deny that there are differences between perception and non-perception, between presentation and representation; such differences, however, are differences of modification and *not* essential ones. This being the case, however, non-presence does not surprise the self-presence of originary impression after the fact (*après-coup*) and the ultimate justification for a self-identity that would be prior to all exteriority and all alterity is thus called into question. If the simplicity of the origin is a myth, the same goes for pure identity. What is destroyed at its root is the very possibility of simple self-identity as such; that is, Husserl's principle line of argument as to the uselessness of the sign in the self-relation of solitary mental discourse. Of course, Husserl does not envision a link between the necessity of retention and the necessity of the sign; as an image, the sign belongs to the genre of representation, without which phenomenology's principle of principles would be overturned. And it is for this reason that Husserl, while describing the constitution of the living now in terms of a continuity with the non-perception of retention, has to reaffirm that the boundary between perception and its other passes *outside* the living now and *not within* its very duration. For Derrida, by contrast, retention and representation are "two forms of the re-turn or the re-stitu-tion of the present" and, whatever the chasm actually separating them, they share a common root: the possibility of repetition in its most general form, that of the *trace* that, rather than being added after the fact (*après-coup*) to the pure actuality of a living now, constitutes it through the move-ment of the *différance* that it introduces:

> The ideality of the form (*Form*) of presence itself actually implies that it be infi-nitely re-peatable, that its re-turn, as a return of the same, is necessary *ad infini-tum* and is inscribed in presence itself. It implies that re-turn is the return of a present which will be retained in a *finite* movement or retention and that primor-dial *truth*, in the phenomenological sense of the term, is only to be found rooted in the finitude of this retention. It is furthermore implied that the relation with in-finity can be instituted only in the opening of the form of presence upon ideality, as the possibility of a re-turn *ad-infinitum.*[74]

The presence of the present is thus thought in terms of the fold of the re-turn, in terms of the movement of repetition and not vice versa. So-called primordial presence is worked by *non-self-identity* at the very heart of the *Augenblick*. This non-self-identity necessary to the very movement of tran-scendental temporalization renders impossible, according to Derrida, the project of reduction in all its forms. There can be no transcendental reduc-tion without the absolute solitude of the *ego*, without the reduction to the monadological sphere of the "proper." From which it follows that there is no possible "solitary mental life." The instant in which the *ego* gathers it-self most closely to itself is already worked by non-self-identity, by a gap. If the *Augenblick* has a duration, solitary mental life is no longer absolutely solitary. All of which allows us better to understand why the reduction to pure expressiveness is in fact a reduction of all language.

The arguments put forward by Husserl in order to disengage this sphere of pure expressiveness focus on a solitary ego. If the ego has no re-lation to indicative communication, it is because it has no relation to the other in the ego; the element of *Logos*, even in its expressive form, is merely a secondary event added to an originary and pre-expressive stratum of sense, a stratum that itself attends the absolute silence of self-relation. In-ner life is devoid of indication because devoid of communication, and devoid of communication because devoid of *alter ego*. Derrida underscores the revelatory character of the example that Husserl gives of false inner discourse: "You have gone wrong. You can't go on like that."[75] The "you" belongs to the order of practical discourse; if it can be reduced, if one can legitimately say that the subject communicates nothing, reveals nothing to itself, if the axiological discourse has nothing productive about it, it is only because language in general, indicative as well as expressive, is determined by Husserl as theoretical language. He is insistent about the reducibility of axiology to its logico-theoretical kernel, referring to the theoretical essence of indication in order to exclude it from an expressiveness that is itself purely theoretical.[76] The proposition "you have gone wrong" is not properly indicative; rather, it is a false communication, one that communicates nothing that the subject might come to know. It is non-logical, non-theoretical. As Derrida points out, moreover, if this proposition is non-indicative by virtue of its being non-theoretical, it is precisely because of such a non-theoretical character that it is also not expressive. What might seem paradoxical is, in reality, profoundly coherent. Expression shares with indication the very thing that it seemed to exclude, the relation to the object as indicative showing, as a pointing-out of what is before the eyes. Between the *Anzeigen* of indication and the *Hinzeigen* of expression, there is an essential unity, the unity of *zeigen* as a relation to the object in visibility, to the object in phenomenality as a state of encounter [*vis-à-vis*] and surface, as intuition and evidence. The separation between *Anzeigen* and *Hinzeigen* is the separation between an external space and visibility and an internal space and visibility.

Now, this separation is only possible thanks to time and to voice. And it is here that we come back to the question of the now that was our starting point and from which we have strayed. The *telos* of expression is the integral restoration of a whole sense presently given to intuition. Expression, as we have already seen, should protect the presence of sense as both the being-before of the object and as internal self-proximity. The ideal object is an object whose showing in *zeigen* can be indefinitely repeated, principally because this showing is divested of all worldly spatiality. Now, the phenomenological voice is the element that allows the object or ideal *Bedeutung* to be shown without venturing outside of ideality, outside of the interiority of a life present to itself. *Zeigen*, "the finger and eye movements," as Derrida writes, is not absent from the voice. On the contrary, voice is what allows them to be *internalized*. Ideal being is only being-before for a look, but this being-before has to be protected from the world. The ideality of the object can only be expressed in an element whose phenomenality does not have worldly form. If the voice is indeed this element, it is because its phenomenon carries no reference to worldliness (something that cannot be said of other signifiers) and because the voice is heard *in the very instant* that it is offered. The subject seems not to have to venture beyond itself in order to be immediately affected by its expressive activity. The ideality of the object depends on the voice at the very point that it appears absolutely free and available. Between voice and phenomena, there is an absolute solidarity. Writes Derrida: "*The phoneme is given as the dominated ideality of the phenomena.*"[77]

Now, this solidarity is played out around the almost absolute proximity that seems to unite the signifier and the signified in the voice. The voice is heard *at the very moment* that it is proffered; as such, its sensible *body* appears thus to be effaced. And it is in this effacement, moreover, that its phenomenological power rests. For not only does the voice carry no reference to the exteriority of the world, it also does without the inner surface, its own body, exteriority in interiority. Nothing about the voice appears to break with the intimacy of life; a signifier, which is no more than an absolutely living breath, renders a sense present to the gaze of consciousness at the very instant it is proffered. The word is given as a pure phenomenon; in it, the thesis of the existence of the world is already suspended. This sense of "hearing oneself speak" is a unique form of auto-affection. Voice guarantees universality. Why? Because the signifiers that appear with it are *de jure* infinitely and identically repeatable and the subject that hears itself speak can be affected by the signifier that it produces without the need for any detour through the world, through what is not its own. In marked contrast, every other form of auto-affection has to pass through the nonproper, through what is not its own, or forego any claim to universality.[78] It is pure auto-affection, therefore, as the operation of the voice, that allows Husserl to carry out the phenomenological project of reduction: in the self-identity of a punctual instant, a transcendental consciousness masters the presence of an ideal sense.

And yet, the auto-affection that generates the originality of the word depends on the purely temporal character seemingly possessed by its very body: auto-affection is, first and foremost, the movement of pure temporalization.[79] In effect, the intuition of time cannot be empirical; otherwise temporality would be the real predicate of a being, but then, as a consequence, the "originary now," the "source point," must be produced by itself, can only be self-generated. The living now, the absolute beginning, is generated through what Husserl terms *genesis spontanea*,[80] and ought only to become past once affected by another originary now in which it can become a not-now as a past-now, and so on. This movement is one of pure auto-affection, since the primordial impression is affected by nothing other than itself, by the absolute newness of an other primordial impression. As Derrida points out, however, this auto-affection is not as pure as it should be, since the self-presence of the living present is only ever constituted by way of difference. The originary now emerges from the possibility of the retentional trace and the retentional trace introduces non-self-identity into its very core, contesting thereby the simplicity of a present whose life would be purely internal. The movement of temporalization cannot be thought in terms of the present; rather, it is the present that appears and that has to be thought in terms of a non-present that, as trace, constitutes it as such. But if such proves to be the case, then there can no longer be any trace of purity in the movement of temporalization, no auto-affection; the living present is always already open to what lies outside it. Temporality itself is *spacing* [*espacement*]:

As soon as we admit spacing both as "interval" or difference and as openness upon the outside, there can no longer be any absolute inside, for the "outside" has insinuated itself into the movement by which the inside of the nonspatial, which is called "time," appears, is constituted, is "presented" itself. Space is "in" time, it is time's pure leaving-itself; it is the outside-itself as the self-relation of time. The externality of space, externality *as* space, does not overtake time; rather, it opens as pure "outside" "within" the movement of temporalization.[81]

And if time can no longer be thought in terms of the present and the self-presence of a present being, it can even less be thought in terms of absolute subjectivity; the "world" is originally implicated in the movement of temporalization[82] and, with it, everything that is excluded by the transcendental reduction.

If we bear in mind that the auto-affection of the word was grounded in the purely temporal nature of expression and that the pre-expressive stratum of sense was itself temporal, only one conclusion can be reached: hearing-oneself-speak refers *not* to the interiority of a within, since time itself constitutes this within only by way of its opening. "Hearing oneself speak . . . is the eye and the world within speech," writes Derrida.[83] Phenomenological time, rather than the time of "an intimate consciousness," is the very opening without which there could be no interiority, no consciousness. But if transcendental time is itself the opening onto the world, it is no longer what is reached through the reduction of the world and its time, through the reduction of this *Weltzeit* with which Husserl opened the *Lectures*. For Derrida, this is what explains the necessity not merely of spoken language but also of the inscription in writing necessary in order for sense to become ideal (and it should be recalled that although Husserl did encounter and recognize just such a necessity, it was to remain somewhat mysterious in phenomenology). Why the need for the body of the word and, stranger still, for the body of writing in order to return truth to itself, if only *Geistigkeit* and *Lebendigkeit*, if only *spirit* could come to give them life? Why the necessity for the body, if the spirit is living? Why would an absolute life need to become incarnate, to inscribe itself within an inert body and a world, that will fundamentally only expose it to death? The necessity for phenomenological truth to pass through the world in order to be free of it remains an inexplicable riddle if one does not recognize the same world at the heart of what should be absolutely severed from it—the Living Present:

But if Husserl had to recognize the necessity of these "incarnations," even as beneficial threats, it is because an underlying motif was disturbing and contesting the security of these traditional distinctions from within and because, too, the possibility of writing dwelt within speech, which was itself at work in the inwardness of thought.[84]

If Derrida calls the movement of transcendental temporalization *arche-trace* or *arche-writing*, it is so as to mark the fact that this temporalization is simultaneously the opening of space, that it is *spacing*, and that this movement, which is itself productive of the difference between the transcendental and the empirical, only produces this difference by rendering it impossible as *pure* difference.[85] For Derrida, the words *writing* and *trace* are those most adequate to mark the impossible division between the transcendental and the world, at least at this moment in the trajectory of his thought.

6. *Widersinnigkeit* and *Sinnlosigkeit*: Ideality of *Bedeutung* and Non-Intuition

Between perception and symbolic representation, therefore, there would be no essential difference. For Derrida, the movement of temporalization as a movement of *différance* or of the primordial *supplement* designates the non-fullness of presence,[86] its being subject, "from the origin," to division and to delay; however, it also designates a function of primordial *supplementarity*, the structure of an "in-the-place-of" that, while characterizing the sign in general, is not, as Husserl and an entire philosophical tradition would wish, limited to the field of signification alone. All self-presence, "all phenomenological self-giving," would be produced by a movement of originary substitution:

> . . . the for-itself of self-presence (*für-sich*) . . . , as phenomenological self-giving, whether reflexive or prereflexive, arises in the role of supplement as primordial substitution, in the form of the "in the place of" (*für etwas*), that is, as we have seen, in the very operation of significance in general. The *for-itself* would be an *in-the-place-of-itself*; put *for itself* instead of itself. The strange structure of the supplement appears here: by delayed reaction, a possibility produces that to which it is said to be added on.[87]

The operation of signification would thus indeed lie beyond the field that philosophy has traditionally reserved for the sign, extending to that of beings as a whole.[88] Guided by such concepts, Derrida will take up the analysis of the first *Logical Investigation* in order to conclude that *idealization, repetition and signification will have to be thought in terms of one and the same opening.*

The structure of supplementarity is complex and diversified. Not only does the signifier represent an absent signified, it also functions thus as a substitute for another order of signifier. Indication is not only a substitute for an invisible indicated term, but also replaces another type of signifier, the expressive sign whose signified—whose *Bedeutung*—is ideal. Expression itself, however, implies non-fullness, and Husserl underlines that the acts of intuitive knowledge that "fulfill" meaning are mere "inessential components" of expression. While the act of meaning, the act that gives *Bedeutung*, always involves the intending of a relation to an object, yet the intention is sufficient to animate the body of a signifier, and there is no real need for an intention to fulfill what was intended in order for discourse to be able to take place. According to Derrida, the originality of the *Logical Investigations* lies in Husserl's recognition of the freedom of expression that can always do without the presence of the object. Husserl demonstrates that neither expression or *Bedeutung*—both of which are ideal—nor the object have to coincide. The central distinction between *Widersinnigkeit* and *Sinnlosigkeit* depends on this non-coincidence.[89] So long as a relation to the object is maintained, an expression can be false, contradictory or absurd without ceasing to have an intelligible sense, without becoming non-sense (*Unsinn*). The difference between *Widersinnigkeit* and *Sinnlosigkeit* is the difference between an expression that intends an object and an expression devoid of any such intention. Falsity is *still* a relation to the object, even if the object is empirically impossible (a mountain of gold, for instance) or impossible for *a priori* reasons (a square circle). Only expressions such as "abracadabra," or "green is where," for example, can be *sinnlos*, since they exclude any intention of an object; this type of non-sense is the only one excluded by logical grammar. *Gegenstandlosigkeit*, therefore, is not the absence of meaning (*Bedeutungslosigkeit*); on the contrary, *the absence of the intuition of the object is the originality of meaning*. Even if this is far removed from Husserl's own conclusions, it is the one forced upon Derrida by the essential distinctions that Husserl himself draws. And once again, he stresses the discrepancy that exists between the content of the Husserlian analyses and the philosophical principle that guides them.

The freedom of language, its capacity to speak in the absence of any object, to be and to remain language even when not speaking the truth, is certainly recognized by Husserl, but it remains subject to an intuitionism that, although not guiding the analyses of a pure logical grammar, nonetheless dictates the *telos* of language. Although one can indeed speak falsely, one speaks well only when one speaks truly; although the originality of language lies in its ability to function without a full intuition, its essence is still that it is fulfilled by intuition. Its *telos* is that of the unity of intuition and intention, a unity in which language would disappear as language once faced with the object that fulfills it.[90] Now, according to Derrida, language, from the moment that it is language, cannot be dissolved into the presence of an object in full intuition. The fact that an intuition can ultimately fulfill significatory intention, whose originality lies in its ability to function while empty, cannot abolish this structural originality. The absence of intuition—and so of the subject of the intuition—is not only *tolerated* by discourse but *required* by the structure of signification in general.

This is what Derrida undertakes to show in the extreme case of statements about perceptions. Such statements, even if one admits that they are made at the very moment that the actual perception takes place, imply that the content of their expression is ideal and that, as a consequence, it is not undermined by the absence of perception here and now. This, for Derrida, is the *very possibility* of language, a possibility that also structures thus the act of the one who speaks while perceiving. The total absence of both the subject and the object of a statement—the death of the writer and/or the disappearance of the object that the writer describes, for example—does not prevent a text from meaning; on the contrary, it is this possibility as such that makes meaning emerge. This radicalization of Husserl's conclusions involves no violence on Derrida's part, but is a necessary consequence of the distinction between meaning-intention (*Bedeutungs-intention*) and fulfilled intuition. What we commonly call writing, which is in fact the name for signs that function beyond or even through the absence of the subject, through the death of the subject, is the very movement of signification. It is at work within the so-called living word, and within the intimacy of a self-presence that one wanted to subsist without signs. We have already seen why the movement of temporalization implies everything that should be foreign to it (spacing, non-presence, world, etc.), rendering it thereby a *trace* partaking of the same condition of possibility as what we think of as signs. Addressing ourselves this time to the side of the *sign*, we will now see why its functioning prevents presence from being pure, from closing in on itself.

The example that Derrida chooses in order to show this is clearly not one among many; at stake is the personal pronoun *I*, the founding "I" of every philosophy of the *ego* and the *cogito*. For Husserl, the first person pronoun is to be classed amongst "essentially occasional" expressions, a *shifter* in Jakobson's terminology; in other words, it is one of those expressions whose *Bedeutung* is oriented to the person or the situation involved in its utterance. This group of expressions needs to be distinguished not only from expressions whose plurivocity is merely contingent but also from "objective" expressions in which the context of their utterance does not affect the univocity of their meaning (and Derrida clearly has theoretical expressions in mind here). The characteristic of essentially occasional expressions is that one cannot replace them by a conceptual objective representation without thereby deforming the *Bedeutung* of the utterance in question. It would clearly be absurd, for example, to replace "I am happy" with "everyone now speaking designates himself or herself as happy." Each time that such a substitution proves to be impossible, we are confronted with an essentially subjective and occasional expression whose function remains indicative. The root of all such expressions is their subjective origin: *I, here, now*. The *Bedeutung* of such expressions becomes an indication whenever it animates real intended discourse for someone else. Yet Husserl himself thinks that, for the one who is speaking, this *Bedeutung*, as a relation to the object (*I, here, now*), is wholly realized. In solitary discourse, the *I* realizes the immediate representation of itself.[91] Now, according to Derrida, even if one admits that such an immediate representation is possible—and in this case, there would be no need for the word "I"—the I also functions in solitary discourse as *ideality*. But then, how can I say *I* without implying, as always, the *ever-present possibility* of the absence of the object of my discourse, in this case myself? As ever, the distinction between signifying intention, meaning, and fulfilled intuition still holds: "whether or not I have a present intuition of myself, *I* express; whether or not I am living, 'I am' *means something*."[92] The ideality of *Bedeutung* excludes the possibility of the *I* naming, depending on the case, a different person by way of an always new *Bedeutung*, as Husserl would like. The possibility of non-intuition constitutes the *Bedeutung* as such of the word *I*, as it does of all other words. The *I* finds itself in the same situation as all statements about perception that depend neither on the actuality nor even on the possibility of a perception: the signifying *I* does not depend on the life of the speaking subject. The meaning of the *I* is wholly indifferent to whether or not life as self-presence accompanies its utterance:

The ideality of *Bedeutung* here has by virtue of its structure the value of a testament. . . . My death is structurally necessary to the pronouncing of the I. . . . The *Bedeutung* "I am" or "I am alive" or "my living present is" is what it is, has the ideal identity proper to all *Bedeutung*, only if it is not impaired by falsity, that is, if I can be dead at the moment when it is functioning. No doubt it will be different from the *Bedeutung* "I am dead," but not necessarily from the *fact* that "I am dead." The statement "I am alive" is accompanied by my being dead, and its possibility requires the possibility that I be dead; and conversely.[93]

Writing, understood as the provisional name for the structural possibility of the *I* that functions even in the absence of both writer *and* reader,[94] reveals better than anything else this possibility of understanding the "I am" in terms of the "I am dead." The autonomy of meaning as regards intuitive knowledge, the same autonomy that Husserl himself had undertaken to show, has its norm in writing and the relation to death; in a writing that is not merely added externally to a word that would not wait for it, to a word whose life sufficed to itself. Indication neither degrades expression nor leads it astray; rather, it dictates it. Derrida underlies that this conclusion depends on the distinctions of pure logical grammar; on the autonomy of the intention of meaning that can always function *emptily*.[95] The displacement that Derrida effects as regards Husserl is extremely subtle; that writing can function in the absence of any subject whatsoever, and so in the absence of all possible subjects, is precisely what is valorized by Husserl, and precisely this functioning of the *virtual level* implies that writing accomplishes ideality by delivering it of any empirical subject. Now, according to Derrida, this same capacity possessed by writing not only frees ideality but also discloses its irreducible origin in the relation to *empirical death*. Ideality, its infinite repetition, is rooted in a *finite* movement of the transgression of death, the world and empiricity.

If Husserl fails to recognize this, then that failure stems from the fact that, so far as he is concerned, *eidos* is always taken up into *telos*. The entire system of essential distinctions set in place in the *Logical Investigations* is purely *teleological*. If the "pure" forms of signification are always forms that can function emptily, this does not prevent form as such from always being the form of a sense, and of a sense, moreover, that opens itself only in the knowing intentionality of the relation to the object. The *telos* of the empty form is its fulfillment by the intuition of the object. The formalism here is wholly regulated by intuitionism. And Husserl concludes accordingly that if there is an essential distinction between subjective and objective expressions, then absolute ideality is on the side of the latter alone and that even in the case of subjective expressions, content can always be replaced by purely objective content. Only the act, therefore, will be lost to ideality. But this substitution is an ideal one and, as ideal, it is *infinitely deferred*. The ideal always being thought by Husserl in the form of an Idea in the Kantian sense, the substitution of ideality for non-ideality, of objectivity for non-objectivity, is a *telos* whose norm rests in a *de jure* necessity, but one that is *de facto* unattainable. Speaking of the replacement of subjective expressions by objective ones, Husserl in fact writes that such a replacement cannot be effected, not only for reasons of practical necessity, but also because "it cannot in the vast majority of cases, be carried out at all, will, in fact, never be so capable."[96] This goes, moreover, for every one of the distinctions proposed here, for the distinction between the sign and the non-sign, between indication and expression, between ideality and non-ideality, etc. The system of essential distinctions being a purely teleological system, it is caught, according to Derrida, in an aporia. Such distinctions, he notes,

de facto and *realiter* [. . .] are never respected, and Husserl recognizes this. *De jure* and *idealiter* they vanish, since, as distinctions, they live only from the difference between fact and right, reality and ideality. Their possibility is their impossibility.[97]

The phenomenological project is one projected onto an infinite horizon. It is a project that, without ever taking the form of a full presence, has the status of a *telos*, an Idea in the Kantian sense. Yet, Husserl never renounces the metaphysical idea of full presence, of a presence that, although always hidden, although always deferred, nonetheless remains an attainable *telos*. As Derrida notes, from this point of view, Hegel's critique of Kant holds equally for Husserl. A positive infinite has to be thought—and it can only think itself—if the indefiniteness of *différance* is to appear as such. But this holds true only if the appearance of the Ideal can be produced somewhere else than in a relation to death in general. For if it is the relation to my own death that produces ideality as the infinite *différance* of presence, at the same time this relation to my own death, compared to the ideality of the positive infinite, becomes the accident of a finite empiricity. Ideality and empiricity appear at the same time; they are produced by the same movement and it is for this reason alone that any attempt to separate them absolutely is doomed to failure. *Infinite* différance *is finite*; a positive infinite does not need to think itself in order for the difference of presence to appear.[98]

PART TWO

DERRIDA BEFORE HEIDEGGER

Finitude is Infinite

2.1

Being is not Gathered

1. On the Epoch of Representation

In "Envoi," a lecture delivered to the 18th Congress of the Societés de Philosophie de Langue Française, held at the University of Strasbourg in 1980 on the theme of *representation*, Derrida analyses the Heideggerian notion of the *epoch of representation*.[1]

For Heidegger, it is modernity that is the epoch of representation. If something like "modernity" can be identified, it is only because each of the traits that characterize it are reducible to an ontologically unitary ground, to the determination of the essence (*Wesen*) of beings and of truth as *Vorstellung*.[2] Modernity, like every other "epoch," is not an historical category in the sense of *Historie*, but a determination of *Geschichte*, of the history of being (in the double sense of the genitive). The event of modernity coincides with a new relation of being to beings and to the essence of truth: first and foremost it denotes a metaphysical shift or, more accurately, a shift *in metaphysics*. This is the reason why *Historie* can provide no real access to any given epoch: as a mode of what Heidegger likes to call research, *Historie* is the project of an objectification of the past, one that reduces the past to an *object* of research, submitting it to the principle of causal explanation. *Historie*, the science of history, is merely a *science*, the twin sister of the natural sciences.[3] As mere *effects* of the shift in the determination of essence, neither one has access to the dimension of the properly historical. In order for science to become possible, there has to be a metaphysical shift. Yet science itself evolves within this new determination of the essence of beings, without ever being able, as science, either to question it or to understand it as an ontological determination. The distinction between ontic and ontological knowledge implies a hierarchy that Heidegger will never call into question. In this regard at least the continuity of his thinking is unfailing: from §3 of *Sein und Zeit*,[4] where the distinction between positive knowledge, on the one hand, and regional and fundamental ontology, on the other, is established, to the end of his work where, although the term ontology is abandoned,[5] the declaration that 'science does not think" is ceaselessly sounded, and where thinking, which can be reduced neither to metaphysics nor to the positive sciences, is, of course, the thinking of being.[6] Within this epochal determination of the history of being, in which the different epochs correspond to different determinations of the essence of beings, the question is raised as to the relation of the epochs to one another: from what common ground are "epochs" detached such that the trajectory of a unitary history can take place and be recognized as such? In "Envoi" Derrida questions the link that gathers the epochs, this singular relation between them that is the sole assurance of something like *Geschichte*.[7] Before turning to this text, however, I want briefly to consider the Heideggerian notion of the *epoch of representation*.

Heidegger identifies five traits proper to modernity.[8] These include, first of all, science and technology, two phenomena to which he ascribes equal importance by recognizing in technology the status of an autonomous transformation of praxis which renders it something more and other than a simple "application" of science, and whose essence ultimately coincides with the essence of modern metaphysics itself.[9] An equally profound transformation affects all other areas of human life: art, religion, and action, are all thought in relation to a subjective experience and in the horizon of a world of values. The work of art becomes an object of a lived experience (*Erleben*)—whence the transformation of art into aesthetics—and human action a striving toward the realization of the supreme values that define a *Kultur*. Even religion, as religious *Erleben*, is possible only on the basis of *Entgötterung*, that double process through which the image of the world (*Weltbild*) is Christianized insofar as the foundation of the world becomes infinite and absolute—and Christianity becomes in turn a worldview (*Weltanschauung*). It is only in the space of an indecision (*Entscheidungslosigkeit*) regarding the gods and God that religion is possible as a form of experience.

Each of these traits have a common metaphysical ground that is particularly visible in the *essence* of science and technology. Whether it is a matter explicating the past or predicting the future, the goal of scientific research is to render beings calculable. For science, nature and history are merely the *objects* of possible explanation. This *objectification of beings* is accomplished in a representing (*Vor-stellen*) that summons all beings before itself in such a way that calculating man can be sure of beings, can be certain (*gewiss*) of them.[10] *Hence science is possible only from the moment that truth becomes the certainty of representation*, the moment of the Cartesian *cogito*. It is with Descartes that beings are determined as the *objectivity* of representation and truth as the *certainty* of representation. Modern science is thus not the process of refining a method of calculation more exact than the objectivity that preceded it; rather, it is with Descartes that science and objectivity come together for the first time.[11] What is at issue in passing from the Greek world and the Middle Ages to modernity is not some sort of progression, but a radical change in the essence of beings. This change in the essence of beings, their becoming-an-object of representation, is inseparable from a change in the essence of man: man becomes *subject*. The word *subjectum*, whose roots in the Greek *hypokeimenon* are recalled by Heidegger, denotes the ground (*Grund*) that gathers everything around itself. Originally, however, this metaphysical notion had nothing to do with man. The becoming "subject" of man is a genuine change in his essence.[12] Man becomes subject at the very moment that beings become an object (*Gegenstand*) brought before him, available to the human-subject who has its representation. The project of calculability as a project of mastery is thus opened up by the all-powerful force of representation. The age of the "world picture" is to be understood in the strongest sense of the term: it is not a matter of deciding *what* picture of the world is given by modernity, but of recognizing the essence of modernity as the *becoming-picture of the world itself*.[13] This becoming-picture is captured perfectly by the term *repraesentatio*, which Heidegger translates, without ever properly explaining why, as *Vor-stellen*:

Here to represent [*vor-stellen*] means to bring what is present at hand [*das Vorhandene*] before oneself as something standing over against, to relate it to oneself, to the one representing it, and to force it back into this relationship to oneself as the normative realm.[14]

For Heidegger, modern representation is completely different from Greek *apprehension* (*Vernehmen*) or from the medieval conception of beings. In the Middle Ages, beings are *ens creatum*: to be a being means to occupy a determinate place in the order of created things. The distance between modernity and the Greek world is greater still: for the Greeks, it is not man's gaze that brings beings to being but *man* who is gazed upon by beings, by what opens itself to presence (*Anwesenheit*). What is decisive in modernity is not some such privileged position occupied by man with regard to beings as a whole, but the fact that this new position is something that he himself produces: man has at his disposal the way he situates himself in relation to beings and so to beings as a whole. Mastery—and calculability: whence the privilege granted by Heidegger to science and to technology—is indissociable from the epoch of representation, from a representation that indeed consists in "[setting] out before oneself and [setting] forth in relation to oneself" [*vor sich hin und zu sich her Stellen*].[15]

Let me now come back to Derrida. His remarks on this text turn on two points, the second of which, as we shall see, is implicated in the first: the equivalence, first of all, that Heidegger establishes between *repraesentatio* and *Vorstellung* and, second, the relation that the epoch of representation maintains with the previous epochs.

Although Heidegger is usually so attentive—and this is an understatement—to what is at stake in the translation of metaphysical terms in their passage from Greek to Latin to German, a passage that, far from being a simple linguistic transposition that leaves meaning untouched, has on the contrary a real ontological bearing,[16] he quite simply "translates" *repraesentatio* by *Vorstellung*. For once, the Latin and the German are placed on the same footing, equidistant from the Greek. As Derrida remarks, however, in both its linguistic usage as well as in common language, the Latin term *repraesentatio* and its English equivalent *representation* seem to imply something not immediately present in the German term *Vorstellung*. *Vorstellen*, as Heidegger ceaselessly reminds us, means to set before oneself; but this sense of being-before is already at work in *praesentatio*, in the "present." The *re-* of *repraesentatio*, like the re- of representation, indicates something extra: it *renders* something present, brings forth the sense of "power-of-*bringing-back*-to-presence."[17] It is a matter not only of setting something before oneself, but also of being always able to set something before oneself *anew*, a power that chimes perfectly, moreover, with the description that Heidegger gives of the epoch of the world picture as an epoch of the technological mastery of beings. Being-able-to-bring-back, this always open possibility of repetition, is marked both in the re- of representation and the German *stellen*, in this *positionality*, this being-able-to-set, to set up, to set in place, described by Heidegger. Now, Derrida points out that to *render present* can be understood in at least two ways, adding that this duplicity is indissociable from the word representation. On the one hand, to render present would mean to bring or to allow something to *come* to presence. On the other, to render present would be to bring or to allow something to *come back*: as with every "rendering," rendering present would also be a restitution, whence the idea of repetition and return that is inseparable from the value of representation. This second sense, however, is already implicated in the first: for how could there be a *bringing* or an *allowing to come* that would not imply the possibility of a *bringing* or an *allowing to come back*? It is clear that, to Derrida's mind, even if he does not say as much, Heidegger fails to question the translation of *repraesentatio* by *Vorstellung* because the relation of presence to its restitution, the relation of coming to presence to the return of this same coming, is far more direct and far less dissociable in the term "representation" than in the German *Vorstellung*. If the idea of being available, of being-before of beings is there in both terms, the German *Vorstellung* interrupts the passage from the bringing to bringing back, a passage that interests Derrida far more than it does Heidegger for reasons that will become clear in the second of our questions, that of the relationship between the epoch of representation and the previous epochs.

What, then, is this relationship? We have seen why, for Heidegger, one can say that there is an epoch of modernity and point to its essence. If representation or *Vorstellung* as such is a far older phenomenon than the modern epoch of Cartesian subjectivity, the latter still has an essential link to representation. Something happens, something arrives to modernity and effects its essential novelty: *the being of beings* is interpreted as representation, everything that is happens in the form of representation. The question is thus one of knowing *how* this has arrived, bearing in mind that, for Heidegger, the domination of representation is not an accident or a misfortune, not a *crisis* of history.[18] If the epoch of the representation of the world truly corresponds to a shift in the essence of beings and of truth, if it is properly historial, it can in no way be the product of chance, of a pure factual contingency that would be the concern of factical history, the *Historie* that, for Heidegger, is only ever the belated and falsely explanatory narrative of a *cause* that always remains on the level of the ontic, blind to the true historial dimension. No more, however, can this epoch of representation be viewed in terms of error, as a false step, and Heidegger takes great care to distance his analyses from any form of ethical judgment. There is no place for ethics in historicality.[19] A shift in essence cannot be reduced to the fault (or merit) of some person or other, to the action or initiative of a *subject*, for the simple reason that it is only in the epoch of the world picture that man becomes subject. Whence, therefore, does the advent of representation come to us? Heidegger does not hesitate in his response: *from the Greek world*. From the Greek world in which, however, there is no question of representation being seen as the affect of a subject. According to Heidegger, the world for the Greeks is not *Bild* in the sense of an available image, in the sense of the spectacular form offered up to the gaze of a subject. Rather, it is man who is invested, gazed upon by presence (*Answesen*). And yet, in the Greek world of presence as *Anwesen*, the world as *Bild* is already announced: this announcement is nothing other than Platonism itself. The determination of the being of beings as *eidos* is not yet its determination as *Bild* but, as aspect, view, and visible figure, *eidos* is the distant condition for the becoming *Bild* of the world:

> That which is, is that which arises and opens itself, which, as what presences, comes upon man as the one who presences, i.e., comes upon the one who himself opens himself to what presences in that he apprehends it. That which is does not come into being at all through the fact that man first looks upon it, in the sense of a representing that has the character of subjective perception. Rather, man is the one who is looked upon by that which is; he is the one who is—in company with itself—gathered toward presencing, by that which opens itself. . . . Greek man *is* as the one who apprehends [*der Vernehmer*] that which is, and this is why in the age of the Greeks the world cannot become picture [*Bild*]. Yet, on the other hand, that the beingness of whatever is, is defined for Plato as *eidos* [aspect, view] is the presupposition, destined far in advance and long ruling indirectly in concealment, for the world's [*Welt*] having to become picture [*Bild*].[20]

For Derrida the whole question is thus one of knowing how to think this distant condition, this long-destined presupposition, this announcement that comes to modernity.

The Platonic world would have destined us for the world of representation. Derrida is careful to make clear that, although he will speak of the "Platonic world," he wants to rule out not only the suggestion that Platonic philosophy produced a world, but also the suggestion that it was, inversely, no more than a simple reflection or symptom—a representation, then—of the world that sustains it.[21] The relation between a world and a philosophy is not a one-way relation, therefore: neither one can be said to produce the other. And it would be difficult, moreover, to think this relation of production outside of a representational schema without turning either the world or the philosophy in question into the simple representative of the other, however one chooses to think this idea of representation: as symptom, reflection, superstructure, signifier, etc. According to Heidegger, then (for whom, however, the sequence of implications is clear: it is Platonism that produces a world), it is the Platonic world that would have prepared us for, destined us for, sent us, the world of representation through successive stages that bear the names Descartes, Hegel, Nietzsche, etc.[22] Platonism would thus have destined us to the whole history of metaphysics and this history would have its presumed unity in an *originary sending*, a singular and indivisible sending. Platonism would have started things off, would have destined from afar the rule of representation, without itself submitting to it. It would have been, Derrida writes, at the limit of this sending, like the origin of philosophy: already and not yet.

Now, the status of this "already and not yet" is difficult to think outside of the dialectic that structures the entire teleology of Hegelian history and that structures, more particularly, the moment of representation (*Vorstellung*) that is already the announcement of what cannot yet be said to *be*, the prefiguration of its overflowing.[23] Yet the historicality of which Heidegger is speaking is not (or ought not to be) a sort of representational and dialectical process.[24] The terms *Geschichte, Geschick, Schicken*, point toward a sending of being that is unthinkable in terms of the history of a series of representations. The epochs are not different representations of a being that would always be the same and that would take place outside of its epochs, outside of representation, so to speak. The epochs are not a modification of beings or of substantial sense, neither a moment nor a determination, in the Hegelian sense of the term. Nevertheless, if Platonism destines the epoch of representation by way of the other "stages" in the history of metaphysics, if representation is already announced in Platonism, there needs to be a unifying presumption that would order a whole multiplicity of modifications and derivations. There needs to be something like "a still-representational pre-interpretation of representation." Now, Derrida thinks that this unifying presumption is at work throughout the strongest and most necessary displacements in Heidegger's thinking.[25] What is in question here is *the very notion of epoch*, a notion which makes sense only in relation to the destiny or gathered sending (*Geschick*) of being. There would be no epoch of representation, with its epochal sense and unity, if it did not belong to the gathering of a more originary and more powerful sending. Without the *Geschick* of being, without its first determination as *Anwesenheit*, no interpretation of the epoch of representation could situate it within the unity of a history of metaphysics. It is clear that the *Geschick* of being, as Heidegger understands it, does not take the form of a *telos* that, determined in advance, would come into play only in the finite or infinite—it hardly matters which—becoming of history. Nevertheless, the sending of being that is given at the origin of history is a sending that gathers with itself, and this self-gathering is the condition of possibility for an epoch's being able to detach and order itself in the unity of a destination or, rather, a destinality of being.

Derrida is careful to emphasize that this gathering does not take the form of a totality, a system or an identity. Such precautions notwithstanding, a fundamental question still remains: the historial or destinal interpretation of the epoch of representation (and this holds true for *every* epoch) orders or derives that epoch from an originary sending of being as *Answesenheit*. That the sense of this order is neither logical nor chronological nor infra-historical only better underlines the role of the sending of being as *origin*. The originary sending of being as *Answesenheit* translates itself into presence and thence into representation according to translations that are mutations within the same, within the being-together of the same sending.[26] All of which implies that this being-together of the originary sending in some way arrives or happens to itself, in proximity to itself, in *Answesenheit*. That is, the *origin arrives to itself, in proximity to itself, at the origin*.[27] And it does so even if it already contains within itself the tensions that can subsequently only distance itself from itself. Why? Because there is dissension, even in the Greek experience of *Anwesenheit*. Heidegger calls this dissension *Zwiespalt*. But the dissension itself is secured and assured, gathered in *legein*,[28] by forming this sort of indivisibility which alone allows the destinal to be thought. On the basis of the indivisibility of the sending of being, Heidegger detaches the epochal figures from his reading of the history of metaphysics right up to this epoch of representation—modernity—that announces itself as the longest and most powerful. In it, presence as *Anwesenheit* is concealed, held in withdrawal; and yet, it is still presence as *Anwesenheit* that has sent us presence as representation, that has destined it from afar. All of which allows Derrida to say that the relation of the epoch of representation to the Greek epoch is still interpreted by Heidegger along representative lines: the *Answesenheit / repraesentatio* couple still dictates the law of its own interpretation:

Behind or under the epoch of representation there would be, drawn back, what it dissembles, covers over, forgets as the very *envoi* of what it still represents, presence or *Anwesenheit* in its grouping in the Greek *legein* which will have saved it, and first of all from dislocation.[29]

Forgetting and even the forgetting of forgetting, as the *forgetting of being*, would be what saves the gathering and the indivisibility of an originary sending.

In point of fact, Derrida's question bears on the very notion of historicality and on the value of *gathering* that the sending of being still carries in Heidegger's text. For it is not so certain that one can think *a* sending, and a sending *of being* (in the double sense of the genitive) without this idea of gathering. Through his analysis of "The Age of the World Picture" (but these same remarks could be extended to all Heidegger's texts on the notion of historicality), Derrida undertakes to show that wherever the sending of being divides itself, and it has to divide itself in order for there to be history, this divisibility challenges the *legein* and the very idea of destination, of a unitary destination. If, according to Derrida, there has always been representation, even before the epoch in which the essence of beings is determined with respect to representation, then being was originarily threatened in its being-together, in the unity of its *Geschick*, by divisibility and dissention, by what he chooses to call *dissemination*.[30] If there is representation and divisibility, the epochal reading, as an ordering reading, becomes untenable. The unity of the history of metaphysics or of the West, is only a presumed unity, therefore:

Can we not then conclude that if there has been representation, the epochal reading that Heidegger proposes for it becomes, *in virtue of this fact*, problematic from the beginning, at least as a normative reading (and it wishes to be this also), if not as an open questioning of what offers itself to thought beyond the problematic, and even beyond the question as a question of being, of a grouped destiny or of the *envoi* of being?[31]

The historicality that Heidegger thinks by way of the *Geschick* of being is not, of course, immune to difference and dissention. According to Derrida, however—and it is here that the idea of gathering becomes decisive— what is at stake for Heidegger is the history of *Anwesenheit*'s difference with itself, of the difference of presence: put differently, the history of *difference as presence*.[32] Heidegger's notion of historicality would be a history of the same, thought, certainly, in its difference from the identical, but in such a way that the difference between the identical and the same serves only to reinforce the value of the latter.[33] The destiny of being is construed thus as a self-relation in which the destination and the sending would always be *unitary* because a self-sending: a sending of the same.

Heidegger's text on the epoch of representation is of particular significance in this regard because the relation between *Anwesenheit* and *repraesentatio* is played out around the notion of presence central to his thought of historicality as the history of being. If there is a destinal gathering, it lies in the modifications in the way in which presence is given. The connection between the notions of *gathering* and *presence* is, according to Derrida, *constitutive*, and remains unquestioned in Heidegger's thought, whatever displacements may be wrought on the notion of presence itself. Now, this idea of gathering is equally indissociable from a certain relation to origin and to *history*, to *temporality* and to *language*. It does not, assuredly, structure anything like a system; what it does structure, however, is something like a configuration of Heidegger's thinking, one with regard to which Derrida will mark a very clear break, as we shall see in a moment. First of all, however, let me try to place the question of the sending of being in a context wider than that of the analyses of "The Age of the World Picture."

2. On Sendings [*Des envois*]

As we have already seen, the idea of gathering in the *Geschick* of being is indissociable from a certain relation to origin and to history, from a certain determination of origin and of history, and from a certain determination of temporality and of language. Before continuing our commentary on Derrida's analyses of—and reservations concerning—Heidegger's thought of *Geschick*, it is perhaps instructive to see just how Heidegger himself characterizes the related notions of *Geschichte*, *Schicken*, *Geschick* and epoch. Among the various texts to which one might refer in order to do so, I have chosen to refer above all to "Time and Being" because of the extreme and problematic density that one finds there as regards these notions.

What, then, is the history of being? If the enigmatic link between being and time is, from a particular moment on, to be thought as a *history*, as the history of being, the difficulties that attend this are clearly going to be gathered around this notion of *Geschichte*.[34] Being cannot "have" a history in the sense that a city or a people have a history, the whole difficulty here resting on our not thinking being as being something "in" time.[35] For a thinking that wants to approach being and time in their particularity, for an originary thinking, the relation between time, being, and history is the most enigmatic of all relations, one that demands the greatest effort from a thinking whose fundamental concern is ultimately this relation.[36]

The difficulty of thinking this relation is what has long since troubled and what sets thus in motion the whole of Western metaphysics. Since the Greek determination of being as *Anwesen*, a word in which, as Heidegger has it, "presence [*Gegenwart*] speaks," being is defined in relation to time and time in relation to being. The temporal is the transitory, what perishes and passes away (*vergeht*). Yet time remains constant in its passing away, and this remaining constant (*bleiben*) means to be present (*Anwesen*).[37] The contradictory statements on the nature of this strange relation are connected to one another, without the resulting aporias leading us to a true thinking of *being and time as such*.[38] Now the first step on the path of such a thinking is to recognize that being and time have something in common, namely the fact that *they are not*: the presence (*Anwesenheit*) of being is not the presence of a thing (*Ding*) *in* time, any more than the permanence of time is the persistence of a temporal thing *in* time. Being and time share the fate of *not being beings at all*. It is not as if we could encounter being and time amongst beings that are. And it is in order to open up a space for a thinking able to take the measure of this difficulty that Heidegger proposes the celebrated formulation: *Wir sagen nicht: Sien ist, Zeit ist, sondern: Es gibt Sein und es gibt Zeit*, "we do not say: Being is, time is, but rather: there is Being and there is time."[39] The question of the *es gibt*, of the gift, of the giving of time and being, leads us to the thinking of history and of epochality that concerns us here. To think being appropriately is first and foremost to abandon its metaphysical determination as the ground of beings (*Grund des Seienden*). Being ought not to be thought on the basis of beings, but on the basis of the giving (*Geben*) from which it stems. Presence as *Anwesen* implies this dimension of letting-come-to-presence (*Answesenlassen*), of a carrying into the open that occurs through the play of a giving:

> To let presence means: to unconceal, to bring to openness. In unconcealing prevails a *giving*, the giving that gives presencing, that is, Being, in letting-presence.[40]

No longer thought as the ground of beings, being, which is nothing (that is), appears to us as a gift, as the gift (*Gabe*) of the *Es gibt*, and the site of this giving is nothing other than *history* (*Geschichte*). The Greek determination of being as *Anwesen* is a strike or imprint (*Prägung*) of being long since decided on and imposed upon us. Since the beginning of Western thought with the Greeks, all saying (*Sagen*) of "being" and of the "is" is held in the memory (*Andenken*) of this determination of being as *Anwesen* and we are tied, consciously or not, to such a provenance (*Herkunft*). The "imprint" of being as *Anwesen* unfolds through what Heidegger terms the abundance of transformations (*Wandlungsfülle*) that constitute *Geschichte* throughout each of the metaphysical determinations of being right up to modern technology which, in its dimension of planetary domination, imposes upon the inhabitants of the earth the final form of being as *Anwesen*: *Anwesen* in the sense of calculable *Bestand*. If the Greek origin opened Western-European thinking, this thinking now dominates all corners of the planet. This unfolding is configured as the *history* of being, a history that refers not to some sort of indeterminate becoming (*Geschehen*), but to the giving (*Geben*) of the *Es gibt Sein* that has the form of a destining, or of a sending:

What is historical in the history of Being is determined by what is sent forth in destining, not by an indeterminately thought up occurrence.[41]

The claim that being is not but that that there is being or that it is given [*ça donne, l'être*], is entirely of a piece with a thinking of the historicality of being itself, according to which being happens or takes place (*geschiet*) only to the extent that it is sent or destined. The gift of being is nothing other than a sending, or a destiny, depending upon which of the available translations one chooses.[42] Yet this *Geben*, which is a sending or a destining, has another essential characteristic. *Schicken*, destining, is a giving that gives only its giving; it is not *itself* given, but holds itself back and withdraws.[43] Being is thus thought by Heidegger as what is destined (*Geschickte*) and its history as the history of its changes. In the history of being, however, which is nothing other than this destination, the giving itself never appears. This is why it is *epochal*. Epoch, in accordance with the Greek sense of the term *epochè*, does not for Heidegger denote a period, a span of time, but this fundamental trait of destining: the *An-sich-halten* of giving that always withdraws in favor of its gift (*Gabe*).[44]

Yet the fact that the epoch is essentially not an isolated period in the course of a history does not stop there from being a *sequence* (*Folge*) of epochs in the destiny (*Geschick*) of being. And the way in which such epochs link up, something that is no more contingent than it is necessary—at least from the perspective of a natural causality—marks nonetheless a unitary character, a certain continuity the nature of which has to be thought. Why? Because it is precisely in the reciprocal belonging-together (*Zusammengehören*) of the epochs that the destinal (*Schickliche*) character of *Geschick* is announced, all the more so because this belonging-together cannot be read in any direction whatsoever; there is an ordering principle. In their succession, the epochs cover one another in such a way that the initial destining (*Schickung*) of being as *Anwesenheit* is progressively more *concealed*. Heidegger describes here a double direction of the gaze toward being: one that sees being turning its gaze toward beings—and this is *metaphysics*, in its quest for a ground—or, one that sees being turning its gaze toward the provenance of being, toward the dimension of this *Es gibt* that sends or destines being to us—the *history* of metaphysics is thus delineated.[45] This history is not a more or less necessary series of events but the strange set of modifications of an originary sending or destining that, as such, is always withdrawn. Now, it is imperative that we not be mistaken as to the nature of this withdrawal, that we do not consider it to be a contingent limit of thinking. The *An-sich-halten* of the *es gibt* is essential. That which gives beings by bringing them into the open is always itself shielded from the light (*Entbergen*).[46] To think being not in relation to beings, but in relation to the *es gibt* whence it comes, means to think a history in which what takes place happens by way of an essential withdrawal, but a withdrawal that is no longer envisaged as something that would have taken place elsewhere, outside of the history that it produces and whose hidden ground it would be. This, if anything, is what is at stake in ontological difference.

As is well known, the Heideggerian gesture of retracing the history of metaphysics in order to refer [*renvoyer*] it in its unity to its originary provenance also works as a way of taking a certain distance, a necessary step back (*Schritt zurück*) in order, finally, to take leave of metaphysics, to abandon it to its destiny.[47] This is one of the major concerns of "Time and Being." For the moment, however, I do not want to dwell on this theme but want instead to concentrate solely on the link that Heidegger establishes between the notions of *Geben*, *Schicken*, *Geschick*, and *Geschichte*. It is on the basis of these notions that one has to understand not only the history of being but also the epochs that punctuate it. And it is around these same notions, moreover, that Derrida addresses to Heidegger a question concerning the relation between the ontological difference and historicity. *What is historicity once seen from the perspective of a thinking of ontological difference?* Can historicity be reduced to *Geschichte?* Can it be thought within the opposition between *Historie* and *Geschichte?*

In order to try to answer these questions, let me take as my point of departure those pages in which Derrida turns repeatedly to the notions of *schicken* and *Geschick.* These pages are to be found in the first part of *The Post Card,* whose title "Envois" (in the plural this time) points again to the heart of our problematic. Given the peculiar character of this text—a series of fragments of postcards or letters sent to an addressee who remains unknown—the decision to concentrate on only a few pages in order to discover Derrida's "thesis" concerning epochality in Heidegger might seem highly arbitrary (and, in *The Post Card,* more than anywhere else, the very possibility of *a thesis* is what is being called into question).[48] Any text whose very form seeks to resist every possible systematization, that seeks to escape generic classification, that plays on a number of different registers— philosophical essay, literary exercise, parody, love letters, etc.—ought to resist being summarized or gathered into a thesis. As, indeed, it does. And yet, what Derrida writes there about the notions of *schicken* and *Geschick* has, to my mind, a genuine theoretical import.[49] To deny this for the reasons already suggested would be to place far too much faith in the distinction between the serious and the non-serious, or between the philosophical and the literary.[50] If at any given point Derrida seeks to call that distinction into question, even in the very style of his writing, it is precisely *not* so as to refuse any sense of legitimacy to the rigor of thinking nor, even worse, so as to suggest that one ought to seek the stakes of philosophy only in certain authorized works. It is a certain idea, a certain *form* of philosophical coherence that is being questioned here, and not the very possibility of a rigorous thought.[51] Such, at least, is the thesis that will guide my remarks.

What, then, does Derrida say regarding *Geschick?* He remarks, first of all, on the central role played by the term: it is through *Geschick* that Heidegger thinks the history of being as the gift of the *es gibt.* Everything seems to turn on a word, *Geschick,* which means not simply "destiny," but also "fortune," "lot," "fate," "address," even "skill" (we will see that for Derrida knowing how to send and knowing how to address oneself require skill, the skill of knowing how to count with time, how to play with the delay).[52] Derrida begins, then, by widening the semantic field of *Geschick* at precisely that point at which Heidegger will want to restrict it. For if *schicken* means quite straightforwardly to send, in the sense that one sends a letter, *Geschick* will quickly come in Heidegger's texts to determine the *unity of a destiny.*[53] Originary *schicken* is interpreted on the basis of *Geschick*, and not vice versa: the sending is a *destinal sending*. Everything begins with a sending whose sole characteristic is that of being a gift (a gift of *nothing*, as Derrida points out, of nothing that is a being, of nothing *present*); however, from the very beginning, *from the origin, Geschick* gathers this sending of *nothing*, this gift of *nothing*, into the history (*Geschichte*) of being—a history which, as we have seen, is constituted as history precisely by its being the unity of the variations within one and the same destination. Between sending and destination, the destinal, destiny, etc., there is for Heidegger no real gap. The same cannot be said of Derrida: between sending and destiny, but already between sending and destination (unless we can speak of a destination without destiny, a destination that would never be assured, a destination of which one retains only the dimension of the address), there is a necessary gap. And it is in order to highlight this gap that he sets up his "postal interpretation" of the destiny of being.

If everything begins with destination, with the destiny or the destining of being (*das Schicken im Geschick des Seins*), why *not* speak of the post? Why not say that the destinal *posts itself*?[54] The first objection seems obvious. What is usually meant by the idea of the post, a certain type of long-distance communication service with its own technology and history, can only ever be a *metaphor* for the *Geschick* of being. An ontic and historic (in the sense of *Historie*) and thus improper metaphor, when it is a matter of thinking the sense of the destinal. But this objection implies, as Derrida points out, that one ought to place great trust, far more than that placed by Heidegger himself, in the notion of metaphor, and in everything that it implies as regards a system of distinctions between figural and literal meaning, between sensible and intelligible, etc.[55] In order to preclude speaking of the post with respect to the sending of being, we would need to turn the post into an image, a figure, a trope, and to be certain of knowing exactly what an image, a figure, a trope *is*. As such, there would be an extremely Heideggerian strategy for speaking of the post with respect to the sending of being. For if, first and foremost, there is a sending, if this sending does not derive from anything, if, "from the moment that there is, from the moment that it is given [*es gibt*], it destines," then it follows that the possibility of the post is always-already-there, in its very withdrawal, and that one can think the postal accordingly on the basis of the destinal character of being rather than vice versa.[56] The situation here is clearly the same as the reversal that Heidegger sets in place when he speaks of language as the house of being, in which it is not a matter of speaking of something un-known—i.e., being—on the basis of something supposedly known—a house or language—but a matter, on the contrary, of rethinking dwelling on the basis of being.[57] Hence the post would no longer be a simple metaphor but, as "the place of all transfers and all correspondences," it would be the very possibility of rhetoric as such.

Now clearly this sort of gesture is not properly Heideggerian. No one should be mistaken about that. But wherein lies the difference, exactly? Why could not the notion of the postal service function, in a given context, in a manner analogous to that of a house or of language? And if it is a straightforward case of a parody, of what, exactly, does the parodic value of this discourse on the postal service consist? Might such a thing as a pure parody, a parody underpinned by no real thought, exist? I do not think so.[58] What *is* certain, however, is that *this* gesture is not truly Heideggerian, not even in its style, for at least one particular reason that pertains to a *properly* Heideggerian theme: that of technology. The postal service, every postal system, is indissociable from a technological determination. Tech-nology, the epoch of technology, is *situated* by Heidegger *within* the his-tory of metaphysics. As such, there can be no question of assimilating tech-nology to the original sending of being that is given to be thought in the *es gibt*. Metaphysics has to be thought on the basis of the *es gibt*, in its desti-nal character and, as a consequence, one ought not to think the *es gibt* on the basis of any metaphysical determination. Heidegger's objection, at least as Derrida imagines it, would thus be that with the postal service one can only construe a metaphysics. Once again, however, the central question here is the question of epoch. It is by way of a certain idea of epochality that Heidegger wants to situate technology as what happens in a given mo-ment in the history of metaphysics, a metaphysics that itself follows upon an even more originary sending. Now, there would be no epochs without the withdrawal proper to this originary destination, without the idea of a break or pause in which being is pulled back, suspended or withdrawn. It is this *Entzug*, this essential withdrawal that Heidegger calls *epochè*, that scans and punctuates the "destiny" of being or its "appropriation" (*Ereig-nis*) which is always also a de-proporiation (*Enteignis*).[59] Now, these ideas, as Derrida notes, are immediately homogeneous with the postal discourse: to post or to send implies a pause or a break, a relay, or a suspensive delay, the possibility of diversion and forgetting:[60]

The *epochè* and the *Ansichhalten* which essentially scan or set the beat of the "destiny" of Being, or its "appropriation" (*Ereignis*), is the place of the postal, and this is where it comes to be and that it takes place (I would say *ereignet*), that it gives place and lets come to be.[61]

Yet the homogeneity of the withdrawal of being and what Derrida terms the place of the postal disturbs what is still derivative in the Heideggerian schema. This homogeneity implies that neither metaphysics nor technology arise [*ne surviennent pas*]. Metaphysics would not arise (*arriver*) in order to determine or to dissimulate, to *conceal* (as Heidegger repeatedly puts it) a sending of being that would not yet be metaphysical (or postal). This is why Derrida writes that neither metaphysics nor technology arrive or happen [*arriver*].[62] They do not arrive from without in order to conceal a first sending, an originary sending that would be pure of them:

> *Technè* (and doubtless he would have considered the postal structure and everything that it governs as a *determination* (yes, precisely, your word), a metaphysical and technical determination of the *envoi* or the destinality (*Geschick*, etc.) of Being; and he would have considered my entire insistence on the posts as a metaphysics corresponding to the technical era that I am describing, the end of a certain post, the dawn of another, etc.); now, *technè*, this is the entire—infinitesimal and decisive—*différance, does not arrive*. No more than metaphysics, therefore, and than positionality; always already it parasites that to which he says that it happens, arrives, or that it succeeds in happening to [*arrive à arriver*]. This infinitesimal nuance changes everything in the relation between metaphysics and its doubles or its others.[63]

But what does it mean to say that metaphysics—and technology—do not arrive? What is at stake in the homogeneity of the place of the postal and the destinality of being if not an improbable metaphysics of postal services or a parody of Heideggerian thought? And why, first and foremost, the post?

If metaphysics, technology or the post, it hardly matters which, are not things that come to surprise or modify the first sending, one could easily imagine that it is *they* that are *originary*. One could easily imagine replacing the phrase "in the beginning was the *logos*" by another: "in the beginning was the post." One *could*, except that what is in question is precisely the idea of beginning and of origin. Equally, to say that metaphysics does not *arrive* is not another way of saying that metaphysics is originary but, on the contrary, a way of saying that there is not *A Metaphysics*.[64] This merits a few words of explanation. If the post is a sending, and by definition a sending at a distance, what determines the sending is the time that separates it from its arrival at its destination. This destination, however, can never be assured, otherwise the time of the sending would be merely a false semblance of time, a fictitious time in which nothing actually happens, the neutral support of a content that, always identical with itself, is merely displaced from one point to another along a line of instants, a fictitious time that renders the sending itself fictive. Imagine that a sending is actually what is normally understood by a process of communication (something of which the handing down of the tradition would be only an expansion): a subject, the addresser, in full consciousness of what he or she means, sends a message that is merely the exact translation of his intention, without remainder, to another subject, the addressee, for whom the message is equally transparent. A subject who knows exactly what he or she means communicates the content of his meaning to another subject who understands exactly and only what it contains. The sending would be thus a transmission, the precise and full exchange of a communication with no remainder.

Does such a sending ever happen? And if it does, would there be a history? Would there be a sending? If sending must reckon with distance, separation and time, it is not in the sense that distance, separation and time would be simple obstacles to be surmounted, accidents always possible, certainly, but inessential nonetheless. Why? Because far from being inessential, these "accidents" constitute the very possibility of a sending being able to take place. There would be no sending without the always open possibility that it could be struck down by a forgetting (a forgetting that is not necessarily homogeneous with the forgetting of being or, still less, with that other notion of forgetting operative in our century, namely the psychoanalytic category of repression, if repression is understood as that which conserves what is forgotten in an unconscious but no less faultless memory.[65] What Derrida writes as regards letters has thus a far more general bearing. A letter can always *not* arrive; no one doubts this. But this possibility is not external or accidental, belonging rather to the essence (which is thus no longer an essence) of the letter.[66] Were a letter always to arrive at its destination it would no longer be a letter since, if one were certain of the destination, there would be no need for a sending. The fact that a letter can *not* arrive is not merely the fate of a particular letter, but the common fate of all letters. And if a letter can always *not* arrive this means that, in a certain sense, it never arrives. What is at stake here is the condition—positive and non-tragic—of sending and so also of the possibility of a letter arriving:

I'm taking notes for the preface. In it I would have (practically, actually, performatively) to make, but for you, my sweet love, my immense one, the demonstration that a letter can always—and thus must—never arrive at its destination. And that this is not negative, it's good, and is the condition (the tragic condition, certainly, and we know something about that) that something does arrive—and that I love you.[67]

There is no contradiction here. We have already seen that were one able to be certain of the destination there would be no need for a sending. The destination, which forms part of the sending, rendering possible the desire to send something, *also* generates the tension of what is not known in advance. The distance and separation implied in every sending is what makes a sending an *address*. Equally, the time of the sending is irreducibly the time of the other, the time of the address to the other. Without a cut, without interruption, there would be neither address nor sending. There would be no relation to the other. How can I address someone if not on the basis of an interruption, a caesura, without which the other would not be an other? The interruption of the address is the address itself, just as the possibility of a letter never arriving is the only chance of it ever arriving.[68] Yet if there has to be a separation and a distance in order for there to be a sending, this separation and this distance are already contained within the sending itself. A letter does not simply risk being lost once it is half-way to its address; the risk is there from the outset, from the inaugural moment when the sending ought to be surest of itself, which, for this very reason, is termed its origin. If everything begins with sending, this sending has nonetheless always been divisible and plural: there is no single *Sending* but only *sendings* without assured destination, without destiny. It should now be a little clearer why we cannot say, unless as a joke, that "in the beginning was the post." What this entire discourse on the post, this parody, if you like, makes clear is that the attempt to arrange the different epochs, pauses and determinations of the history of being according to *one* unique destination is an illusion. Just as there is no single *Sending*, no single *Metaphysics*, so there is no Central Post Office:

The postal principle is no longer a principle, nor a transcendental category; that which announces itself or sends itself under this heading (among other possible names, like you) no longer sufficiently belongs to the epoch of Being to submit itself to some transcendentalism, "beyond every genre." The post is but a little message, fold (*pli*) or just as well. A relay to mark that there is never anything but relays.[69]

Between this divisible sending and the sending of being a fundamental difference as to history is being played out.[70] Heidegger's thinking of ontological difference is also, without a shadow of a doubt, a thinking of history. It is the ontological difference that dictates, amongst other things, what Heidegger takes to be a fundamental distinction between *Historie* and *Geschichte*. In *Being and Time* it is because Dasein has a constitutive relation to being that it is essentially *geschichtlich* and the possibility of *Historie* as a narrative of events, as historiographical science, is rooted in this *geschichtlich* being of Dasein.[71] Later it is *being itself* that is being thought as historical. As such, history ought not to be confused with an empirical or ontic sequence of events: it is first an ontological characteristic of Dasein, and then the giving of being itself. In the strictest sense of the term, therefore, there will be no other history than the history of being, which is itself nothing outside of this history. Being only arises (*arrive*) in its history, which, as we have already seen, is nothing other than the history of an essential withdrawal. Hence the reason why some readers of Heidegger have sought to interpret the thinking of the ontological difference as a thinking of difference as such: the difference between being and beings, the impossibility of reducing being to some given being, of making it into a ground of beings, would mean that being is but a *gap*, the opening of all possible history.[72] Derrida's position is rather different: *ontological difference does not open history but closes it*; if there is history, it cannot be gathered and thought in terms of the Heideggerian concept of *Geschichte*, in terms of the opposition between *Geschichte* and *Historie*.

Heidegger's notion of the sending of being, even if it has no *telos*, is still sufficiently indivisible and gathered to itself to provide the origin of a *single history*, to the history of the different forms of the same forgetting that constitutes, according to Heidegger, metaphysics as such. The sending of being is still sufficiently indivisible and gathered to itself to *have an origin*. Despite its being constituted by an essential withdrawal, it is in closest proximity to itself at its origin and, for this very reason, the history to which it gives rise, the history of the transformations in being as *Anwesen*, the history of the epochs in their belonging together, takes the form of an always more profound concealment.[73] For Derrida, what is questionable in Heidegger's notion of epochality is clearly not the fact that there are changes. What is problematic in the history of metaphysics as narrated by Heidegger—even if, for Heidegger, it is precisely *not* a matter of narrative [*récit*][74]—is the suggestion that everything that has taken place arrives to us from an originary beginning that already contains within itself all possible transformations, which are thus only subsequently unfolded (precisely what Heidegger means by the notion of *Wandlungsfülle*, the abundance of changes). What arises, and what has arisen, arrives to us from the origin, and the form of this becoming—although the word "becoming" is perhaps a little inappropriate here—is a progressive *distancing* that is, in effect, a progressive *concealment*. Now, according to Derrida a history that begins from a proximity to itself is not really a history. And the epochs that derive from it, ordered as they are and all stemming from the same provenance, merely submerge all the differences, scansions and mutations that have taken place. To oppose the divisibility of all sending to the initial gathering of the sending of being means to *deny sending the possibility of functioning as an origin*, to gather oneself up in order to reduce history, what has or could have taken place and so what will be able to take place, *to the unity of a destiny*:

I have tried to retrace a path opened on a thought of the *envoi* which . . . did not as yet gather itself to itself as an *envoi* of being through *Answesenheit*, presence and then representation. This *envoi* is as it were pre-ontological, because it does not gather itself together or because it gathers itself only in dividing itself, in differentiating [*différant*] itself, because it is not original or originally a sending-from [*envoi-de*] (the *envoi* of something-that-is or of a present which would precede it, still less of a subject, or of an object by and for a subject), because it is not single and does not begin with itself although nothing present precedes it; and it issues forth only in already sending back: it issues forth only on the basis of the other, the other in itself without itself. Everything begins by referring back [*par le renvoi*], that is to say, does not begin.[75]

This divisibility of the sending is not negative, not a lack. On the contrary, as we have already seen, it is the condition for there being sendings and, possibly, the condition also for the sending of being, of the gift of being and time. It is the condition for there being history, the very possibility of history.[76] If we call this *différance*, we can see how Derrida can write that, *as soon as there is, there is* différance,[77] a *différance* that is older than the ontological difference, older in a sense that is clearly neither logical nor chronological, that harbors no reference to an origin, to an older or earlier *archè*, to an *archè* more withdrawn than the origin of ontology.[78] If *différance means* anything,[79] it is precisely the putting into question of this logic of the origin, a logic that is always also a logic of destination and sometimes of destiny.

The divisibility of sending, of *différance*, is thus not an event that could undermine the unity of an origin. To think division, *différance*, as something that happens at a particular moment *in* history is, for Derrida, the most fundamental of metaphysical gestures.[80] What happens *in* history, *as* history,[81] or in histories, are always singular divisions and differences preceded by no origin, and above all not by *différance* "itself":

> What is written as *différance*, then, will be the playing movement that "pro-duces"—by means of something that is not simply an activity—these differences, these effects of difference. This does not mean that the *différance* that produces differences is somehow before them, in a simple and unmodified—in-different—present. *Différance* is the non-full, non-simple, structured and differentiating origin of differences. Thus, the name "origin" no longer suits it.[82]

This is why one can say that *différance* does not happen or arrive, that it is "older" than the ontological difference between being and beings,[83] or even that it is always-already-there, according to another of deconstruction's more celebrated expressions. This is possible, however, only if one is attentive to the context from which such affirmations derive their sense, to the strategy to which they conform. For although *différance* does not arrive at a particular moment within a given history, this does not mean that it should be understood as an atemporal and synchronic structure commanding history.[84] Rather is it the dimension of *historicity in general*, something that ought not to be confused either with an ahistorical eternity or with some empirically determined moment in the course of factical history. The opening of history, its condition of possibility, is neither within history nor outside of it. *Outside* of history, it would still function as the ahistorical origin; *within* history, it would be reduced to merely one empirical fact amongst others.[85] Now, the gap between factical history, *Historie*, if you will, and historicity in general, does need to be sustained. But this gap is not the one that Heidegger can conceive through the distinction between *Geschichte* and *Historie*. The holding back (*Ansichhalten*) of sending (*Schicken*), the gap, if you will, from which *Geschichte* stems, is thought by Heidegger as origin; nothing precedes it—and in this sense it is, in effect, *pure* opening—and nothing exceeds it in the history to which it gives rise. Now, if nothing either precedes or exceeds it, the history that it opens up is, in a certain sense, programmed in advance; its form can only be that of a progressive concealment:

> The epochs overlap each other in their sequence so that the original sending of Being as presence is more and more obscured in different ways.[86]

The originary sending sends us history, but as a destiny. Indeed, it is hard to see how it could be otherwise. For what can come to us from an origin that is preceded by nothing if not the origin itself? Whether it arrives to us in the form of an infinite progress, a teleological movement or, on the contrary, in the form of a progressive—and finite—concealment, as is the case for Heidegger, *the origin can transmit only itself.* Thus historicity, at least as Derrida thinks it, has no origin, does not begin.[87] Why? Because *the origin is not a category of history.* Which is not to say that everything would have been in place from the start; rather is it to say precisely the opposite: nothing can truly take place on the basis of a pure beginning. Which implies a certain logic of the event. I shall come back to this. For the moment, however, I want to remain a little longer with the concept of origin as it functions in Heidegger's text. Indeed, it seems to me that it is precisely here that we find the confirmation of everything that we have said regarding the fact that the origin cannot be a category of history.

3. The Paradox of the Origin in Heidegger

For Heidegger, the gesture of raising anew the fundamental question "How does it stand with being?" is nothing other than a repetition (*Wieder-holung*) of the origin or the inception (*Anfang*) of what he calls our historical-spiritual (*geschichtlich-geistig*) Dasein.[88] In order for such a repetition to be carried out, one has to go back to the original sources of metaphysics, to those sources that the tradition has concealed to the point of rendering incomprehensible the very necessity of this return. Accordingly, therefore, one has to render newly accessible that which the tradition has concealed rather than handed down.[89] Only by questioning this essential provenance anew does the link with tradition become a *lösende Bindung*, a liberating link. As such, it is always in the horizon of the future that thinking turns back, back toward its provenance. Thinking as *An-denken* is inseparable from thinking as *Vordenken*.[90] The look or step back is always oriented toward the future; turning toward what *has been thought* is the only way of turning toward what is *still to be thought*.[91] The past, the authentic past, arrives to us from the future: this is the structure of ek-static temporality of Dasein explored in *Being and Time*,[92] but is also the form of every authentic relation to tradition. Now, it is precisely this relation of the past to the future that explains the return to the inception (*Anfang*), the extreme paradox of the function of the origin in Heidegger's thinking. As we have already seen, the "return" is always a repetition. Yet the only way of repeating the origin is by taking it up more originally. *The function of the origin is to clear the path toward another origin.*[93] What Heidegger is looking for in the Greeks is not a model to be repeated,[94] but the inaugural force of the origin. That alone is what is to be repeated. The return to the inception can only be a new inception. And it for this reason alone that, as we said earlier, *the origin can only produce another origin.* Or its *degeneration*:[95]

To ask: how does it stand with Being?—this means nothing less than to *repeat and retrieve (wieder-holen)* the inception [*Anfang*] of our historical-spiritual [*geschichtlich-geistigen*] Dasein, in order to transform it into the other inception. Such a thing is possible. It is in fact the definitive form of history [*Geschichte*], because it has its onset in a happening that grounds history [*Grundgeschehnis*]. But an inception is not repeated when one shrinks back to it as something that once was, something that by now is familiar and is simply to be imitated, but rather where the inception is begun again *more originally* [*ursprüng-licher*], and with all the strangeness, darkness, insecurity that a genuine inception brings with it.[96]

Outside of origin as pure springing forth (*Entspringung*), there can be only a fall. And such is the destiny that befalls the originary words that opened the *Geschichte* of the West, that opened it as a *fall out of truth.* If Parmenides' words have long been considered the guiding principle of Western philosophy, it is only insofar as they ceased to be understood:

The saying became the guiding principle of Western philosophy only after it was no longer understood, because its originary truth could not be held fast. The Greeks themselves began to fall away from the truth of the saying [*das Heraus-fallen aus der Wahrheit des Spruches*] right after Parmenides. Originary truths of such scope can be held fast only if they constantly unfold in a still more originary way [*indem sie ständig noch ursprünglicher zur Entfaltung kommen*]—never, however, by merely applying and appealing to them. The originary remains originary only if it has the constant possibility of being what it is: origin as springing forth [from the concealment of the essence] [*Ursprung als Entspringen (aus ver Verborgenheit des Wesens)*].[97]

The origin is thus only ever the origin of itself. Or of its concealment. Beyond its inaugural moment, history is produced as concealment. And it should be pointed out that this inaugural moment becomes for Heidegger ever shorter until it lasts no longer than a flash of lightning. If, in *Being and Time*, which begins with a citation from Plato's *Sophist*, the origin has a real duration—the highpoint of Greek philosophy, from Plato to Aristotle, after which the forgetting of fundamental questioning as to the sense of being accordingly begins[98]—in the years following 1927 things are rather different. From the 1930s onward, the moment of rupture is moved back, as it were, to mark off those who are usually, although inaccurately, termed the Pre-Socratics from all subsequent thinkers.[99] In certain passages from *Introduction to Metaphysics*, like the passage on Parmenides cited above, Heidegger appears to suggest that during a particular period, precisely the period of the origin, an original experience of being in fact took place, albeit implicitly, lodged in language. The fall out of truth (*Herausfallen aus der Warheit*) would be subsequent, would come after, even if immediately after. Yet the duration of this experience, already implicit and fragile, is quickly reduced by Heidegger. In "Logos" of 1944 he writes:

What would have come to pass had Heraclitus—and all the Greeks after him— thought the essence of language [*das Wesen des Sprache*] properly [*eigens*] as Logos, as the Laying that gathers [*lesende Lege*]! Nothing less than this: the Greeks would have thought the essence of language [*Wesen der Sprache*] from the essence of being—indeed, as this itself. For Logos is the name for the Being of beings. Yet none of this came to pass. Nowhere do we find a trace of the Greeks having thought the essence of language [*Wesen des Sprache*] directly from the essence of being [*Wesen des Seins*]. . . . *Once, however, in the beginning of Western thinking, the essence of language flashed in the light of Being—once, when Heraclitus thought the Logos as his guiding word, so as to think in this word the Being of beings. But the lightning abruptly vanished. No one held onto its streak of light and the nearness of what it illuminated.*[100]

Then even the lightning itself vanishes. In one of his last texts, "The End of Philosophy and the Task of Thinking," Heidegger refuses to extend any privilege to the Pre-Socratics. The translation of *aletheia* by *Unverborgenheit* no longer has anything to do with etymology, but concerns the matter (*Sache*) of thinking.[101] Not only did the Greeks *not* think *aletheia* explicitly as *Unverborgenheit,* they entirely lacked the implicit experience with which Heidegger had previously credited them. *Aletheia* has always been thought as the conformity of the proposition (*Richtigkeit der Aussage*), not merely in philosophical language, but in poetic language, too.[102] The history of Greek philosophy—and with it the history of metaphysics in general—is reunited. If, in *Being and Time*, the Pre-Socratics had been assimilated to Plato and Aristotle, the opposite is now the case. The moment of rupture is suppressed; the division between the originary and the derivative no longer divides history. *The withdrawal of the origin is its withdrawal from history.*[103]

The parting between the originary and the derivative, between the origin and its concealment, runs throughout—or, rather, underpins—the whole of Heidegger's thinking. In *Being and Time* it is the phenomenological model of original structures (which contain both their own possibility *and* the possibility of their concealment) that guides the entire analytic of Dasein and the project of the destruction (*Destruktion*) of the history of ontology. Throughout, it is a matter of starting from a concealed, derivative, or inauthentic form so as to move toward the proper, authentic, or original, of returning the derivative to that from which it derives, of returning it to the originary possibility that can be read through *its own* concealment. This model continues to function on the level of historicality, even when the withdrawal of the origin becomes so profound that it can be seen as a withdrawal from history. If the originary has never taken place, not even in the earliest moments of Greece, it nonetheless continues to impose its law on everything that does take place. History is readable only in relation to the withdrawal of its origin.

Two questions arise at this point. The first concerns the problem of knowing whether the origin-concealment model actually allows one to think something like historicity. The second concerns the phenomenological status of this model. The first of these questions was clearly at the forefront of the preceding analyses, analyses that might well have led one to suspect that the origin-concealment model is not, in fact, compatible with a thinking of historicity, at least if one understands by historicity the possibility of a becoming that is irreducible to a series of changes or modifications *within the same*. Indeed, it is difficult to think origin as anything other than a pure opening absolutely independent of that to which it gives rise. As we have already seen, however, historicity does not, in fact, arise from such a *pure* opening, a concept that seems to me far too theological to be in accordance with a thinking of historicity; nor do I believe that historicity can be reduced to changes within the same. This said, we would need to look closer at precisely how the notion of origin operates in Heidegger's thinking of temporality, of historicity and finitude, for *original temporality* alone is finite. Other analyses would be necessary, therefore, in order to confirm the suspicions being raised here. All the same, it should not be forgotten that, from the outset, Heidegger's thinking of being and time is inscribed within a thinking of history.[104]

The second question, which intersects with the first, concerns the difference between the way in which Heidegger and Husserl put the concept of origin to work. Let me explain. The notion of origin (and of concealment) is doubtless present—and operative—in Husserl's phenomenology. The crisis of history of which Husserl speaks is a crisis of the forgetting or the concealment of originary sense, that is, of the *origin* of sense. But the problematic of origin in Husserl continually intersects—and is ceaselessly complicated by—a problematic of genesis. The same cannot be said for Heidegger who, guided as he is by a preoccupation with a more originary thinking of being and time, displaces the origin-concealment model—the opening-closure model, if you like—from the level of the analytic of Dasein to that of the historicity of being. Yet no genetic question can complicate an essentially *static* model. Dasein is born and Dasein dies, of course, but it does not *become*. Dasein *is* according to one of its possibilities (or their modal absence).[105] It is authentic or inauthentic, proper or improper, but the question of becoming, of the movement from one possibility to another, is never raised,[106] still less the question of *becoming Dasein*.[107] Of course, one can always object that the *very being* of Dasein lies in its existence (without essence) and that one cannot accordingly turn the being of Dasein into an essence and even less into a *static* essence. This is obviously true. Nonetheless, the elimination of any genetic dimension seems to me to prompt questions and to pose problems that will have to be addressed. Every genetic question is delegitimized *a priori*. According to Heidegger, the only possible horizon for dealing with genetic questions is that of causal explanation, borrowed from the natural sciences, ruling out thereby any relevance to an inquiry concerned with being: with the being of Dasein or with being as such. The same goes for the history [*Geschichte*] of being: the forgetting that befalls it has neither becoming (progressive concealment being only a *distancing* of the origin) nor cause; it is only—and can only be—a destiny. To the contrary, the question of genetic becoming continues to haunt Husserl's phenomenology. Now, it is precisely this genetic dimension that, through the question of passivity, allows Derrida to address not merely the limits of phenomenology but also that toward which these limits themselves point as a positive possibility for thinking. The limits of phenomenology indicate a *project* for thinking, a project which is not the project of Heideggerian ontology. My hypothesis here is that the notions elaborated by Derrida through his putting into question of phenomenological time and transcendental historicity in Husserl are still at work, now as a theoretical backdrop, in his confrontation with Heidegger. And in this confrontation the question of passive genesis, insofar as it is opposed to any possible concept of origin, leaves more than a trace.

In order to show this—and this will be the subject of the following chapter—we need first to recall that the question of historicality (*Geschichte*) is always tied in Heidegger to the question of an originary temporality, whether it is a matter of the temporality (*Zeitlichkeit*) of Dasein or of the temporality of being itself.[108]

2.2

Whence the Future?

1. Originary Temporality and Originary Historicality

In *Being and Time* the project of raising anew the question of the meaning of being involves a twofold task: on the one hand the elaboration of the analytic of Dasein, on the other the destruction (*Destruktion*) of the history of ontology. The first of these is carried out, the second only announced. Nonetheless, both are placed under the banner of a struggle against dissimulation, both intended to open a path through concealments.[1] This is why the new ontology is possible only as phenomenology and why phenomenology is in turn possible only as hermeneutics. If one must return to the things themselves then this is because there can be no immediate access to them, because forgetting and concealment are indissociable from all showing.[2] This is the sense of the "Greek" interpretation that Heidegger gives of phenomenology in §7 of *Being and Time*. Phenomenon (*phainomenon, phainesthai*) means that which shows-itself-from-itself, the manifest (*das Sich-an-ihm-selbst-zeigende, das Offenbare*). Yet such a self-showing always implies the possibility that beings can be given as something that in themselves they are not, that they can be given as semblance or appearance (*Scheinen*).[3] Between phenomenon, as that which shows itself, and semblance there is, Heidegger insists, a structural unity but also an "order" of derivation. The ability to show itself is the ground of all dissimulation. Thus, appearance is a privative modification (*privativen Modifikation*) of manifestation.

The structure of phenomena is thus a structure of manifestation-concealment[4] to which the structure of *logos* itself corresponds. If *logos* is understood as discourse (*Rede*) then this is only because *legein* is first of all *apophainesthai*: the making manifest of the beings about which one is speaking by wresting them from their withdrawal (*Verborgenheit*). When this is the case: because the power of discovering (*entdecken*) that belongs to discourse is always accompanied by the power of covering over (*verdecken*). The parallel between phenomena and *logos* is an exact one: to the way in which a being "shows itself from itself," which always implies the possibility of that being showing itself as "something that it is not," there corresponds a "letting-be-seen" which, as originally disclosive, harbors within itself the possibility of concealment. If being is the phenomena *par excellence*, it is precisely because, in the first place and for the most part, it does not show itself; the depth of its withdrawal and its concealment is unparalleled.[5] As the "original" and "intuitive" seizure of phenomena, phenomenology is the opposite of a naïve and immediate seeing; phenomenological letting-be-seen will never be reducible to the pure passivity of mere reception. From which it follows that ontology is won only at the expense of a hard-fought battle against the powers of dissimulation and concealment and the path toward what is original won only at the expense of a struggle against forgetting.

The manifestation-concealment structure of all phenomena guides the very problematic of the interpretation of being from out of the horizon of time. The temporality (*Zeitlichkeit*) and historicality of Dasein make their appearance in the analyses of *Being and Time* at the very moment that Heidegger posits the need for the ontological interpretation to be originary.[6] If, in accordance with its methodological demands, the work begins with the way in which Dasein is given in the first place and for the most part, that is, in the mode of everydayness, there can be no possible guarantee that the analyses will have dealt with Dasein as a whole. Indeed, they would seem even to exclude such a possibility: existence is defined first and foremost as the potentiality-for-being of a being that is always mine and that is free for authenticity or inauthenticity or their modal indifference. Now, in everyday life, one does not encounter the authentic potentiality-for-being of Dasein that can alone assure that the analysis of the meaning of the being of Dasein will attain the necessary level of originarity.[7] The analyses of everydayness aim to bring to light the unitary structural of Dasein as care (*Sorge*) but they fail in this because they have still not articulated the mode of being proper (*eigen*) to Dasein, its possible authenticity

(*Eigentlichkeit*), a possibility that Heidegger will find in the celebrated analyses of Dasein's potentiality for being-a-whole (*Ganzsein*), a potentiality founded on its being-toward-death (*Sein-sum-Tode*).[8] It is only on the basis of this authentic possibility of being a whole that the ontological sense of care can be revealed as temporal. If the interpretation of the being of Dasein can attain the necessary level of originality only once Dasein's authentic potentiality-for-being has been attested then this is not only because any such interpretation has to be *complete* and authenticity shown to be part of existence, but also because the possibility of Dasein being-a-whole is attested only in the mode of authenticity, the mode of originary being.

At this point in the analyses, the two modalities of authenticity and inauthenticity seem to be indissociable from a double schema of the original and the derivative,[9] as well as being essentially of a piece with the structure of manifestation-concealment with which we began. Indeed, if the mode of the authentic and the originary are concealed, it is because the level of *Eigentlichkeit* is founded upon itself and, at the same time, accounts for the inauthentic as its derivative possibility. The authentic is the possibility both of itself and of the inauthentic: closing off is only a (privative) mode of opening up. This is why Heidegger, once he has shown the temporal meaning of *Sorge*, will repeat the analyses of everydayness in order to establish that they are possible only as modifications of original temporality, and why he will undertake to show that the ordinary conception of time—the "vulgar" time that is nothing other than the metaphysical conception of time, from Aristotle to Bergson and beyond[10]—finds its possibility in original temporality. Because if it is "vulgar," it is above all derivative. Both the critique of metaphysics that the Heidegger of *Being and Time* identifies as a *Destruktion* of the history of ontology, as well as his thought of finitude, are placed under the sign of *originary temporality*. What are the consequences of this decision for the historicality—also originary—of Dasein and the irreducible passivity of time that—from genesis to trace—lies at the heart of Derrida's work? Before returning to Derrida's texts on Heidegger, it seems to me necessary to pause for a moment on the Heideggerian notion of the originary past and its implications for historicality.

From whence comes the future? Derrida and Lévinas would probably respond: from the past. From an immemorial past that was never present. And Heidegger? Let us see.

If being-toward-death and resoluteness (*Entschlossenheit*) are the authentic modalities of care, the possibility of Dasein being a whole, is there not then a paradox? The being always ahead-of-itself (*Sichvorweg*), the potentiality-for-being (*Seinkönnen*) that defines existence in *being-toward-death* seems opposed to any sense of closure. But the temporality that underpins the unified structure of *Sorge* has nothing to do with this conception of time as a linear succession of instants. It is in *Sorge* itself that Heidegger finds the principle for the pluralization of time.[11] The sense of care is originarily a potentiality-for-being: the anticipatory resoluteness (*vorlaufende Entschlossenheit*) is nothing other than a being-for one's own-most potentiality-for-being.[12] Yet this is only possible because of the originary phenomena of the future or the future as coming toward (*Zu-Kunft*)[13], itself in no way a non-present present but the possibility for Dasein to let itself come toward itself (*sich auf sich zukommen-lassen*):

> By the term "futural" [*Zukunft*] we do not here have in view a "now" [*Jetzt*] which has *not yet* become "actual" and which sometime *will be* for the first time. We have in view the coming [*Kunft*] in which Dasein, in its ownmost potentiality-for-Being, comes toward itself [*auf sich zukommt*]. Anticipating [*das Vorlaufen*] makes Dasein *authentically* futural [*eigentlich zukünftig*], and in such a way that anticipation itself is possible only in so far as Dasein, *as being*, is always coming toward itself—that is to say, in so far as it is futural in its Being in general.[14]

It is on the basis of this new meaning of the future [*à-venir*] that Heidegger brings out the reciprocal implication of the three dimensions of time. The authentic dimension of the future demands that Dasein take over its thrownness (*Geworfenheit*). Dasein can only happen to itself [*advenir à soi*] in the mode of a return. The authentic future implies thus an equally authentic return, what Heidegger calls the existential past. From the future and from the having-been (*Gewesen*) there also arises the originary present which, far from being thought along the lines of the presence of things, refers to the existential notion of situation.[15] Thus the present does not generate the past and the future as modifications of itself but is, on the contrary, "deduced" on the basis of them. *Zeitlichkeit* is the ek-static unity that unfolds in the mutual implication of the ek-stases (future, having-been and present), the ek-static character of which marks temporality as "the pure and simple original outside-of-itself [*Ausser-sich*]": temporality (Dasein, then) is not a being that can step outside itself but is from the outset the *outside-of-itself*.[16] If the temporalization of the ek-stases is co-original, however, and if it can be determined on the basis of one or the other, it nonetheless remains the case that, according to its authentic mode, it is temporalized on the basis of the future: the primary phenomenon of original and authentic temporality is the future. As Heidegger puts it: "the primary phenomenon of primordial and authentic temporality is the future" (*das primäre Phänomen der ursprünglichen und eigentlichen Zeitlichkeit ist die Zukunft*).[17] This accords with the proper sense of *Sein-zum-Tode*, which does not simply imply that Dasein has an end, that at a particular moment it ceases to exist; rather, the end of Dasein as its ownmost possibility means that it exists in a finite manner. The temporality that arises in Dasein's coming toward itself is thus originally finite; it has an end that does not befall it from without, at the moment when existence ceases, but opens it from within itself. Are we now in a position to respond to the question: Whence the future? Not yet. What we *can* already say, however, is that it does not come from the past. And why not? Because it is the past itself that arises from the future:

> Only in so far as Dasein *is* as an "I-*am*-having-been" [*ich* bin-*gewesen*], can Dasein come toward itself futurally in such a way that it comes *back* [zurück-*kommt*]. As authentically futural, Dasein *is* authentically as "*having been*." Anticipation of one's uttermost and ownmost possibility is coming back understandingly to one's own most "been." Only so far as it is futural can Dasein *be* authentically as having been. The character of "having been" [*Gewesenheit*] arises, in a certain way, from the future.[18]

It is on the basis of the future alone that Dasein turns toward the past, toward a past that is never something by-gone "in" time but something that *has* passed [*il est* passé] only in so far as it *is* past [*il* est *passé*]. Is there a hint of *passivity* in the originary past? Perhaps. Yet *Gewesenheit* seems to exclude everything that is passively received from the sphere of the originary, something that is confirmed by the analyses of Dasein's historicality (*Geschichtlichkeit*). Heidegger introduces a dimension of anteriority necessary to every possible thought of history. This anteriority, however, is precisely *not* the anteriority of a past; it is the anteriority of birth. Just as temporality was introduced through the question of the possibility of Dasein being a whole, so the same goes for the question of its historicality. Death is but one of the ends of Dasein; there is another: its inception (*Anfang*), its birth. Dasein cannot be grasped in its being-a-whole without the extension (*Erstreckung*) that constitutes its existence between (*zwischen*) birth and death.[19] Insofar as it exists, Dasein exists in its ex-tension. Its birth is thus never a past, an event that is no longer present, just as death is never a future event.[20] *Sich-erstrecken*, the ex-tension that pulls the existence of

Dasein between birth and death is precisely what Heidegger sees as constituting its becoming-historical (*Geschehen*). In this way, Heidegger derives
historicality from originary temporality, the notion of *Erstreckung* being
comprehensible on the basis of *Sorge* alone. There are just two more things
that he needs to show, therefore: firstly, that what we habitually call history,
as well as all historiography, finds its basis in the *Geschichtlichkeit* of Dasein
and, secondly, how we can pass from one to the other. Now this passage
from one to the other is played out around the notion of the past: between
the past of the vulgar concept of time and the originary past of Dasein, a
past that is originary only insofar as it does not truly pass, as it continues
to exist, at least as long as Dasein exists. The finitude of originary time also
implies the impossibility of the authentic past being a past that is over.
Heidegger ponders the primacy of the "past" (*Vergangenheit*) in the constitution of historicality, but does so in order to turn away from its importance, in order to show its origin in this past of Dasein that is never over.
The example that Heidegger takes in order to clarify the character of the
past proper to history is a particularly instructive one: antiquities in a museum. In what sense are they *past*? They are still there. So what is it that
renders them historical? By what right do we call something that has not
yet passed historical? What is it that such things were and are no longer?
What is it that they lack? Heidegger's answer is that they lack the *world*:

> What *were* these "Things" which today they are no longer? . . . What is "past"
> [*vergangen*]? Nothing else than that *world* within which they belonged to a context
> of equipment and were encountered as ready-to-hand and used by a concernful
> Dasein who was-in-the-world. That *world* is no longer. But what was formerly
> *within-the-world* with respect to that world is still present-at-hand.[21]

The historical (*geschichtliche*) character of things is founded on Dasein's
past, and the world, we should remember, is one of Daseins' existentials.
Yet this remains the case only insofar as the past is understood in its originary sense: otherwise only the "past" (*vergangene*) Dasein could be historical (*geschichtliche*). Now, Dasein is never past. This is to say not that it is
imperishable but that its mode of being, existence, is irreducible to the
mode of being of other beings. A Dasein that no longer exists is not something past, but something that *has been-there* (*da-gewesen*).[22] This is why it
is unnecessary for Dasein to be no longer there in order for it to become
historical: Dasein is historical in the very manner of its existing, and
nowhere else. The past (*Vergangenheit*) is no more a category of history
than it is a category of existence because, according to Heidegger, it con-

cerns only beings that are *vorhanden* or *zuhanden*. The dichotomy between being past and having-been is one of two irreducible modes of being: the mode of being of "things" and the mode of being of the beings that we ourselves always are. It is only because Dasein does not think what is proper to it that it interprets itself in terms of the things that it encounters within the world. Of course, such inauthenticity is still one of the possible modalities of existence, and is to a certain extent inevitable, but it is founded on possible authenticity. It is only because Dasein is not a thing that it can think itself—improperly—in terms of things. *The question that needs to be asked, therefore, is whether what is irreversible and irreducible in the past can simply be left on the side of the past of things. Or, in more Husserlian terms, whether Dasein's past, as* an originary past, *is always reactivatable.* For Heidegger the answer is probably yes, thanks to the finitude of time and its essential bond with authenticity. We have already seen that it is on the basis of the future that the original past comes to be temporalized. Now that it is a question of historicality,[23] the implications of this provenance ought to be a little clearer. We have seen that the ground of Dasein's historicality has to be located in care. In anticipatory resoluteness toward death Dasein takes on its potentiality for being, which implies that it takes on its facticity, that it decides as to the situation. Now, the actual possibilities of existence do not stem from the possibility of death, all the more so since the anticipation of the possibility of death means nothing other than Dasein's being referred to the place where it is, to its own factical (*faktisch*) *da*, that is, to the world in which it always exists. In resoluteness, Dasein turns back in on itself in order to open itself to the factical possibilities of an authentic manner of existing in terms of a heritage that it takes on, a taking on that is *also* the taking on of a destiny (*Schicksal*):

The resoluteness in which Dasein comes back to itself, discloses current factical possibilities of authentic existing, and discloses them *in terms of the heritage* which that resoluteness, as thrown, *takes over.* . . . Only by the anticipating [*Vorlaufen*] of death is every accidental and provisional possibility for being driven out. Only Being-free *for* death, gives Dasein its goal outright and pushes existence into its finitude. Once one has grasped the finitude of one's existence, it snatches one back from the endless multiplicity of possibilities which offer themselves as closest to one—those of comfortableness, shirking, and taking things lightly—and brings Dasein into the simplicity of its *fate.* This is how we designate Dasein's primordial historizing [*ursprüngliche Geschehen*], which lies in authentic resoluteness and in which Dasein *hands* itself *down* [*überliefert*] to itself, free for death, in a possibility which it has inherited and yet has chosen.[24]

The past appears thus by way of resoluteness, and if it does, of course, take on the form of a heritage, then this heritage is so freely chosen that it constitutes a transmission of the self to the self, a *self-heritage*, one could say, and, in this sense, a *destiny (Schicksal)*: *"Das in der Entschlossenheit liegende vorlaufende* Sichüberliefern *an das Da des Augenblicks nennen wir Schiksal."*[25] What constitutes authentic historicality is the repetition of a given possibility. This repetition, however, stems from a resolute self-projection (*entschlossen Sichentwerfen*) that resists the seductions of a past. Indeed, this repetition resists being seduced by the past to such a great extent that it could only be described as its disavowal (*Widerruff*). What is repeated is fundamentally nothing other than *possibility*:[26]

The resoluteness which comes back to itself and hands itself down [*die auf sich zurückkommende, sich überlieferten Entschlossenheit*], then becomes the *repetition* [Widerholung] of a possibility of existence that has come down to us. *Repeating is handing down explicitly* [ist die ausdrückliche Überlieferung]—that is to say, going back into the possibilities of the Dasein that has-been-there. . . . Arising, as it does, from a resolute projection of oneself, repetition does not let itself be persuaded [*überreden*] of something by what is "past," just in order that this, as something which was formerly actual, may recur. Rather, the repetition makes a *reciprocative rejoinder* [*erwidert*] to the possibility of that existence which has-been-there. But when such a rejoinder is made to this possibility in a resolution, it is made *in a moment of vision; and as such* it is at the same time a *disavowal* [*als augenblickliche der* Widerruf] of that which in the "today," is working itself out as the "past."[27]

Access to the originary past involves the disavowal of the past as such. Historicality has no after effect [après-coup].[28] Its roots lie neither in the past nor in the present but in the future: it is authentic being-toward-death—the finitude of temporality—that constitutes the hidden basis of Dasein's historicality (*Geschichlichkeit*).[29] But this grounding of history in the constitution of the being of Dasein poses several problems. If authentic being-toward-death, the finitude of Dasein's temporality, is the hidden ground of Dasein's historicality, then historicality is defined first and foremost in an eminently "individual" way. Death, which is always mine, refers Dasein back to the *solitude* of its decision.[30] Even the heritage that it takes on is placed thus under the sign of this coming back to itself that Heidegger immediately defines as a *self*-transmission, a heritage *passed down from the self to the self.* The collectivity necessary to all history appears only, and somewhat elliptically, thanks to some essential structures of Dasein's constitution such as being-in-the-world and being-with. The world and others are summoned by originary historicality only on the basis of Dasein's absolute singularity. Indeed, it could hardly be otherwise given that historicality originates in being-toward-death, which is, remember, *always mine*: *sein-zum-Tode* is for Heidegger the site of absolute singularity and irreplaceability.[31] All of which chimes perfectly with the strange heritage passed down from the self, in which one inherits only what is *taken on*, and with this notion of the originary past, in which everything that is irreducibly past is disavowed in the always open possibility of repetition. The originary past is nothing more than the past that one can always summon anew. *Vergänglichkeit*, the possibility of disappearing without trace, seems to belong to things alone, to beings whose mode of being is that of *Vorhandenheit* or *Zuhandenheit*. *The historicality that stems from Dasein and from its future is truely finite, and finite, too, in the sense that the past and the future summoned by Dasein remain caught within the limits of* its *project.*

Whence the future, therefore? From Dasein itself, from this ecstatic and originally finite opening that is its own being-toward-death.

It seems to me necessary to return to *Sein und Zeit* at the very point at which our question bore on the historicality of being in the final figure that it assumes in Heidegger's thinking: that of the gift (*es gibt*) of being and of time. Why? Because at its core, the critique that Derrida addresses to the Heideggerian notion of epochality concerns the *gathering* to itself of the sending of being, a gathering that makes a *destiny* of being. Now, this gathering only occurs as such because the sending of being is *originary*. This sending has *an* origin, *one* origin: the fact that this origin is not full but is, on the contrary, more and more withdrawn, and that this withdrawal is essential, changes nothing on this point. It is a *single* origin, and produces only a *single* history that has the form of a series of modifications that are as many necessary concealments of itself. But, according to Derrida, historicity is precisely that which cannot be thought within the horizon of an origin. *Origin is not a category of history.* It is for this reason that what Heidegger thinks as historicality is, in fact, a *form of the reduction of history*.[32] Now the model of an origin and of its concealment does not appear in Heidegger's thinking with the introduction of the historicality of being. It already guides the analyses of *Being and Time*; it is the very definition of phenomena in the sense of phenomenology. The finitude of Dasein, of its ownmost temporality and historicality, are thought *as* originary. On this point, at least, there is no *Kehre*: whether it is a matter of the temporality and the historicality of Dasein or of being itself, this temporality and this historicality are *originarily* finite. Now what Derrida has tried to think as the movement of temporalization and as historicity is precisely what cannot be derived from an origin. We saw in the first part of this study how Derrida deploys these themes by way of a reading of Husserl. I shall now want to come back to this. Derrida's refusal to think historicity through the categories of origin and concealment is rooted in his interpretation of the *genetic dimension* of Husserlian phenomenology, a dimension that will not cease to haunt and to contradict the project of an *originary foundation*. If, according to Derrida, the question of genesis thwarts the project of a pure phenomenology and the project of a philosophy as "rigorous science," it remains a constitutive theme of this project itself. Such is, it seems to me, the principle difference between Husserlian phenomenology and that of Heidegger, from the point of view of the relations that Derrida maintains with these two modes of thinking. The putting into question of Husserlian phenomenology, far from being a "deconstruction without remainder," has been for Derrida the point of departure in the elaboration of questions central to his own reflection. This is demonstrated, I believe, by the notions of the contamination of the empirical and the transcendental and of ideality (without presence) that traverse and underpin his entire thinking.[33] And which remains operative in his uninterrupted dialogue with Heidegger. This is what I shall want to try to show in the following pages as regards the Heideggerian conception of the temporality, historicality and being-toward-death of Dasein.

2. Genesis and Origin of Time

We have seen the central role played by the theme of genesis in Derrida's first work on Husserl and, in particular, in the interpretation that he puts forward of the *Lectures on Internal Time Consciousness*. If Husserl's project is to retrace the phenomenological origin of time, that is, its purely constituting origin, every genetic problematic seems for this very reason to be excluded, genesis being, at this point in Husserl's thinking, confined to the level of the empirical and the constituted. According to Derrida, however, although genesis may well be excluded on principle, it nonetheless returns to haunt Husserl in the form of the *passive synthesis* necessary for the appearance of temporality, a synthesis that Husserl wants to be purely phenomenological but that—still according to Derrida—is just as *ontological* and *empirical* insofar as it reintegrates the constituted into the constituting and marks thus the impossibility of a pure phenomenology. The originary now, which appears by way of a passive synthesis of time with itself, through a retention—however immediate this may be—of the past, is constituting only because rooted in a constituted past. The present appears thus on the basis of a passive continuity with the prior moment. *What marks the difference between genesis and origin is the question of passivity.* The purely phenomenological origin of time ought to be purely constituting, the ground of phenomenological time a self-foundation.[34] Now, genesis introduces an *irreducible passivity* that is at the same time an *irreducible alterity*. The transcendental subject, as temporal subject, encounters the uncrossable limit of its power of pure self-constitution. The past is constituted *before* the present can be constituting: the genesis of time points toward this fundamental passivity that the very concept of origin would seek to deny.

Subsequently, Derrida will no longer employ the concept of genesis, but everything that he has elaborated thus far by way of the concept of passive genesis—the passivity of time in its connection with alterity and spacing—will be taken up once again in the notion of the trace:

The general structure of the unmotivated trace connects within the same possibility, and they cannot be separated except by abstraction, the structure of the relationship with the other, the movement of temporalization, and language as writing.[35]

Trace replaces genesis once the theme of writing appears, but it should not be forgotten that the theme of writing also first appears in the context of an interpretation of the movement of temporalization in Husserl.[36] Nor should it be forgotten that the trace will also mark the impossibility of every origin.[37] In *Voice and Phenomena*, the trace, as the common root of retention and re-presentation, constitutes the pure actuality of the now, thus rendering uncertain the boundary that separates the sphere of the originary certainty of the now (to which, according to Husserl, retention still belongs) from the non-originary sphere of every re-presentation. As such, this boundary no longer separates a pure present from a non-present, the actuality of the living now from the inactuality of the non-present, but the two forms of the re-turn or the re-stitution of the present: retention and re-presentation. The originary truth of phenomenology can only be constituted or wished to be so after the fact of the non-originary, of the trace as the finite movement of all retention and so of all temporalization.[38] First and foremost, therefore, finitude is the relation to an irreducible passivity that could be called time insofar as it refers to an absolute past, a past that has never been present: in this relation, the always-already-there marks the impossibility of reactivating the same origin that could bring it to presence:

This passivity is also the relation to a past, to an always-already-there that no re-activation of the origin could fully master and awaken to presence. This impossibility of reanimating absolutely the manifest evidence of an originary presence refers us therefore to an absolute past. That is what authorized us to call *trace* that which does not let itself be summed up in the simplicity of a present.[39]

The past is absolute because it cannot be envisaged simply as a *present* that is now past in the linear connection of successive nows. What is in question in the deconstruction of the privilege of the present is also, and perhaps above all, the classical idea of time as a *homogenous and successive* modification of the present. It is not enough to follow Husserl and simply complicate the structure of time; showing that the past present and the future present originarily constitute the form of the present by dividing it, is not yet grasping what is essential. To say that *Now* B is constituted by the retention of *Now* A and the protention of *Now* C leaves the linear model of the course of time unchanged; however complicated the structure of *Now* B, it is preceded by nothing if not *Now* A. And no present experience can ever be determined by a past that did not directly precede it, by a past that would be considerably anterior to it.[40] But why the reference to an absolute *past*? Why the need to speak of the *trace* in order to designate temporality? Could one not contest the homogeneity of the succession of time thought as a series of presents modified on the basis of the future? In the unfactorable synthesis of temporalization, protention is just as necessary as retention, and what is anticipated in protention is no less disjunctive of the self-identity of the present than that which holds itself back in the trace. Doubtless this is true. Yet any privilege accorded to anticipation inevitably runs the risk of effacing the passivity of time, its always-already-thereness.[41] Now, the always-already-thereness of time does not of course mean that everything has already taken place; rather, it means that what has taken place cannot be mastered, neither by Husserl's transcendental subject nor Heidegger's Dasein, to mention only those figures that concern us here.

Something about the past is irrevocable; just as no resolute decision can ever disavow the entire past of Dasein on the basis of the future that it has available to it, so no reactivating reduction can ever make the origin reappear or summon it back in an act of memory. Why? Because no present is ever simple, in tune with itself. All of which amounts to saying that it is not only the finitude of memory that means that the origin cannot be reactivated (as Husserl clearly recognized); were this to be the case, the impossibility of summoning something back would be merely a factual, empirical and accidental impossibility. *This* finitude—of memory, of time—fails to call the concept of origin into question. *The origin cannot be reactivated because it never took place.* Nothing begins in the fullness (or in the withdrawal) of an originary instant gathered to itself. What could happen on the basis of such an origin if not its infinite unfolding, already programmed in advance as a *telos*, or, on the contrary, its concealment, its *degeneration*? The absolute past, the past that has no origin, is thus the sole possibility of the future. The passivity of a past that is not a past-present is *also* the relation to a future that is not a future-present. Were this not so, the future would not truly be a future; it would remain within a horizon of anticipation; it could be anticipated and calculated, hostile to anything that might arrive: first and foremost, to the coming or the event of the other.[42]

By putting into question Husserl's "dialectic" of temporal synthesis, Derrida finds thus not the model of a complication of the structure of the present but the idea of a temporality marked by an irreducible *anachrony*,[43] an anachrony that he elaborates first through the notion of genesis and then through that of the trace. We have already seen the sort of continuity that regulates the passage from one to the other. What needs now to be noted, therefore, is that Husserl's phenomenology, shot through as it is by the tension between the level of the constituting and that of the constituted, is caught immediately within a genetic problematic, static analyses being only one stage of the investigation. The very position of the question of the transcendental would prevent Husserl from being indifferent to the possibility of a certain becoming. Now, as we have seen in regards to both *Being and Time* and the later work on the historicality of being, this genetic dimension is wholly absent in Heidegger's thought. This raises the question of what possible relations there might be between a temporality thought on the basis of the trace (a temporality that maintains the "heritage" of a problematic of genesis) and Heidegger's originary temporality. Although it goes without saying that both are finite, the concept at finitude at work here is not the same in each case. The question, therefore, is also a question concerning finitude.

On the basis of all that has been said, the differences are relatively easy to spot: they are played out around the notions of genesis and origin. Temporality thought by way of the trace is finite[44] because it resists being gathered to itself in any of its dimensions: both in the past, which in order to be absolute will never have been present, that is, will never have been *one* with itself, gathered to itself, and in the future, which will never be a present to come [*un present à venir*]. And, more emphatically, in the present "itself," if by present is meant the absence of any gap, the simplicity of a non-divided presence.[45] This is what Derrida terms anachrony.[46] It, too, denotes the impossibility of origin, since origin cannot be thought outside the notion of gathering. *Finitude marks thus the impossibility of the origin, precisely the opposite of what happens in Heidegger, where temporality is finite only insofar as it is originary.* Not only, moreover, in the sense that it would in some way come "before" infinite time, the sense in which it would be the forgotten foundation of infinite time, but also because the authentic temporality of Dasein—and the possibility of its sheer authenticity—is only thinkable within the horizon of its finitude: it is from this finite future that being-toward-death, which temporalizes the ekstases of temporality, is opened. The privilege that Heidegger accords to the future is indeed founded on finitude, but is tied essentially to the themes of authenticity and the originary.[47] Only once Dasein has decided in favor of its ownmost possibility, in favor of its mortal and finite future, does it turn toward its own past and take it over. The finitude of time guarantees thus the possibility of Dasein's taking on its *ownmost* past; as Heidegger himself puts it, in being-toward-death the past is "disavowed." The past freely taken over by Dasein is thus something entirely different from the absolute past to which the notion of the trace refers. The same can be said for the future. The resolute decision is devoid of all passivity; in the decision it is a matter of taking over a destiny, but between destiny and the passivity of time the choice is radical.[48] If the past and the future of which Heidegger and Derrida are speaking are not the same past and future, then we need to attend to the difference that is played out around the present, the precise point at which the proximity between them would seem to be the most acute. Heidegger will never cease to question the strange privilege of the present.[49] But just as there is an authentic future and an authentic past in Heidegger, so there is an authentic present: the *Augenblick*, the moment in which nothing happens (*vorkommen*, in the sense that things "happen" in the *Jetzt*, the now) but that first renders possible the encounter with beings as things that are present- or ready-to-hand.[50] Authentic temporality is a unitary phenomenon:

Coming back to itself futurally, resoluteness brings itself into the Situation by making present. The character of "having been" arises from the future, and in such a way that the future which "has been" (or better, which "is in the process of having been") [*die gewesene (besser gewesende) Zukunft*] releases from itself the Present.

This phenomenon has the unity of a future which makes present in the process of having been [*gewesend-gegenwärtigende Zukunft*]; we designate it as "*temporality.*" Only in so far as Dasein has the definite character of temporality, is the authentic potentiality-for-being-a-whole of anticipatory resoluteness, as we have described it, made possible for Dasein itself. *Temporality reveals itself as the meaning of authentic care.*[51]

Rather than signaling disjunction, time is a gathering. And finitude, then, far from preventing Dasein from being a whole is precisely what allows it to grasp itself in an ownmost way.[52] Finitude, therefore, rather than being the impossibility of the originary, is the originary itself.[53]

But what is at stake in the difference between the anachrony of the trace and the originary finitude of temporality? To my mind, the difference is essentially an ethical or arche-ethical one; that is, one that concerns the condition of all possible engagement for an ethics. For Derrida, from *The Problem of Genesis* right up to the most recent texts, the movement of temporalization is unthinkable outside of a relation to alterity: to the alterity of the other, of course, but also to the alterity inscribed within the subject's own relation to itself. And just as the notion of gathering threatens the possibility of a future beyond any anticipatory horizon, so, too, does it threaten this relation to alterity. In *Specters of Marx*, the theme of the disjunction of time, Hamlet's "the time is out of joint" is interpreted as the very condition of justice, an interpretation that leads Derrida, perhaps unsurprisingly, to address those passages from "The Anaximander Fragment" in which Heidegger considers the relation of time to *dikè*. I cannot reconstruct here the whole of those analyses, and so will limit myself to drawing attention to just one of its traits. *Dikè*, justice, is interpreted by Heidegger as *Fug, Fuge*: jointure, alignment, harmonious accord, ordering articulation, etc., and this alignment is thought on the basis of being as presence.[54] From which it follows that injustice will be thought as "disjointure" or "disjoining":

Dikè, thought on the basis of Being as presencing, is the ordering and enjoining Order [*ist der fugend-fügende Fug*]. *Adikia*, disjunction, is Disorder [*die Un-fuge, ist der Un-fug*].[55]

As Derrida points out, Heidegger, as always, comes down on the side of the "ordering and enjoining Order."[56] And yet, neither order nor harmony are without their attendant risk:

. . . is there not a risk of inscribing this whole movement of justice under the sign of presence, be it of the presence to meaning of the *Anwesen*, of the event as coming into presence, of Being as presence joined to itself, of the proper of the other as presence? As the presence of the received present, yes, but appropriable as the same and therefore gathered together? Beyond right, and still more beyond juridicism, beyond morality, and still more beyond moralism, does not justice as relation to the other suppose on the contrary the irreducible excess of a disjointure or an anachrony, some *Un-Fuge*, some "out of joint" dislocation in Being and in time itself, a disjointure that, in always risking the evil, the expropriation, and injustice (*adikia*) against which there is no calculable insurance, would alone be able to *do justice* or to *render justice* to the other as other?[57]

Now, whether finitude is the name of the impossibility of the origin or, on the contrary, the originary itself, this marks, one suspects, a very significant gap as regards time and history. No less significant, moreover, is the consequent break as regards the history of metaphysics. For Heidegger, historicality and intratemporality, two structures of Dasein's temporality founded on its ecstatic existence, respectively give rise to two derivative possibilities, the ordinary concept of history on the one hand and the "vulgar" concept of time on the other. The metaphysical way of thinking time is not severed from the "vulgarity" of the concept; on the contrary, it is both its captor and captive. This is why Heidegger, having shown how the vulgar concept of time derives from—and thus presupposes—intratemporality,[58] devotes the following section of *Being and Time*, the penultimate of the book, to a discussion of the Hegelian concept of time and of the relation of time to Spirit. The stakes here are twofold: on the one hand, it is a matter of dispelling the ambiguity that attends the proximity between the existential analytic and Hegel's own reflections on time; on the other, it is a matter of highlighting Hegel's continuity with the entire tradition that precedes him. It is only by showing that, from Aristotle to Hegel, time has always been thought in terms of a *point* (*Punkt*), a now that has been leveled off, that Heidegger can refer the entire metaphysical tradition to its forgotten origin: the vulgar concept of time as an inauthentic and derivative form of the temporality of Dasein. Hence, too, can he confirm, *a contrario*, the necessity of the existential analytic as the proper point of departure for a new *gigantomachia peri tes ousias*. The analytic of Dasein alone can account for the originary phenomenon of time and its concealment in an inauthentic modality. By accounting for the proper and the improper, the originary and the derivative, the existential analytic renders possible both a new ontology *and* an understanding of the straying of classical ontology. The section on Hegel announces thus what would have to be the first step (back) through this *Destruktion* of the history of ontology announced at the very start of *Being and Time*.

Now, in "*Ousia* and *grammè*," Derrida deals at length with a note appended to the paragraph in question, a note in which Heidegger advances the arguments that will have to justify the affiliation that he wants to establish between the Aristotelian concept of time and its Hegelian counterpart. Derrida's choice here is a significant one: although his explicit concern is with the general axiomatics of the Heideggerian question of time, and notably with the idea of a "vulgar" concept of time, he takes as his point of departure *not* the purely phenomenological analyses of §81, but the history of ontology, a move that has several distinct advantages. Derrida intends to show that the distinction between an originary and a derivative temporality is not in fact operative within the history of ontology. From which it follows that it is simply inoperative; if it is impossible to refer the whole of metaphysical thinking to its "vulgarity," that is, to its forgotten and concealed foundation, then it is just as impossible that a new point of departure for thinking might allow for an experience of the originary. Centering the question around the putative "vulgarity" of the history of metaphysics also allows Derrida to highlight a certain continuity within Heidegger's thinking. If, after *Being and Time*, the question of time, along with all the themes that had depended upon it (principally the themes of Dasein, of finitude, of historicality), will no longer constitute the *transcendental horizon* of the question of being,[59] it will nonetheless be reconstituted on the basis of the theme of the *epochality* of being in which, as we have already seen, the distinction between the originary and the derivative is still at work. From this perspective, Derrida can, with total coherence, conclude "*Ousia* and *grammè*" with a commentary on the early trace (*die Frühe Spur*) of difference identified in "The Anaximander Fragment." As we shall see, the difference that is here played out around time is the same as the one that was played out around history. And it comes as no surprise, therefore, to rediscover the theme of the trace opposing itself to any sense of origin, however finite that may be. Nor does it come as any surprise, moreover, to see Derrida distancing himself from Heidegger at a point where their proximity seems at its most extreme.

In the note with which Derrida's commentary will deal, Heidegger remarks that, in the *Jena Logik*, one already finds precisely that interpretation of time that will subsequently be developed by Hegel in the *Encyclopedia*, pointing out that "even the roughest examinations reveals that the section on time is a *paraphrase* of *Aristotle's* essay on time."[60] The "*paraphrase*" consists in Hegel's reprising the key terms that had, in that treatise, defined the essence of time: Aristotle sees the essence of time in the *nun*, Hegel in the now (*Jetzt*); Aristotle takes the *nun* as *oros*, Hegel takes the now as limit (*Grenze*); Aristotle understands the *nun* as *stigmè*, Hegel interprets the now as a point.

Rather than follow the detail of Derrida's analyses, which would necessitate a discussion of the problem of time in Aristotle and Hegel—a task that lies beyond the scope of this study—I want merely to draw out the strategy of Derrida's commentary. He begins by recalling that, in the *Physics*, Aristotle opens the question of time by way of an aporia, an exoteric aporia.[61] Time is something that is not, or which is only "barely and scarcely." If the *nun* is the essence of time, the form it can never leave behind, this essence will be problematic insofar as the *nun*, in a certain sense, *is* not. The *nun*, the now, is given simultaneously as what no longer is and as what is still not yet. In one sense it has been and is no more; in another, it will be and so is not yet. Time, which is made up of a succession of *nun* moments, is thereby made up of non-beings. Now, whatever is made up of non-beingness cannot participate in presence, substance, beingness itself (*ousia*). This is the first phase of the aporia, which involves time being thought in terms of its divisibility. Time is divisible into parts, and yet none of these parts can be said to be in the present. In the other phase of the aporia Aristotle will maintain the reverse hypothesis: the now is *not* a part of time, time is *not* made up of the *nun*.

Derrida begins with the first phase of the aporia. His first move is to underline the strange relation of the now to time. Although the *nun* is the elementary part of time, it is not in itself temporal; it is temporal only by *becoming* so, that is, by ceasing to be, by passing into no-thingness in the form of the past or future being. If the now is the kernel of time, it is so only insofar as it is atemporal, the non-modifiable form of temporal modification, the inalterable form of temporalization. Time, therefore, is what happens to this kernel by affecting it with the nothing [*né-ant*]. Which is the same as saying that in order to be, in order to be a being, something has to be unaffected by time; in order to be, it must not become:

To participate in beingness, in *ousia*, therefore is to participate in being-present, in the presence of the present or, if you will, in presentness. Beings are what *is*. *Ousia* therefore is thought on the basis of *esti*. The privilege of the third person present of the indicative here yields all its historical significance. Beings, the present, the now, substance, essence, are all linked in their meaning to the form of the present participle. . . . And later it will be likewise for the form of presence that *consciousness* itself is.[62]

Hence, beings that are, the presence of the present, do not refer to a mode of temporality, but to the *atemporal form* of time. Temporal becoming—and without becoming there would be no time—refers to a non-being present, which is itself simply a non-being.

According to Derrida, Hegel actually takes up this first phase of the Aristotelian aporia in both the *Jena Logik* and in the *Encyclopedia* (§257). In each case, moreover, as Heidegger continually reminds us, the question of time is raised in the sections that relate to the philosophy of nature. Time and space are the fundamental categories of nature, that is, of the self-externality (*Aussersichsein*) of the Idea, of the Idea as immediate, abstract and indeterminate exteriority (*das ganz abstrakte Aussereinander*). For Hegel, space is the self-externality of nature, the abstract universality that knows neither mediation nor difference nor determination. Nothing is related to nothing: such is the origin of nature. Now, in accordance with this dialectical logic, space in its undifferentiated immediacy will be able to take on determination or differentiation only as a negation of this original purity. Pure spatiality is determined by negating the indeterminacy that constitutes it, that is, by negating itself. This negation can thus be thought as the negation *of* space *by* space. The first such spatial negation of space is the *point*: the point is space that takes up no space, the place that does not take place. As a first determination and negation of space, the point *spatializes* or *spaces*; it negates itself by relating itself to itself, that is, to another point. The negation of the negation, the spatial negation of the point, is the *line*. The point sublates itself into the line through *Aufhebung*, the line constituting thus the truth of the point.[63] Through the same process, *Aufhebung* and the negation of negation, the truth of the line is the *plane*. Space thus becomes concrete by retaining the negative within itself. It has become space by determining itself, by foregoing its original purity. From which it follows that spatialization, the fulfillment of the essence of spatiality, is a *de*spatialization.[64] Now, as Derrida points out, time is already situated in this dialectic genesis of space: the no-longer-being and the being-still that relate the line to the point and thence to the plane, this negativity in the structure of the *Aufhebung*, is already time. At each stage in the negation, time is necessarily at work: the space that is produced by its negation of itself *is* time. If space is to be thought as time, therefore, it is because space is determined on the basis of the negativity of the point. And Heidegger is thus correct, according to Derrida, in saying that, for Hegel, time has to be thought on the basis of the point. *Stigmè*, punctuality, is the concept that, in Hegel as in Aristotle, determines the now (*nun, Jetzt*). Up to a point, therefore, Heidegger is correct in his account of the Hegelian definition of time as a *paraphrase* of the Aristotelian aporia. But only up to a point. And Derrida finds the reason for this limitation in precisely that passage of the *Encyclopedia* that appears to confirm Heidegger's hypothesis of the paraphrase, the hypothesis of "the brilliant formulation of a vulgar paradox," as Derrida has it.[65] Here is the passage in question:

> Time, as the negative unity of self-externality, is similarly an out-and-out abstract, ideal being. It is that being which, inasmuch as it *is*, is *not*, and inasmuch as it is *not*, *is*; it is Becoming *directly intuited* [*das* angeschaute *Werden*]; this means that differences, which admittedly are purely *momentary*, i.e. directly self-sublating [*unmittelbar sich aufhebenden Unterschiede*], are determined as *external*, i.e. as external to themselves.[66]

Wherein lies the problem? The answer is very simple: if Hegel repeats Aristotle, the Kantian concept of time is included in this repetition. Intuited becoming in itself, without sensible empirical content, is the purely sensible, Kant's nonsensuous sensuous (*das unsinnliche Sinnliche*), as Hegel paraphrases it in the *Encyclopedia*.[67] Contrary to what Heidegger appears to think, therefore, Kant would fall squarely into the lineage that leads from Aristotle to Hegel. But there is another difficulty. Hegel's own position will always seem to be very close to some of the theses developed by Heidegger in *Kant and the Problem of Metaphysics*. Hegel's conclusion that "time is the same principle as the I=I of pure self-consciousness" is not unrelated to the affirmation of the temporal character of the self, to the identity of time and the *I think* with whose discovery Heidegger credits Kant before adopting it in his own fashion.[68] So, too, the conclusion that "it is not *in* time [*in der Zeit*] that everything comes to be and passes away, rather time itself is *becoming*, this coming-to-be and passing away,"[69] a remark that appears strangely close to the Heideggerian critique of intratemporality. But what is the significance of this reintroduction of Kant into the line that runs from Aristotle to Hegel? For Derrida, it is certainly not a matter of denying to Kant what Heidegger accords to him, namely, a break with respect to a problematic that thinks time by way of "spatial" concepts. What is in question is not the fabled "generosity" of Heidegger's interpretation of Kant but his lack of generosity as regards

Aristotle and Hegel. Derrida's gesture here is extremely complex: it is a matter of showing that it is the more radical, less metaphysical, if you like, aspect of Kant's thought of time that marks its continuity with Aristotle's aporetic. Put differently: if in Kant metaphysical fidelity organizes and arranges itself with the rupture, this refers to the inaugural ambiguity of Aristotle's text and more generally to what is usually called metaphysics.

Let me try to sum up as briefly as possible Derrida's line of argument, before turning to the broader scope and consequences of this complicated strategy of intersecting readings. Derrida begins by recalling the two questions that organize Aristotle's treatise on time: 1. Is time a being, a part of *ta onta*? 2. What is its *phusis*? Now, the very formulation of the first of these questions determines in advance the being of time on the basis of the now and of the now as part. This tacit presumption is never called into question, not even when Aristotle appears to reverse the initial hypothesis in order to raise the possibility that the now is not a part or that time is not composed of nows. Now, if Aristotle does recall the reasons why it may well be thought that time is not in fact a being, he leaves the question unanswered and moves on to address the question of the *phusis* of time. What will be addressed, therefore, is the *phusis* of that whose belonging to being remains still undecidable. But to raise the question of time in terms of its belonging to being or to non-being already involves an omission; it is already to *avoid the question*. The same question and the same avoidance, moreover, that Heidegger puts into play at the very start of *Being and Time*: the prior temporal determination of beings as being present. The effects of this omission, this avoidance of the question, are spread thus across the whole history of metaphysics—or, more accurately, constitute it as such. Time would be only the nothing, or the accident foreign to the essence of truth. It is as if metaphysics as a whole were plunged into the exoteric discourse on the aporia that opens book IV of the *Physics*.[70] And this would be visible even in Kant, visible at the very point of his most fundamental advance, that advance dictating that it is because time is, as Aristotle says, neither a being nor a determination of beings that it has to be made a pure form of sensibility. Derrida points out that if one compares book IV of the *Physics* to the "Transcendental Exposition of the Concept of Time" a decisive common trait emerges: the non-beingness of time.[71] But the relation that can be established between Kant and Aristotle is not limited to this still very general trait, and concerns also the specifically Kantian definition of time as a *form of inner sense*. In his question concerning the *phusis* of time, Aristotle raises the question of what it is about movement that constitutes time, since time, which is neither change nor movement, is related to both. He replies: "it is together that we have the sensation of movement and time."[72] It is in *aisthesis*, therefore, that Aristotle unites time and movement. And he does so without the need for any external sensible content: time is the form of what occurs only *en tè psykhè*. Which is why Derrida can say that the Kantian rupture that Heidegger undertakes to point out only to repeat and deepen it in its own way was already prepared for in book IV of the *Physics*. Hence the destruction (*Destruktion*) of metaphysics remains, up to a certain point, *within* metaphysics, and explicates only one of its motifs:

> What Aristotle has set down, then, is both traditional metaphysical security and, in its *inaugural ambiguity*, the critique of this security. In anticipating the concept of the nonsensuous sensuous, Aristotle furnishes the premises of a thought of time no longer dominated simply by the present (of beings given in the form of *Vorhandenheit* and *Gegenwärtigkeit*).[73]

All of which allows Derrida to conclude that the originality of the Kantian breakthrough, as it is repeated in the *Kantbuch*, transgresses the vulgar concept of time only by making explicit something already hinted at in book IV of the *Physics*, something that *equally* depends on the hitherto avoided question that Heidegger wants to reawaken. For if the now is not, in fact, a part, if time is not composed of nows, if the unity and identity of the now are always problematic, then this will depend on the very presupposition that has thus far gone unquestioned. It is only by temporally determining beings as being-present that time can be determined as nonpresent, as non-being. The present now is not time because it is present and time is not (a being) precisely because it is not (present).[74]

Yet, to say that the transgression of the vulgar concept of time is already hinted at in book IV of the *Physics* amounts to saying that there is no vulgar concept of time. From which it follows that there can be no originary concept of time either. The concept of time, Derrida writes, is part and parcel of metaphysics; it names the domination of presence. Throughout its history, the whole system of metaphysical concepts develops the "vulgarity" of the concept, something with which Heidegger would not disagree. Yet the consequence that Derrida draws from this is that one can produce no *other* concept of time. Time belongs to metaphysical conceptuality in general; the construction of another concept of time could be no more than a reorganization of other metaphysical predicates.[75]

In a sense, this is precisely what Heidegger himself experienced with *Being and Time.* The shaking undermining of classical ontology undertaken in that work is still caught within the vocabulary and grammar of metaphysics. Such, at least, is the reason Heidegger gives for the incompletion of the book,[76] even if it is unlikely that Heidegger saw the insufficiency of the analyses of *Being and Time* and the necessity of another point of departure in the same way as Derrida. For according to Derrida, what is at stake in the axiomatic of *Being and Time* is the fundamental distinction between the authentic and the inauthentic in its link to that of the originary and the derivative, a distinction that structures all the analyses of that work, and principally the analysis of temporality. What is in question is this originary temporality that, constituting the horizon of time, ought to open the way to the question of the sense of being. Now, as we have already seen—and I will come back to this in due course—although Heidegger recognized the need to abandon the question of the transcendental horizon of the sense of being, he does not abandon the axis of the opposition between the originary and the derivative. On the contrary. According to Derrida, however, it is precisely this opposition that remains metaphysical.[77] Taking up Heidegger's objection to Hegel's assertion regarding the fall of spirit into time, Derrida points out that what is metaphysical is less this idea of a fall *into time* than the idea that there is a *fall* in general, an idea to which Heidegger himself will not be immune. If spirit does not fall into time it is because factical existence "falls" as a falling from (*"fällt" als verfallende*) originary temporality.[78] Despite all the precautions that Heidegger takes, it is difficult to shield *Verfallen* from a certain Platonic connotation.[79] To use the idea of a fall in order to indicate the passage from one temporality to another is hardly a neutral gesture. And the same can be said for the concepts of *Eigentlichkeit* and *Uneigentlichkeit,* concepts whose ethical connotations are difficult to avoid even though they intervene at a level of analysis where all ethical preoccupations ought to have been suspended.

The "inaugural ambiguity" of book IV of the *Physics*—but the same would be true of any metaphysical text—renders thus impossible the project of returning to an originary concept of time, over and above the "vulgar" concept; equally, it renders impossible the very opposition between the originary and the derivative, of which vulgarity is but one instance. But if the reference to an inaugural ambiguity is indeed opposed to the axiomatic of *Being and Time,* what happens in the later Heidegger? Before turning back to more general considerations, let me stay for a moment

with the questions raised by "*Ousia* and *Grammè.*" If no conceptual construction is able to guarantee a move outside metaphysics, to take a step
beyond, what possible form of excess can there be? What place can it have?
Here, as one might well expect, we come back to the theme of the *trace:*
"In order to exceed metaphysics it is necessary that a trace be inscribed
within the text of metaphysics. . . ."[80] The whole difficulty here is one of
knowing what the mode of inscription of this trace might be. Now, if
metaphysics is indeed a thinking of presence, the trace can thus be neither
absent nor present, since absence either gives nothing to be thought or is
only a negative mode of presence. The inscription of the trace can only be
described, therefore, as the effacement of the trace itself. *The trace produces
itself as its own effacement.* Now, this seems to be very close to a certain
thought of Heidegger. The difference between being and beings is forgotten in the determination of being as presence and of presence as present.
This forgetting, moreover, has gone so far as to efface the very trace of this
difference. Such, at least, is what Heidegger suggests in "The Anaximander
Fragment":

> *The oblivion* (l'oubli) *of Being is the oblivion of the distinction between Being and
> beings* . . . The distinction collapses. It remains forgotten. Although the two par-
> ties to the distinction, what is present and presencing [*das Answesende und das An-
> wesen*], reveal themselves, they do not do so *as* distinguished terms. Rather, even
> the early trace (*die frühe Spur*) of the distinction is obliterated when presencing ap-
> pears as something present [*das Answesen wie ein Anwesendes erscheint*] and finds
> itself in the position of being the highest being present [*in einem höchsten Anwe-
> senden*].[81]

What is marked thus in the text of metaphysics is not the trace but its effacement. Rather than think the trace referring to a presence, presence has
to be thought as *the trace of the trace*, as the trace of the effacement of the
trace. Even at this point of extreme proximity, however, a significant difference remains. Once again, moreover, the difference will be played out
around the question of the originary. If the texts of what are usually called
the history of metaphysics are thought on the basis of the notion of the
trace, the trace no longer needs to be sought only in thinkers of the originary. There is no longer any need for the effacement of the trace to be
sought in the words of Anaximander and not in the later texts of our tradition of thinking. Thought in all rigor, *the trace will never be early*; it is
not progressively effaced by its being distanced from the origin. If the trace
is a trace, it cannot be said to be in closest proximity to itself at the inau-

gural moment of its emergence, something that is simultaneously its inscription *and* its effacement; its inscription *as* its effacement, if you like. Why? For the simple reason that there is no trace itself, no proper trace, no *as such* of the trace. Heidegger, too, says that difference can never appear as such, a remark to which Derrida, in his own account, will take on as his own, with the difference that he shifts the emphasis from *difference* to the *as such*:

> The trace of the trace which (is) difference above all could not appear or be named *as such*, that is, in its presence. It is the *as such* which precisely, and as such, evades us forever.[82]

What this amounts to saying is not only that difference never appears as such but that there is no *as such* that could be assigned to difference in its originary form as ontological difference:

> Thereby the determinations which name difference always come from the metaphysical order. This holds not only for the determination of difference as the difference between presence and the present (*Answesende/Anwesen*), but also for the determination of difference as the difference between Being and beings.[83]

Let me try now to gather all the threads unraveled thus far in order to come back to our initial question. I have tried to describe the opposition that separates an anachronic temporality thought by way of the trace from a temporality the finitude of which falls under the sign of the originary, a finitude that appears as the impossibility of either origin or end[84] from a finitude that, on the basis of the possibility of an end, refers back to the origin. I have tried also to show how the anachrony of time, as Derrida understands it, is rooted in an interpretation of Husserl and, in particular, in the genetic dimension of Husserl's thinking, a dimension wholly absent from Heidegger's own phenomenology. As we have seen, moreover, the same opposition can be found on the level of history in a way that illuminates the reasons for Derrida's reservations, already discussed at the beginning of the second part of this study, concerning the epochality of being. And no less clear by now should be the complement to this hypothesis, namely, that in the movement from *Being and Time* to his later works, Heidegger retains something that was at work in the earlier text, something that guides his later developments of the idea of originary temporality.

Given this context, some consideration of "*Ousia* and *Grammè*" was always going to be unavoidable. Even if, as has to be said, among all Derrida's texts, "*Ousia* and *Grammè*" would be one of those with the least claim to underwrite our hypotheses, for reasons that, to my mind, pertain not only to the necessities of a strategy determined by a very precise context but also to a certain formalization not entirely absent from Derrida's work.[85] As we saw in our commentary on "*Ousia* and *Grammè*," to Heidegger's attempt to delimit the metaphysical concept of time in relation to an originary temporality that it would only conceal, Derrida opposes the *inaugural ambiguity* of the text of metaphysics. The critique of the opposition between the originary and the derivative does not refer directly to temporality, but to the notion of *text*. Why? Because the text of metaphysics works according to the structure of the trace, thus harboring within itself an ineffaceable tension. As we have already seen, however, the question of writing and the question of temporality are inseparable in Derrida's thinking. Once again, moreover, it is the functioning of the *text as trace* that allows Derrida both to follow the more audacious moves of the Heideggerian thought of difference *and* to break with it at a very specific point, namely, the point at which the difference as trace, as Heidegger understands it, nonetheless remains anchored in "its early origin," an anchorage that irrevocably determines it as ontological difference, as the difference between being and beings. The impossibility of difference appearing as such seems not to affect the *as such* of the ontological difference.

With this, we are back (in a different "rhetoric," the reasons for and consequences of which will need to be considered) with the same critique as the one already seen at work in "Envoi" and *The Post Card*: the impossibility of evoking something like Metaphysics in the presumed unity of its history. What is being called into question, therefore, is the possibility of referring the whole of metaphysics (or metaphysics as a whole) to its origin, whether this takes the form of a *Destrucktion* (which is not deconstruction) of the history of ontology, or the later form of the *Schritt Zurück*, a step back that, once the exhaustion of the destiny of metaphysics has been grasped, ought to allow the tradition to be left behind, abandoned to its fate. To carry out a task of endless mourning, if you will. The step back, behind or beyond the origin, is a step that always implies the possibility of a last reprise, the possibility of an *end* of philosophy.[86] And only that which has *an* origin can have *an* end.

Recall, in this context, the central place that the *Introduction* to *The Origin of Geometry* accorded to Husserl's notion of *Rückfrage*, that other great attempt to relate to the adventure of Western thought as a whole.

Through *Rückfrage*, inquiring back, Husserl thought to reach the new constituting origin of sense, to re-establish, beyond any possible forgetting,[87] the link between the production and the transmission of truth, a link that alone constitutes a tradition. Derrida's analyses were aimed at showing that, through the impossibility of a total reactivation of sense, through the impossibility of reaching the end of the *Rückfrage*, something like *historicity* could be thought. This impossibility, that Husserl wants at any price to be a merely empirical impossibility, is, for Derrida, a *transcendental* one. Or, better perhaps, the point at which the transcendental touches its limit, the point at which the transcendental can no longer make the break, can no longer keep itself pure of all empiricity. And were it to be precisely here that something like historicity could be thought, it would only be because the impossibility of *returning to* the origin, itself the impossibility of *beginning with* the origin (the question always asked in return), was the sole condition for something like history, something like becoming, actually being able to take place. As such, the "crisis" is no longer the empirical and inexplicable danger that threatens the transcendental historicity of truth but the form, the very condition of the possibility of this passage that we call historicity, a passage that alone is absolute. Origin and end, *archè* and *telos*, are no longer points of departure and arrival, even thought in the always distant form of regulative ideas, but the reciprocal and endless return of one to the other, a return that can only be produced in this *absolute that is the passage*. The *Wechselsspiel* between *archè* and *telos*, this sort of coming and going between origin and end, far from being produced by that *archè* and that *telos*, is what produces them. It is never definitive, therefore; there is no possible final reprise, no *Schritt Zurück* or consummated mourning.

We see, on the level of history, the difference that we have already seen with respect to temporality: the difference between, on the one hand, an anachrony of the time in which the future (that which will come but not as a *present* future—as a future that, as *present*, could be anticipated and thus *calculated*) comes (back) only from an absolute past, that is, a past that cannot be summoned back by an act of totalizing memory, and, on the other hand, that time which can be described as originarily finite insofar as it can gather, on the basis of the finitude of the future, the whole of the past in the present (*Augenblick*) of a decision. If, with the step back it is no longer a question of decision but of a completed destiny, the possibility of gathering is not, for all that, called into question. *And it would be necessary, moreover, to ask what an incompletable destiny, a destiny that could not be gathered would be.* Without an already assigned end (*telos*), there could be no destiny. As was the case with the movement of temporalization, Derrida finds in Husserl's critical interpretation of the notion of crisis a "positive paradigm" for a thought of historicity and the event. Thought in terms of its *necessity* and so shielded from any negative connotations, the crisis or the forgetting of sense that always oscillates in Husserl between the status of an empirical accident, an eidetic necessity and an ethical failure, points toward the contamination of the empirical and the transcendental that is the—positive—condition of possibility for an event being able to take place. If, like Derrida, one understands by the event the enigma of that which happens for the first time, in a singular time and place, the empiricity or absolute singularity that destines the first time to be also the last, the unique and so what is destined to the return of that which will never return, *to the spectral ideality of the transcendental.*[88] An event that retains empiricity (absolute singularity) on the paradoxical condition that the first and unique time of its event is destined to return as that which can never return. Thus the absolute past is also the past of others that do not stop returning, without the return being the return of the same. If the past comes from the future, the future also comes from the past: the *Wechselspiel* is endless.[89] And this is why the question of the address and its singularity becomes decisive. Time is not gathered; it is "always already" the time of the other and of justice.[90] The dialogue that ends *Of Spirit*, in which Derrida gives voice to a disagreement between Heidegger and certain imaginary theologians, needs to be read in this light; what is at stake in the impossibility of "deciding" upon what is beyond or behind "metaphysics" is also the possibility of other voices, other addresses,[91] and not the thesis of the "always already there" in the sense in which everything would already have taken place and in which nothing new would be possible, forever.

2.3

Dasein's Life

It is the alternative between the (passive) genesis of time and its origin that leads Derrida to focus on what, in *Being and Time*, opens originary temporality as such, namely Dasein's being-for- or being-toward-death. The question here is whether time stems from my own death or from the death of the other. This alternative would sum up the difference between Heidegger and Lévinas regarding the question of the relation of time to alterity, an alternative between a thinking in which time stems from the finite future of my own being-toward-death and a thinking in which time stems from infinite alterity, from the absolute past of the other. To the auto-affection of Dasein's temporality, which opens the future as a *coming to self* in the projection of one's ownmost potentiality for being,[1] Lévinas opposes the hetero-affection of absolute passivity, opening time as the relation to what is infinitely other. But is the alternative that confronts us here the same as the one between the (passive) genesis of time and its origin? Does the alternative between the genesis or the trace of time and its origin intersect with the one that exists between Heidegger and Lévinas, with all the various oppositions that they themselves bring into play (the opposition between activity and passivity, between finite and infinite, between my death and the death of the other, etc.)? I think not. Here, as elsewhere, Derrida's thought is a thought of *contamination* more than *opposition*; the passive genesis of time implies, amongst other things, that there is indeed no simple opposition between activity and passivity, the finite and the infinite, the *Selbst* and the Other, etc. And so, too, that there is no simple opposition between my death and that of the other. At the—unassignable—origin of time there is, according to Derrida, neither the other, nor myself, but *mourning*. And so the alternative is no longer between a thought of life, as was the case in Husserl's phenomenology, and a thought of death, whether the death in question be my own or that of the other. Just as nothing happens to (or in) a pure life, so nothing happens to (or in) a pure death. There is no life *proper* and, even less, no death *proper*.

Although this unavoidable confrontation with *Sein-zum-Tode* has been addressed explicitly by Derrida in *Aporias*, it had actually been broached long before through the question of *originary mourning*, a theme that has become—and hardly by chance—progressively more insistent in Derrida's reflections.[2] Before turning to the text of *Aporias*, however, I want to recall some of the traits of Heidegger's analysis of *Sein-zum-Tode* in order to show how it comes to be defined by a series of *suspensions*.

1. Dasein Does Not Pass Away

Following the analyses of everydayness, the existentiale of being-toward-death is introduced by Heidegger in order to respond to the demand for completeness and originality in the interpretation. Everyday Dasein "lacks" something, principally that mode of possible existence, established at the very outset of the book and never again addressed, that Heidegger terms authentic or proper (*eigen*).[3] In order for the analysis to grasp Dasein *as a whole*, it will need thus to question that being's ownmost potentiality for being.[4] But how is it possible, if possible it is, for a being that has existence as its mode of being, for a being that *can* be, for a being that *has* to be, to be a whole? The structure of existence seems to exclude *a priori* the possibility of *Ganzsein*, therefore. Insofar as it exists, Dasein is never a whole. Insofar as it exists, Dasein has not yet done with its possibilities. Once it reaches the end, its end, however, far from becoming a completed totality it simply no longer exists: reaching its end, Dasein is no longer *there*. Far from paralyzing the analysis, however, this difficulty encourages the question of what possible end there might be for a being that has Dasein's mode of being.[5] Now, to draw conclusions regarding the impossibility of its being a whole from Dasein's being-ahead-of-itself (*Sich-vorweg-sein*), identified by Heidegger as constitutive of care, would be to interpret Dasein as a *vorhanden* being and so miss the existential meaning of being-ahead-of-itself and of being-toward-the-end that Heidegger needs to establish. If Dasein's end is undeniably death, the *ontological sense* of death has to be addressed.

What, then, is Dasein's death? Such a question can only be understood if one remembers that, when it comes to Dasein, the only form of question appropriate to the matter at hand is not What is Dasein?, but Who is Dasein?[6] If the possibility of being-a-whole is bound up with death, this requires that Dasein's death be thought in its specificity, that it be thought in terms of its existential sense. But how is the existential sense of death to be approached if death is the no-longer-being-*there* of a being whose essence resides in its being precisely *there*, in its being the *da* of *Sein*? One answer springs immediately to mind: although Dasein has no "experience" of its *own* death, it does have experience of the death of others. To the extent that *Mitsein* belongs essentially to Dasein, to the extent that being-with is constitutive of its mode of being, might it not be that, whilst its own death remains inaccessible, Dasein can always have access to the ontological meaning of death by way of the death of those others with whom it always is? Yet Heidegger only advances this hypothesis, of course, in order to exclude it categorically. *Mitsein*, evidently, renders possible an experience of mourning; those who remain *are* indeed with the dead in the intimacy of thought and of mourning. Yet whilst they may well *be* with the deceased, the deceased are no longer there. Only those who are left *are-with*, since *Mitsein* always means being-with in the same world, and it is only on the basis of *this world* that one can be-with.[7] So whilst it is always possible to be with the deceased in the experience of mourning, it can in no way constitute the experience of Dasein's authentic being-toward-the-end.[8] We can never truly experience the dying of others. Yes, we can accompany them to their death, recall them once they are dead, weep for them now they are gone; doing so, however, we remain inexorably on the other side of death, *on this side*; we remain in the world, *there*, a *there* that is itself the only possible place of mourning, if by mourning we understand *merely* the experience of the death of others. And yet, it is not only the other who dies that remains thus inaccessible to us; even were one to attain the putative clarity of a "psychology of the dying," this would be of little help in understanding the mode of being in question, this being-to-the-end whose existential meaning has to be grasped: "We are asking about the ontological meaning of the dying of the person who dies," writes Heidegger, "as a possibility-of-being [*eine Seinsmöglichkeit*] which belongs to *his* being. We are not asking about the way in which the deceased has Dasein-with or is still-a-Dasein [*Nochdaseins*] with those who are left behind."⁹ If one could ever grasp the ontological sense of death by way of *Mitsein*, it would only be because the latter harbors the possibility of replacing one Dasein with another. Yet although such replaceability (*Vertretbarkeit*) is indeed constitutive of Dasein's being-with-one-another in the world, it is also what is radically lacking once it is a matter of what confers on that being its being-a-whole [*Ganzsein*], namely its coming-to-the-end (*Zu-Ende-kommen*). In death, it would seem, there can be no possible substitution:

> *No one can take the Other's dying away from him* [*Keiner kan dem Anderen sein Sterben abnehmen*]. Of course someone can "go to his death for another". But that always means to sacrifice oneself for the other "*in some definite affair*". Such "dying for" [*solches sterben für . . .*] can never signify that the Other has thus had his death taken away in even the slightest degree [*dass dem Anderen damit sein Tod im geringsten abgenomen sei*]. Dying is something that every Dasein itself must take upon itself at the time [*Das sterben muss jedes Dasein jeweilig selbst auf sich nehmen*]. By its very essence, death is in every case mine, in so far as it "is" at all. And indeed death signifies a peculiar possibility-of-Being in which the very Being of one's own Dasein is an issue. In dying, it is shown that mineness [*Jemeinigkeit*] and existence are ontologically constitutive for death.¹⁰

Within the confines of this framework, not only is death always my own and hence inaccessible through the experience of mourning, but the very mineness of existence is itself possible only through the possibility of (my own) death. It is only in the face of death that Dasein is properly irreplaceable and referred to its selfhood, to its *Selbst*. If, in the mode of everydayness, Dasein is not itself but They, *Man Selbst*, and hence no one, death forces it to take upon itself what is proper to it, its irreplaceable singularity:

> Death does not just "belong" to one's own Dasein in an undifferentiated way; death *lays claim* [beansprucht] to it as an *individual* Dasein. The non-relational character [*Unbezüglichkeit*] of death, as understood in anticipation, individualizes Dasein [*vereinzelt*] down to itself [*auf es selbst*]. This individualizing is a way in which the "there" is disclosed for existence. The entity which anticipates its non-relational possibility, is thus forced by that very anticipation into the possibility of taking over from itself its ownmost Being, and doing so of its own accord [*das Vorlaufen in die unbezügliche Möglichkeit zwingt das vorlaufende Seiende in die Möglichkeit, sein eigenstes Sein von ihm selbst her aus ihm selbst übernehmen*].¹¹

The relation to death functions thus as a principle of individuation: it is death alone—my death—that shelters me from the They and refers me to this *Selbst* prior to any form of subjectivity. Only an "I" can take over my death and, that being the case, every form of *Mitsein* is suspended since, its co-originarity with all other structures of existence notwithstanding, the mineness of existence presupposes the absolute singularization, the pure and isolating individuation (*Vereinzelung*[12]) of Dasein faced with its own death:

Death is a possibility-of-Being which Dasein itself has to take over in every case. With death, Dasein stands before itself in its *ownmost* potentiality-for-being [*Mit dem Tod steht sich das Dasein selbst in seinem eigensten Seinkönnen bevor*]. This is a possibility in which the issue is nothing less than Dasein's Being-in-the-world. Its death is the possibility of no-longer-being-able-to-be-there [*Nichts-mehr-dasein-könnens*]. If Dasein stands before itself as this possibility [*Wenn das Dasein als diese Möglichkeit seiner selbst sich bevorsteht*], it has been *fully* assigned to its ownmost potentiality-for-Being. *When it stands before itself in this way, all its relations to any other Dasein have been undone* [*so sich bevorstehend sind in ihm alle Bezüge zu anderem Dasein gelöst*].[13]

Being-with, although constitutive of Dasein, is only possible on the basis of mineness, the always being mine of existence that can be taken over only through the essential solitude of being-toward-death.[14]

Yet even if being-toward-death, which is always mine, *does* individuate Dasein, *does* refer Dasein to its *Selbst*, through the—provisional[15]—suspension of any form of *Mitsein*, we are still far from having elucidated the ontological meaning of death. What is Dasein's dying? What does it mean for Dasein to die? How does Dasein die? How does Dasein die a death that is always its own?

Let me begin to answer these questions by pointing out that, despite §10 of *Being and Time* having already carefully distinguished the project of the existential analytic from anthropology, psychology and biology as fields of research, once the issue becomes that of death, Heidegger seems to feel the need to return to precisely these fields. The analytic began with the "epochè" of all metaphysical interpretation, of all prior (and unquestioned) knowledge of the being that we always are and that Heidegger calls Dasein precisely in order to avoid reintroducing with the name man a metaphysical determination that fails to raise the question of being in an appropriate manner.[16] Whether implicitly or explicitly, anthropology and psychology, like every science, are founded on an ontology. As such, there can be no question of crediting the results of their researches once it comes to the difference between the being of Dasein and that of other beings, a difference that metaphysics has never questioned. Now, although this is true of all science, Heidegger nonetheless pays particular attention to biology as the science of life, the proximity between Dasein and living beings requiring a certain kind of caution:

> In the order which any possible comprehension and interpretation must follow, biology as a "science of life" is founded upon the ontology of Dasein, even if not entirely. Life, in its own right, is a kind of Being; but essentially it is accessible only in Dasein. The ontology of life is accomplished by way of a privative Interpretation; it determines what must be the case if there can be anything like mere-aliveness [*sie bestimmt das, was sein muss, dass so etwas wie Nur-noch-leben sein kann*]. Life is not a mere Being-present-at-hand [*Vorhandensein*], nor is it Dasein. In turn, Dasein is never to be defined ontologically by regarding it as life (in an ontologically indefinite manner) plus something else.[17]

Biology is unable to clear a path in the direction of an ontology of life; rather, it presupposes one. And presupposes too, therefore, the analytic of Dasein.[18] Would Dasein be the living being par excellence? Heidegger's answer is unequivocal: by no means. *Dasein is essentially not a living being.* Only by severing it from everything essential, everything that constitutes Dasein *qua* Dasein, could an ontology of life be derived. Such is precisely the direction in which that line of inquiry characterized here as a "privative interpretation" tends.[19] If there is a chasm between Dasein and *vorhanden* or *zuhanden* beings, the gulf between Dasein and other living beings is no less gaping. Yet if all this has already been established at the very outset of the existential analytic, why does Heidegger return to it once the issue of being-toward-death hoves into view?[20] He does so because if Dasein is essentially *not* a living being, if the specificity of its being is drawn not from life but *from death*, a supplementary question has to be raised: *How are we to understand the death of a being that is essentially* not *a living being?* Heidegger does not dispense with this question. He recalls that the biologico-ontical line of inquiry considers death in its broadest sense to be a phenomenon of life and Dasein a pure living being, engaging thereby its researches into the "mechanisms" of death. As such, therefore, the ontology upon which it rests goes unclarified. On the other hand, however, if one begins with the ontological constitution of Dasein, it does become possible to grasp an ontological sense of death that resists confusion with any biological notion of end. It is at precisely this point in the analyses that Heidegger introduces his celebrated distinction between the three senses of ending (*enden*): *sterben, verenden,* and *ableben.* The ending of a living being that he terms perishing (*verenden*) is a physiological and biological death that is of no relevance to Dasein qua Dasein.[21] Although Dasein does indeed "have" a biological death—one that, moreover, can never be isolated and is always determined by its originary mode of being—qua *Dasein* it never really, or never simply, perishes; rather, it deceases (*ablebt*). Deceasing, the second mode of ending, is introduced by Heidegger as an intermediary phenomena (*Zwischenphänomen*). Deceasing is an ending that, without being a dying (*sterben*) in the "proper" sense of the term, is no less irreducible to the ending—the perishing—of a purely living being. Heidegger summarizes as follows these (decidedly problematic) distinctions between the various senses of ending: *Dasein verendet nie. Ableben aber kann das Dasein nur solange, als er stirbt.*[22] Dasein never perishes. Dasein, however, can decease only as long as it is dying. There is no "biological" death of Dasein qua Dasein. What is proper to this being that we always are is not what ties it to life, to the life of a living being, to a life of which it would thus be only the most evolved form in the great chain of being. Rather, what is proper to Dasein is what sinks the chasm between it and other beings, between it and every possible form of animality: *its relation to being as being*.[23] The death proper to it, most proper to Dasein qua Dasein, the death that constitutes the very possibility of its propriety, its absolute singularization, the absolute irreplaceability inscribed forever within its very being, would have nothing to do with the end of life, therefore. Dasein's death would have nothing to do with the cessation of a life that, in any case would never have essentially defined Dasein qua Dasein, a life that would always have been, so to speak, outside an existence that is played out in the relation to being in general and to its own being in particular[24]. What is at stake for Dasein in the ontological sense of death is less its *being*-toward-the-end (*Zu-Ende*-Sein) than its being *for* the end (*Sein zum Ende*).[25] Dasein does not die once, at a given moment, at the moment that its life ceases, at this undetermined moment that will surely happen but that has not, for the moment, yet happened. Dasein does not die as if death were an external event that might at any point affect life from without, that might come to affect it at a future instant in time that cannot be known in advance and that has no relation to the other instants in time, the instants of the past and the always singular instants of the present. It is the inauthentic They that considers death in this way, as an event that surprises a life that, for the time being, knows nothing but its future ineluctability. This attitude of the They, however, is merely a concealment, a flight in the face of the true ontological bearing of death, in the face of a certainty incomparable to any other certainty, most of all to some sort of "empirical" knowledge of the death of others.[26] Everyday knowledge of death has exactly the same structure as "vulgar" temporality. It is a knowledge that concerns a future event; that is, an event that will take place at a particular moment "in" an instant that will be present one day, but that, for now, has not yet come to pass, is not yet present. Perhaps one could say, therefore, that vulgar, inauthentic temporality, derived through a leveling out of originary temporality, has its most basic impulse in Dasein's flight from its being-mortal; it is Dasein's being-for-its-own-death that constitutes the only possible *experience* of an originary temporality.[27] Dying, properly dying, death in the ontological sense, has nothing to do with the (future) end of life. Rather, it concerns the being of Dasein, its essentially mortal being. Dasein does not just die once, once and for all, at a single moment at the end of its life; rather, it dies insofar as it exists.[28] *Sterben*, dying proper, does not bring about the end of existence from the *outside* but is inscribed *within* it; Dasein's existence is a finite existence within itself. Dasein is mortal (and native) insofar as it exists and not merely on the day of its (empirical) death.

But what does it mean to die properly? What is meant by *sterben*? Having carefully distinguished it from the end of a living being, how does Heidegger determine it? What is meant by the finite existence he describes? Answer: being toward the *possible*. In §53 of *Being and Time*, entitled "Existential Projection of Authentic Being-toward-death," Heidegger offers his own "definition" of *eigentlich sterben*. In authentic being-toward-death Dasein relates itself not just to death, but to death as a *possibility* that has to be sustained as possibility. This is not a matter of awaiting death, still less of suicide. Quite the contrary, in fact. Being-toward-death, where death is grasped as possibility, excludes from the outset any suggestion of an implementation or "realization" of death, this relation to possibility implying, rather, an anticipation (*Vorlaufen*). Once again, however, this sense in which Dasein anticipates death involves no reference to actuality. Instead, it should be understood as a rendering possible, as what frees the possibility of the possible. Why? Because if death is indeed Dasein's ownmost possibility, it is so only insofar as it is understood as *the possibility of the impossible*. As if impossibility alone could allow Dasein this anticipation into possibility (*Vorlaufen in die Möglichkeit*) that is its own death, the "truth" of a finite existing that opens onto itself:

The closest closeness which one may have in Being toward death as a possibility, is as far as possible from anything actual. The more unveiledly this possibility gets understood, the more purely does the understanding penetrate into it as the possibility of the impossibility of any existence at all. . . . Being-toward-death is the anticipation of a potentiality-for-Being of that entity whose kind of Being is anticipation itself. In the anticipatory revealing of this potentiality-for-Being, Dasein discloses itself to itself as regards its uttermost possibility [*seiner äu·ersten Möglichkeit*]. But to project itself on its ownmost potentiality-for-Being means to be able to understand itself in the Being of the entity so revealed—namely, to exist. Anticipation turns out to be the possibility of understanding one's ownmost and uttermost potentiality-for-Being [*als Möglichkeit des Verstehens des eigensten äu·ersten Seinkönnens*]—that is to say, the possibility of authentic existence [*eigentlicher Existenz*].[29]

Each one of the traits of the ontological constitution of death is gathered together thus. Death is Dasein's *ownmost* possibility and, as such, what pulls it back from the They. Equally, it is absolute possibility, absolute being understood here in the sense of an absence of all relation: *unbezüglichkeit*, Dasein's taking over of what it can-be is purely and simply a matter of its ownmost potentiality for being. This, then, is what makes death the root of Dasein's irreducible singularization, the *unsurpassable* possibility that *frees it*. Frees it from what, precisely? From any and all contingency. Faced with the unsurpassable possibility that death is, Dasein for the first time authentically chooses the factical possibilities of its existence.[30]

The problem, however, is that this *existential* projection of Dasein's authentic potentiality-for-being-a-whole (*eigentliches Ganzseinkönnen*) requires *existentiell* attestation (*existenzielle Bezeugung*), the very method of phenomenology demanding that it move beyond ontological constructions that cannot be attested by the phenomena themselves.[31] The *existential* project ought to unveil the ontological conditions of possibility for an *existentiell* possibility. Heidegger undertakes to clarify and interpret this existentiell possibility, attested by Dasein,[32] as resoluteness (*Entschlossenheit*). Now, it should be recalled that, for Heidegger, resoluteness is the pre-eminent mode of Dasein's openness (*Erschlossenheit*), that is, of its primordial truth (*ursprüngliche Wahrheit*).[33] And it is at precisely this point in the analysis, when it is a matter of showing what unites two phenomena as apparently disparate as anticipation and resoluteness, that he introduces originary temporality as accounting for the unity of the two phenomena, and that is, more generally, the ontologically unitary sense of care. As the pre-eminent mode of Dasein's openness (*Erschossenheit*), and thus as *originary truth* in its most authentic existentiell tendency, resoluteness (*Entschlossen-*

heit) refers to anticipatory resoluteness as its most authentic possibility. Resolution would not be what it is were Dasein to project itself toward any sort of possibility whatsoever, rather than toward the extreme possibility that is death—a possibility, remember, that, as Dasein's extreme possibility, precedes any and all of its factical possibilities.[34] The *existential project* of Dasein's potentiality-for-being-an-authentic-whole (the anticipation that marks being-toward-death) and the *existentiell attestation* of this same potentiality-for-being-an-authentic-whole (resoluteness as openness and as originary truth) are the same phenomenon: the anticipatory resoluteness that is, in turn, nothing other than the *originary* temporality of Dasein. It is only in anticipatory resoluteness, in authentic being-a-whole, that Dasein has an *originary experience* of temporality.[35] The link between death and temporality—in their originary sense—could hardly be more direct; in fact, the two actually involve one and the same experience of the originary. The experience of an essentially finite existence, as the temporality that opens such an existence, is originarily finite. And how could it be otherwise, when openness to the possibility of the possible is simultaneously, and indissociably, openness to the possibility of (the) impossibility (of existence)?

It comes as little surprise, therefore, that, in the analyses of being-toward-death, we again encounter precisely what it was that we saw to characterize originary temporality: a privileging of the future that cannot but go hand in hand with a reduction of the past—or, more accurately, of the *passivity* of the past. This privileging of the future and reduction of the passivity of the past seems to me profoundly of a piece with a conception of temporality that, whilst ekstatic, is still thought as *auto-affection*.[36] Let me try to explain.

If originary temporality is what renders possible anticipatory resoluteness [*vorlaufende Entschlossenheit*], it is only through such anticipatory resoluteness that Dasein experiences originary temporality. Now, this experience, this resoluteness in which Dasein anticipates by coming back-before itself, has the ontological meaning of a *project* of a *possibility*, and of Dasein's ownmost possibility at that. Originally temporalizing itself, Dasein does nothing other than give itself the possibility of openness to *Eigentlichkeit*.[37] The future, which is opened by Dasein's project of taking on what is proper to it, and which is nothing other than this opening itself, is thus the very possibility for Dasein to come [*venir*]—or happen [*advenir*]—to itself. The fact that the ekstases of past and present are co-originary with that of the future does not efface the latter's primacy in the matter of authentic temporalization: originary temporality temporalizes itself as the future. We have already seen that the past called forth by the future, that the past which comes from the future (from the future as *project*), is not only devoid of all the hallmarks of the "vulgar past" but also, and more fundamentally, appears "purified" of all passivity, of everything that points in the direction of the irrevocable and the unmasterable. Now, it appears to me that this effacement of passivity in the originary "past" is confirmed by the (authentic) being-toward-death that opens the (finite) temporalization of time. Yes, the originary past springs from a future; above all, however, it springs from a future which, as being-toward-death, as the decision for the possibility of the possible (that is, according to Heidegger, for the only true possibility: the ownmost), is a future that has *come to itself* and that, as such, has involved a series of exclusions or, more accurately, *suspensions*. As we have already seen, authentic being-toward-death suspends first and foremost any form of *Mitsein*. For Dasein to open itself to its own possibility, to its truth or to its future, there has to be an essential isolation. In its originary being-toward-death, Dasein knows no more of the experience of mourning than it does of the experience of a certain *Vergänglichkeit*. The past that springs from this future cannot and, above all, *should not* reintegrate what has been thus suspended. No more, however, can it refer to Dasein's being *perishable*, to the death of its life, to living pure and simple, to empirical death, to its fragility, if you will.[38] Dasein can attain its *Selbst*, which is also its singularity, only through resoluteness for its own death, a resoluteness that is itself possible only insofar as it is wrested from all being-with, only insofar as the irreplaceability which is its experience in authentic being-for-death refers it to an essential individuation and an essential solitude. In order to reappropriate for itself a *mit-sein* that is not simply the loss of a *Selbst* in the everyday and inauthentic They, Dasein has first of all to suspend all relation to the other in order to come back to itself (*auf sich zukommen*), in order to project itself for its ownmost and unsurpassable possibility, to project itself for its sole possibility: the possibility of its death. Dasein can come to itself (and this is the future: it is only the self that comes) only by appropriating the inappropriable: its death. The sole possibility proper to Dasein is its death, even if this possibility is the possibility of the impossible. Dasein can only appropriate the impossible for itself—a position that is not so very far removed from heroism. Everything else is subordinate to or suspended in favor of this confrontation with death. Time, above all. But then originarily finite time would have nothing to do with the (admittedly everyday) experience of a certain irreversibility, of a certain irrevocability of time that simply passes. And death, the experience of death in its ontological import, would never be in the first place the experience of the no longer being-there of others, or of certain others, or of something that has itself disappeared. The originary past is, like Dasein, precisely what does *not pass away*: it is what one can remember, re-evoke, re-call anew. Dasein does *not pass away*: at least, it does not do so *as long as it is* and, as Heidegger insists time and again, when Dasein is no longer there, it *is* been. Hence there is no passivity in originarily finite temporality other than the bare passivity of being-thrown.[39]

But does Heidegger's notion of being-toward-death account in the most radical manner possible—does it account *ontologically*—for the transcendental sense of death that Derrida's readings of Husserl have brought forth as what phenomenology *ought to* and *cannot* reduce? The passage from a transcendental phenomenology to a phenomenological ontology is, amongst other things, a passage to a thinking of originary finitude in which death is no longer placed between parentheses, is no longer confined and reduced to the level of an empirical event. And yet: what shows through the ontological meaning of death is, according to Derrida, the *irreducibility* of the empirical, the constituting contamination of the empirical and the transcendental. Now, if the Heideggerian distinction between the ontological and the ontic does not correspond to that between the empirical and the transcendental, it nonetheless shares with it a fundamental trait, namely, a certain hierarchical ordering of levels and a certain *de jure* uncrossable distinction between levels.[40] To this, moreover, being-toward-death is no exception. On the contrary, to the extent that it is what opens originary temporalization, all the distinctions made in *Being and Time*, to say nothing of its very project, will have to depend on it. Originary finitude is rooted in—coincides with—being-toward-death; *eigentlich sterben* is precisely *not* the end of the life of a living being. And it is wholly unsurprising, therefore, that Derrida, having addressed the question: What is a (transcendental) life that is never thought in terms of an (empirical) death? to Husserl, addresses to Heidegger the following: What is a death that is never thought in terms of life?

But does Dasein have experience of death *as such*, even by anticipation? What could that mean? What is being-for-death? What is death for a Dasein that is never defined *essentially* as a living thing? This is not a matter of opposing death to life, but of wondering what semantic content can be given to death in a discourse for which the relation to death, the experience of death, remains unrelated to the life of the living thing.[41]

2. Is My Death Possible?

I want now to follow in some detail Derrida's own analyses of being-toward-death. The question around which the various stakes that Derrida will want to raise can most economically be gathered is this: "Is my death possible?" But what are the stakes? First and foremost, they concern the status of the phrase "my death." *Whose* is the death thus named? The quotation marks surrounding the phrase allow us to keep open the possibility that the death in question is not necessarily "my own," that it can be the death of anyone whatsoever. If death, as Heidegger maintains, names the very irreplaceability of absolute singularity—the fact that no one can die in my place or in place of the other—it is left to Derrida to remark that any example whatsoever could serve to illustrate the point. The possibility of saying "my death" is placed under the sign of the irreplaceable; yet, and herein lies an unresolvable paradox, *all* examples are exemplary of this sort of irreplaceability. In this sense, therefore, the phrase "my death" also does the job, as does everything that undertakes the grammatical form of the first person.[42] "My death," like "my life," is indeed irreplaceable; yet the very phrase that defines absolute singularity also articulates a death (and a life) of everyone. "Every other is completely other" [*tout autre est tout autre*], Derrida concludes,[43] something Heidegger, still less Lévinas, would probably not want to contest. With this, however, Derrida begins to displace not only the logic in which singularity is constituted in relation to the *Selbst*, but also the logic (or, since it is Lévinas who is central here, we should perhaps say the *ethics*) in which singularity is constituted in relation to the other that, in order to be truly other, has to be wholly Other.[44] Whatever the status of singularity and its constitution, what concerns Derrida with the question of the possibility of "my death" is the possibility of establishing, within the context of *Being and Time*, a rigorous distinction between what Heidegger terms authentic dying, *eigentlich sterben*, and other forms of ending. This distinction is fundamental since, as we have already seen, it orchestrates the analyses of being-toward-death and so, too, the notion of authentic temporality that lies at the very heart of the project of *Being and Time*.[45]

The possibility of establishing an *eigentlich sterben* is preparatory to the possibility of developing an ontology of life. Preparatory to, but not independent of, however, for Heidegger is able, in fact, to determine the ontological characteristics of *vorhanden* and *zuhanden* beings simply by presupposing their difference from Dasein's own mode of being before even having brought this latter to light. How? Put rather briefly, by noting that men and things have nothing in common. Now, the same cannot be said when it comes to the ontology of life. The ontology of Dasein remains prior to any ontology of life, of course, but the latter cannot be addressed unless the question "Who is Dasein?" has already been answered and so what is meant by *eigentlich sterben* has already been grasped. The question "Who is Dasein?" can only be answered in terms of Dasein's *death*, which, we must remember, will never be the death of a living being. So why, then, is it necessary to pass through the ontological constitution of Dasein in order to arrive at the being of life? According to Derrida, Heidegger's explanation, which thematizes the necessity of this passage as a *privative interpretation*, merely underlines the difficulty rather than resolving it.[46] Dasein shares nothing with *vorhanden* and *zuhanden* beings; as such, there is no need to subtract anything from its mode of being in order to reach that of those other sorts of beings. On the other hand, however, Dasein *has* to share something with other living beings if it is only on the basis of a sufficient determination of the essence of Dasein that the essence of life can be ontologically determined. Life would be what remains once Dasein has been divested of everything essential to it, of everything that makes it a Dasein. The chasm separating it from *vorhanden* and *zuhanden* beings is no less vast than the one separating it from other living beings. No less vast, but not the same. If one grasps the *who* of Dasein only by way of its own death, which is never the death of a living being, Dasein is nonetheless *living* enough that one has to subtract its essence from life in order to determine *pure life*. The boundary that separates Dasein from other living beings is one that traces out the possibility of an *eigentlich sterben*; it is authentic death that separates Dasein from life, from a life that, as *pure life*, can know nothing of death, nothing of the only death worthy of the name and worthy of having an ontological sense, namely *Sterben*. The possibility of this uncrossable boundary is the very possibility of death, of death understood as *the possibility of the impossible*. And it is this celebrated definition that Derrida will want to confront but also, and above all, he will confront the entire Heideggerian logic presupposed by the idea of being-toward-death:

I'll explain myself with some help from Heidegger's famous definition of death in

Being and Time: "the possibility of the pure and simple impossibility for *Dasein*" [*der Tod ist die Möglichkeit der schlechthinnigen Daseinsunmöglichkeit*].[47]

The possibility of being-toward-death, to say nothing of the possibility of all the possibilities dependent upon it, is the *possibility of the impossible*. As might be expected, moreover, it is with a discussion of this possibility of the impossible that Derrida's own confrontation with the notion of *Sein-zum-Tode* will culminate. But let us not get ahead of ourselves.

Derrida begins by recalling that the existential analytic of death can and ought to precede any metaphysics of death as well, and even more so, as any biology, psychology, theodicy or theology of death. All such disciplines necessarily presuppose a pre-understanding of what death is or of what is meant by the word "death." The explication of ontological pre-understanding in general is the task of the existential analytic: the delimitation of the domains or regions of knowledge presupposes an onto-phenomenology that is itself non-regional. Onto-phenomenology, Derrida writes, is not caught within the boundaries that mark out the different fields of knowledge or within cultural, linguistic, national or religious boundaries; equally, it oversteps the sexual boundaries that cross all such others.[48] It is this logic of presupposition (*Voraussetzung*) that allows the boundaries of the existential analytic to be delimited, a logic whose legitimacy and force Derrida wants to follow right up to the point at which the rigor of any such delimitation vacillates. What point is this? The point, precisely, of authentic dying. Now, according to Derrida, this logic of presupposition is not specific to Heidegger but, whether in its dialectical, transcendental or ontological form, in fact runs throughout the entire philosophical tradition.[49] §49 of *Being and Time* is a renewed call to attend to the proper order of questioning. In their haste to decide on the essence of life, the ontic sciences have always-already decided on the essence of death as no more than the end of life. Now, this undue haste on the part of the ontic sciences respects neither the *dignity* of the question (such sciences resting on an pre-understanding that is never explained, never questioned as to its ontological sense, and working, accordingly, with a response never posed as a question) nor the *order* of questioning, the two clearly going hand in hand. For questioning to be done in an appropriate manner, things have to be done in the right order: the anthropological and biological sciences naively employ more or less obscure conceptual presuppositions (*Vorbegriffe*) as to life and death, requiring thus a new preparatory sketch (*Vorzeichung*) made on the basis of an ontology of Dasein that is itself prior to any ontology of life. To such an ontology of Dasein, which thus has absolute priority, even an existential analytic of death will be subordinate. Derrida summarizes as follows the hierarchy being proposed here by Heidegger:

> This characteristic, that is, the existential analysis of *Dasein*, is thus an *absolute priority*, and then an existential analysis of death, which is itself a part of this ontology of *Dasein*, comes to be subordinate to it. In turn, this ontology of *Dasein* is presupposed by an ontology of life that it thus legitimately precedes.[50]

This *programmatic order*, so insistently emphasized by Heidegger, is in no sense external to the project of *Being and Time*, a sort of scholarly habit of which this great thinker had still not managed to rid himself, but wholly essential to it. As Derrida points out, if Heidegger uses the term "Dasein" rather than "man" it is in order to secure a point of departure based on no philosophical knowledge of what man is. Every definition of the essence of man, whether as *animal rationale*, as consciousness or as subject, is no more than a presupposition stemming from metaphysics and the ontic sciences. The analytic of Dasein will have to be severed from all such presuppositions and, in order to do so, it has to delimit the fields occupied by such sciences so as to be certain of itself and its own field. Only then can it ensure the rigor of its elucidation of the fundamental constitution of Dasein and show that this ontological constitution is also the condition of possibility, until now forgotten and concealed, of all the presuppositions with which we have been dealing. This delimitation of fields is thus based on the only possibility of Dasein's authentic dying (*eigentlich sterben*):

> According to Heidegger, these regions are legitimately separated by pure, rigorous, and indivisible borders. An order is thus structured by *uncrossable* edges. Such edges can be crossed, and they are *in fact* crossed all the time, but they *should* not be. The hierarchy of this order is governed by the concern to think what the death proper to *Dasein* is, that is, *Dasein's* "properly dying" [*eigentlich sterben*]. This "properly dying" belongs to the proper and authentic being-able of *Dasein*, that is, to that to which one must testify and attest (*Bezeugung*, §54). At stake for me here is approaching a certain enigmatic relation among dying, testifying and surviving. We can already foresee it: if the attestation of this "properly dying" or if the property of this death proper to *Dasein* was compromised in its rigorous limits, then the entire apparatus of these edges would become problematic, and along with it the very project of an analysis of *Dasein*, as well as everything that, with its professed methodology, the analysis legitimately [*en droit*] conditions.[51]

The attestation of Dasein's properly dying involves not just a delimitation of ontological fields, but also a *delimitation of the limit itself*, one made through a questioning of the different modes of ending.[52] Dasein's own death presupposes a secure limit between simple ending (*enden*) and authentic dying (*eigentlich sterben*), the distinction between the end of a living being, perishing and Dasein's authentic dying, between death (*der Tod*) and the sort of ending proper to a living being (*verenden*). Such a distinction is far from being merely *terminological*, however; rather it is a determinate *conceptual* delimitation. Only thus can one understand what it is for Dasein to die authentically, for Dasein to become what it properly is by *testifying* to its own being in the anticipation of death.[53] Indeed, so little is it a matter of a purely terminological difference that, with *eigentlich sterben*, it becomes a matter of a difference *of* language itself, of the uncrossable chasm that separates Dasein *qua* speaking being from all other living beings. Dasein is mortal not because its life comes to an end, but because it undergoes death *as* death, because it undergoes death *as such*. Further, this possibility of the *as such*, and so also of death *as such*, is, according to the Heidegger both of *Being and Time* and well beyond it, tied to the very possibility of speech. In this context Derrida refers to the passage from *On the Way to Language* in which Heidegger, having defined mortals as those who are capable of the experience of death, defines the animal in terms of its inability to undergo the same experience. To this inability of the animal, Heidegger juxtaposes another inability: the animal, he writes, is incapable of speech. The essential relation between speech and death flashes thus into view, but as-yet remains unthought.[54] Now, the fact that, for Heidegger, the animal no more attains speech than it does death, allows Derrida to push this logic to its limit: the living being, *qua* living being, is not mortal if by mortal we understand the possibility of undergoing the experience of death as such:

Heidegger never stopped modulating this affirmation according to which the mortal is whoever experiences death *as such*, as death. Since he links this possibility of the "as such" (as well as the possibility of death as such) to the possibility of speech, he thereby concludes that the animal, the living thing as such, is not properly a mortal: the animal does not relate to death as such. The animal, the living thing as such can come to an end, that is, perish (*verenden*), it always ends up kicking the bucket [*crever*]. But it can never properly die.[55]

Everything here depends on the *as such* of death, on the possibility of undergoing the experience of death as death, an experience of which Dasein, unlike the animal, is capable. But how does Dasein undergo the experience of death as death? What is it that renders Dasein thus capable? Whence Dasein's access to the *as such* of death? It is clearly not life that renders Dasein capable of death; the life of the living being, as we have seen time and again, can involve no experience of death as death. Death as such will never be the end of life, the living being is not mortal, and Dasein is not (essentially) alive. Perhaps it is language, then, that gives Dasein access to the possibility of death, the fact of speech of which it, unlike the animal, is capable in the same way that it, unlike the animal, is capable of the experience of death. Yet the essential link between death and the word that "flashes thus into view" cannot yet be made explicit; it is not yet thinkable. And still more to resist being defined in terms of a dependency of death on speech. Derrida dwells at some length on this point, on this careful juxtaposition that allows Heidegger to leave open several different possibilities: *before* or *after* the flash, if you like. The juxtaposition allows us to see—this is the first possibility—that there is no irreducible link between death as such and speech, that an experience of death is still possible for a being *without language* and is so, moreover, at precisely that point at which the word is broken, at which the word fails.[56] Yet this failure of the word, as Heidegger constantly reminds us, still belongs to language. The "without language" of death, the silence that breaks the word, would still be a possibility of language.[57] Yet one could also say—and this is the second possibility—that the experience of death as such is only possible *in language*, that it depends on the ability to speak and to name. And yet, Derrida inquires, what assurance do we have that the ability to name is what gives us the experience of death as death, as if it were enough merely to *say* death in order to have access to it as such? Surely the best that language can do is give us the *illusion* of the experience of death and not death as such. From which it would follow that it is *in* and *through* language that death loses its as such.[58] In each hypothesis, death is refused *as such* both to language *and* to what overflows it. The "as such" of death is held neither in language nor in that which, for a speaking being, overflows language, in the silence of the broken word, for example. If such proves to be the case, however, then the boundary between the animal and the Dasein of the speaking human, a boundary established by the possibility of death as death, would become unassignable.[59] This is one of the principle reasons for Derrida's objection to the possibility of an experience of death as death and all that it entails. Yet he will also raise a slightly different objection, much later on in the same text, by addressing the question, still keeping in mind the theme of death as the possibility of impossibility, of the possibility of the *as such in general* and so of *the possibility of phenomenology itself*. As we shall see, the two objections are basically the same. I will come back to this in due course but, for the moment, let us continue to follow Derrida's text.

Having problematized Heidegger's distinction between perishing and properly dying, Derrida turns to that other mode of ending that complicates Heidegger's line of argument on this point: deceasing (*ableben*). For Heidegger, *ableben*, as we have already seen, is an intermediary phenomena between *verenden* and *sterben*. In German, *ableben*, to depart from life, to leave life behind, has a medico-legal connotation that more than justifies its translation by the archaic verb "to decease."[60] To decease, which is neither so-called biological death nor the dying proper of Dasein, is defined through the play of a supplementary distinction between the other two figures of ending. Dasein alone deceases when its physiological or biological "death" comes to be certified according to the conventional medical or legal criteria. Dasein is thus *declared* to be dead, which never happens to an animal. Deceasing, therefore, is as proper to Dasein as dying; yet it is not identical to it. Dasein can decease only *because* it can die. Deceasing, in other words, even if it is not authentic death, presupposes *sterben*. Derrida recalls the Heideggerian formulation, cited earlier, that gathers together the various relations between the three distinct figures of ending: "Dasein never perishes [*Dasein verendet nie*]. Dasein, however, can decease [*ableben*] only as it is dying [*nur solange, als er stirbt*]."[61]

Now, Derrida suspects that the possible chiasmi between these three modes of ending could well be what reconciles the existential analytic with the twentieth century's two other great, competing discourses on death, those of Freud and Lévinas. If the distinction between *sterben* and *verenden* is taken into account, Heidegger's statements would no longer be irreconcilable with the double Freudian postulate dictating that, the irreducible death drive notwithstanding, neither biological science nor the unconscious testify to our necessary and intrinsic mortality. And the same could be said for the reproach leveled by Lévinas against Heidegger's claims for the irreplaceable mineness of death: the primary death, Lévinas insists, is not mine, but that of the other for whom I am infinitely responsible precisely because of that mortality. Now, remarks Derrida, it is only in what is properly termed dying, in *sterben* alone, that mineness is irreplaceable, that no one can die for the other in the experience of being hostage or of sacrifice, at least if "dying for the other" means "in the other's place" and not "in place of the other." Lévinas' pronouncements on this issue can hold for the experience that I have of the death of the other in deceasing alone and not in *sterben*. Or, rather, they presuppose, as does Heidegger himself, the co-originarity of *Mitsein* and *Sein-zum-Tode*, a co-originarity that does not contradict but supposes a *mineness* of dying or of being-toward-death which is not that of an I or of an egological sameness.[62]

However it stands as regards the debate between Lévinas, Freud and Heidegger, which Derrida only begins to sketch, what is interesting in this particular context is that the introduction of the category of *ableben* allows Heidegger, within the architechtonic of *Being and Time*, to trace out a supplementary limit. Not only does he construct a distinction between the biological end and the authentic dying of Dasein, he also constructs a distinction between being-toward-death and all the legal, cultural and medico-anthropological phenomena of deceasing. We will see shortly the importance of this for the status of the existential analytic but, first, let me turn once more to Derrida's own version of the various possible intersections between the three figures of ending.

The distinction between deceasing and dying is made *within* Dasein's being-toward-death. It is only because it exists *toward* death that Dasein can decease; although Dasein never merely perishes (*verendet nie*) *qua Dasein*, it can still decease (*ableben*), it can still end without either perishing or properly dying:

> Deceasing is not dying but, as we have seen, only a being-toward-death (*Dasein*) that is, a being-destined-to-death, a being-to-death or tending-toward-(or up-to)-death (*zum Tode*), can also *decease*. If it never perishes (*verendet nie*) as such, as *Dasein* (it can perish as living thing, animal, or man as *animal rationale*, but not as Dasein), if it never simply perishes (*nicht einfach verendet*), Dasein can nevertheless end, but therefore end without perishing (*verenden*) and without properly dying (*das Dasein aber auch enden kann, ohne dass es eigentlich stirbt*). But it cannot decease without dying. Thus there is no scandal whatsoever in saying that *Dasein* remains immortal in its originary being-to-death, if by "immortal" one understands "without end" in the sense of *verenden*. Even if it dies (*stirbt*) and even if it ends (*endet*), it never "kicks the bucket" (*verendet nie*). *Dasein*, *Dasein* as such, does not know any end in the sense of *verenden*. At least from this angle and as Dasein, I am, if not immortal, then at least imperishable: I do not end, I never end [*je n'en finis jamais*], I know that I will not come to an end. And with a certain knowledge I know, Dasein says, that I can never perish [*je ne saurais périr*].[63]

From this long passage, I want for the moment to retain only this: Dasein *qua* Dasein, in its originary being-toward-death, is *immortal.* At least if, by immortal, we intend a reference to *verenden,* to the end of the life of a living being, to the end of this life of a simply living being of which Dasein *qua* Dasein, the Dasein in man (as Heidegger sometimes likes to put it), can know nothing. And yet, the whole force of this system of distinctions stems from the fact that it is established solely so as to exclude any possible contamination between the end of the life of a living being and the ontological meaning of the death of Dasein *qua* Dasein; from the fact that it is established, adopting for a moment a more Husserlian vocabulary, so as *to bracket or to reduce my empirical death.* Dasein's death has nothing to do with empirical death; being-toward-death is *originary* only insofar as it reduces any empirical sense of ending. If Heidegger, like Husserl, cannot deny empirical death *de facto,* he nonetheless distances it from sense: there is no sense to the end of a living being, *ontological* sense being on the side of properly dying, assuming, at least, that one can speak of Dasein *qua* Dasein, precisely what is ultimately at stake in *Aporias.*

For the moment, let us come back to the latter distinction, the one rendered possible through the introduction of ending as deceasing. If deceasing supposes properly dying, what becomes possible is a rigorous distinction between everything indicated, on the one hand, by anthropology, in the description of the various cultural differences affecting death, by a "history of death,"[64] and, on the other, the results of an existential analytic of death which, by definition, is devoid of all boundaries. If the various forms of deceasing change as we cross the boundaries that separate one place from another, one culture from another, one epoch or language from another, properly dying has no such boundaries—or, what amounts to much the same thing, cuts across them all. These sorts of differences, as well as all other imaginable differences, concern only deceasing, which, as we have already seen, presupposes a *sterben* untroubled by any anthropological difference. The distinction between perishing and dying, and hence, turning now to what lies within the existential field, the distinction between properly dying and deceasing, allows Heidegger to trace out the boundaries of a problematic closure. Deceasing marks a twofold break: a break with the life thus left behind but also, and more importantly, a break with living beings in general because animals are incapable of deceasing. Equally, however, it marks a break as regards properly dying. Anthropology accounts for the various ethnologico-cultural differences that affect deceasing, illness and dying; *first and foremost*, however, there is an onto-logico-existential problematic that all anthropology has to presuppose, a problematic that concerns Dasein's being-toward-death over and above any cultural, religious, historical, sexual borders whatsoever.[65] In other words, if there are different cultures of deceasing, there is no culture of death it-self, no culture of properly dying. Dying is neither natural (biological) nor cultural, at least not wholly so. The distinction between perishing, deceas-ing and dying allows Heidegger to separate, order and subordinate various problematics; it allows him to establish a hierarchy between the various on-tic sciences on the one hand and ontology on the other, as well as allowing him to order such a hierarchy within the ontological domains themselves. But this distinction is only possible because Dasein is presupposed. It is only possible because it is presupposed that Dasein *is* and can be identified *qua Dasein*. It is only possible because it is presupposed that Dasein *can it-self testify* to its being Dasein, that is, to its potential being for death.[66] Be-fore turning to Derrida's analyses of the question, on which everything is going to depend, of the possibility of Dasein's being for its own death, and so, ultimately, of the possibility of Dasein being Dasein, we need to follow his remarks on another methodological presupposition made by Heidegger in his analyses of *Sein-zum-Tode*. This time, the presupposition concerns the "metaphysics of death" and is strictly tied to the question of method and so to the question of phenomenology itself.

Now, the same methodological presuppositions that govern the ontic sciences clearly govern the entire metaphysics of death. The analytic of Da-sein is prior to, neutral as regards and independent of any relation to the question of survival, of immortality, of what lies beyond (*das Jenseits*) or short of this side of things, the hither side (*das Diesseits*). For Heidegger, there can be no room for doubt on this point: one can only start from here, from the side on which Dasein is, since it is only in terms of this *here* that Dasein can then distinguish between the opposition between the here and the there, the short of and the beyond. The whole question of what comes after death is only possible *de jure*, only makes sense, if the ontological con-cept of death has already been elaborated. According to Derrida, the ges-ture made here by Heidegger is the same as the one that, at the very start of *Being and Time* (§2), was used to justify the ontico-ontological primacy of Dasein. The best point of departure is the point from which we *can* start and that point is always *here*, where we are.[67] As mortal, Dasein can only start from its own mortality, which means that the whole question about being can only be addressed in terms of this exemplary being that we always are, this being that is the only one able to ask this sort of question. *Where to begin if not from here?* Derrida summarizes thus the apparently invincible force of Heidegger's way of proceeding. However, he does so in order to ask what it is that makes this apparently unshakable decision problematic. Heidegger, at the very moment that he takes the decision to begin on this side of the boundary, makes a strange confession: "Whether such a question is a possible *theoretical* question at all must remain undecided here [*bleibe hier unentschieden*]."[68] The theoretical question of the *here* as a point of departure is not simply undecided, but *must* remain so;[69] the question, in other words, has been decided prior to and without any theoretical question whatsoever, and so, too, without proof. A decision is forced on us before any recourse either to logic or proof is possible; the theoretical space is opened by a decision whose necessity is not on the level of theory but of *testimony*.[70] Derrida underlines that it would be hard to overestimate the import that such a decision will have, and this for three reasons.

On the one hand—first reason—it is this decision that, presented as *methodological*, hierarchizes all the delimitations about which we have been speaking. If, in the order of method, the existential analytic precedes any biology, psychology, theodicy or theology of death, if it precedes any ontic content, it might well seem purely formal and empty. So far as Heidegger is concerned, this is merely an appearance that ought not to blind us to the richness of the phenomenological structures described by the existential analytic. It is precisely here, however, that Derrida raises the question of whether the phenomenal or ontological content of the analyses do or, indeed, can actually remain pure of all ontic content or whether, on the contrary, Heidegger does not surreptitiously reintroduce in *ontological repetition* theorems or theologemes that pertain to the disciplines that he would want to describe as founded and dependent.[71]

Next—second reason—Derrida emphasizes that Heidegger does not interpret death in terms of a decision that consists in privileging "this side of things." Rather, it is the *originary* and *underivable* character of death, as well as the finitude of temporality in which death is rooted, that requires him to decide to begin here. A mortal can only start from mortality; any belief in immortality, interest in what lies beyond, in the gods and spirits, however irresistible it may be, stems, according to Heidegger, *first and foremost* from his mortality. Hence, and still according to the logic underpin-

ning Heidegger's discourse, the *survival* [*survivance*] that structures each instant, "a retrospective anticipation that introduces the untimely moment
and the posthumous in the most alive of present living thing,"[72] is *secondary*, stemming as it does from mortality, from being-toward-death, which
alone is *originary*. For Heidegger, only a being that exists toward death can
project, think or desire immortality or any other form of survival [*survie*]
or return [*revenance*]. Survival, therefore, is not opposed to being-toward-
death; rather, its very possibility is conditioned by it and, at best, it confirms the originary being-toward-death that founds it.[73]

The third reason, and the one that brings us to the question of phenomenology, stems from the fact that the prevalence of the here, of the
"hither side," is equally a prevalence of the *phenomenological tradition*.
What is at stake here, in other words, is the preference given to the pre-
archic originarity of the proper, of the authentic, of the *eigentlich*, a preference that is not simply one hierarchical valorization amongst others, but
the very choice that generates every evaluation and every possible hierarchy. As such, the decision to decide from the here is not simply a methodological decision but *a decision about method*,[74] an absolute decision, therefore, since it marks the *very decision to decide*. It is an absolute decision that
is obliged—and how could it be otherwise?—to decide what is not decid-
able [*décider de ce qui ne se décide pas*]:

> The decision to decide from the *here* of this side is not simply a methodological
> decision, because it decides upon the very method: it decides that a method is pre-
> ferable, and better, than a non-method. It is not surprising to see this absolute de-
> cision turn into a non-decision, since it is an unconditional decision concerning
> the place and the taking-place of the decision. In fact, it is not even, not yet, or al-
> ready no longer a decision because, on the one hand, it relies on a prevalence
> rooted in precisely what cannot be decided, that is, in death, and, on the other
> hand and for that very reason, it leaves undecided (*unentscheidet*) the theoretico-
> speculative questions that could impose themselves, the questions that would
> make one hesitate between decision and non-decision, as between the two poles of
> one alternative.[75]

Heidegger's whole discourse on being-toward-death—which, as we have
repeatedly seen, shores up the very possibility of the existential analytic—
has a privileged *figure* or schema: that of the *crossing* or *passage over a line*,
the line between existence and non-existence, between Dasein and non-
Dasein. Being-toward-death would have no boundaries as regards historical, cultural or sexual differences; it would be universal, then, but univer-

sal only within those boundaries that separate Dasein from all other beings and particularly from all other living beings. And it is because death has no boundaries in this sense that it is possible to establish not merely the boundary between two problematic closures, between the existential analytic of death on the one hand and all regional knowledge on the other, but also to establish a logical demarcation between all the concepts involved in this problematic. If death has no boundaries, it is because it has itself established the boundaries that separate Dasein from non-Dasein, existence from non-existence (and so not, it should be noted, living from dying). We have already enough proof of this. What still needs to be shown, however, is that there is another consequence arising from the boundaries thus traced out, a consequence that will prove to be of fundamental importance to Derrida's account.

The existential analytic, in its decision to begin "from the here," as it were, wants nothing to do either with *returning* [*revenant*] or with *mourning*. So far as Heidegger is concerned, everything involving mourning either comes from derivative disciplines like psychoanalysis, metaphysics or theology, or else is founded in the experience of deceasing [*Ableben*] rather than in the experience of death in the proper sense of the term. Now, according to Derrida, mourning, ghosting [*revenance*], surviving, etc., are "non-derivable categories, or non-reducible derivations,"[76] something that implies, once again, that the debate between Heidegger and Lévinas has been displaced. The alternative between my death and the death of the other no longer has any relevance once one grants, as Derrida does, that Dasein's or my own *Jemeinigkeit* (regardless of whether this "I" or this "ego" is taken in the psychoanalytic or Lévinasian sense of the term) is *constituted* in its very selfhood in terms of an *originary mourning*. Just as any relation to the other will be indistinguishable from a *bereaved apprehension* so, in the hypothesis of an originary mourning, any self-relation presupposes a welcoming of the other within oneself as different from the self ("in itself outside me, outside me within me").[77] The "I," what we call the "I," only emerges, is only delimited, not just through the experience of the other, but through the experience of the other *as mortal.* The other is the one who can die, thus leaving nothing more than its memory in me. The terrible solitude that strikes us is opened up not through the ineluctable possibility of our death but through the death of the other, through the death of the other that, moreover, constitutes the self-relation that we term "me," "we," "subjectivity," "intersubjectivity" or "memory." In order for this to take place, however, one does not need to wait for the "actual" death of the other: the *possibility* of death precedes all such instances and renders them possible. It is through the *possibility* of the death *of the other and of mine* that my relation to the other and to the finitude of memory can first arise:

We weep *precisely* over what happens to us when everything is entrusted to the sole memory that is "in me" or "in us." But we must also recall, in another turn of memory, that the "within me" and the "within us" *do not* arise or appear *before* this terrible experience. Or at least not before its possibility, actually felt and inscribed in us, signed. The "within me" and the "within us" acquire their sense and their bearing only by carrying within themselves the death and the memory of the other; of an other greater than them, greater than what they or we can bear, carry, or comprehend, since we then lament being no more than "memory," "in memory." Which is another way of remaining inconsolable before the finitude of memory. We know, we knew, *we remember—before the death* of the loved one—that being-in-me or being-in-us is constituted out of the possibility of mourning. We are only ourselves from the perspective of this knowledge that is older than ourselves; and this is why I say that we begin by *recalling* this to ourselves: we come to ourselves through this memory of *possible mourning.*[78]

But why is the only experience of the other in which the "I" arises the experience of mourning? Why does the other only come to us *as mortal*? Derrida's response is clear: because finitude, and so the finitude of memory, cannot be thought in the form of a limit, in the form of a limited faculty or capacity, in the form of a power that is precisely not an infinite power but that is still thought in terms of the infinite. The finitude in question here is that of the *trace* that is always the trace of the other. If there is a finitude of memory, and thus also a coming [*venir*] or a memory [*souvenir*] of the future, it is because there is some other: memory as the memory of the other, memory coming from the other and returning to it.[79]

The alternative between my death and the death of the other has little relevance here, therefore; there is no subjectivity, intersubjectivity or alterity that could be constituted without the experience of mourning, without the experience of a mourning that, although sometimes "real," is still, in its general possibility, always constitutive. This logic of *originary mourning* is what makes possible all my relations to the other as other, that is, any relation *of one mortal to another*. My "own" mortality is indissociable from that of the other:

A logic or an a-logic, of which we can no longer say that it belongs to mourning in the current sense of the term, but which regulates (sometimes like mourning in the strict sense, but always like mourning in the sense of a general possibility) all our relations to the other *as other*, that is, as mortal for a mortal, with one always capable of dying before the other. *Always one before the other*. Our "own" mortality not dissociated from this. . . . The death of the other, if we can say this, is also situated on our side at the very moment when it comes to us from an altogether other side.[80]

The "hither side" of which we are still speaking is never wholly distinct from the "other side;" "boundaries" are always being crossed. For Derrida, moreover, the boundaries thus crossed are the same as those that separate the world of the living from the world of the dead. The crossing of boundaries cuts both ways; it is a two-way ticket, there and back again. If we can only ever begin "from the here where we are," as it were, and so if there is no real choice in the matter, this *here* where we are is itself never actually acquitted of the past that constitutes it, of the forgetting that, by the very fact of its being forgotten, always involves an appeal to memory. The here where we are is never *only one place* that *only one* ego can inhabit and answer for.

With this, then, we reach the final step, if I can put it that way, of Derrida's *Aporias*. If the entire axiomatic of *Being and Time* stems from the *possibility* of death, what needs *also* and *above all* to be interrogated is this concept of possibility. Derrida's account of possibility in *Being and Time* has two stages: first, he ponders the double value that Heidegger gives to the notion of possibility; second, he turns to the determination of possibility as the *possibility of the impossible*. Let me again follow the analyses in some detail.

The possibility of the possible has two senses. On the one hand, the possible has the sense of the *impendence of the future*, of the "that can always happen at any instant."[81] On the other hand, however, the possible has the sense of *ability*, the possible, this time, in the sense of that of which I am capable. At the end of his delimitation of the existential meaning of death in relation to its other interpretations, Heidegger confirms that each one of these other problematics mistakes or forgets the essence of Dasein (and so mistakes or forgets the essence of its death). Dasein is not a ready- or present-to-hand sort of being, a *verhanden* being, but one whose essence lies in its existence, in *possibility*, in *having*-to-be, in being-possible (*Möglichsein*). It is only because they remain ignorant of this dimension of possibility that other spheres of knowledge, and philosophy more than most, enclose Dasein into an ontological determination that is not its own, and that they ignore the ontological distinction between Dasein, on the one hand, and *vorhanden* or *zuhanden* beings, on the other. If being-possible is what is proper to Dasein, the ontological account of death will have to be a horizon of possibility. The sense of death will have to be possibility. But given that death is the exemplary figure of the existential analytic, it cannot simply be one possibility amongst others; rather will it have to be *possibility par excellence*. Now, so far as this sense of possibility is concerned, Heidegger establishes two series of ontological statements, which, according to Derrida, articulate each other as two moments of a single aporia. The first series characterizes death as Dasein's ownmost possibility, as the possibility most proper to Dasein: being-possible properly belongs to the being that Dasein is and death is its ownmost possibility, a possibility of being that is not, in accordance with this sense of possibility, a characteristic that one would have merely to remark or describe. The essential impendence of possibility can only be *assumed*; one can only *testify* to it on the level of a phenomenological attestation that entails an *irreducibly prescriptive character*:

Death is a possibility-of-Being which Dasein itself has to take over [*zu übernehmen hat*] in every case. With death, Dasein awaits itself [*bevorstehen*] in its ownmost potentiality-for-Being.[82]

As one might expect, Derrida comments at length on his translation of *bevorstehen* by *s'at-tendre*, "to await" or "to expect." Now, whilst what is at stake here is indeed the possibility, at least in French, of crossing between several different transitives, of playing thus on the effects of an idiom,[83] what is also and above all at stake is the necessity of showing that the solitude of death, even of death in the proper sense of the term, is not, in fact, the solitude described by Heidegger. On the one hand, *s'attendre* can mean "I await myself, and nothing else [*je m'attends moi même et rien d'autre*]." As such, it would be a matter of the most identifiable and the most identifying form of self-relation: the *ego*'s memory or promise of itself. Yet the other syntax of this transitivity refers *to* something: one awaits or expects *something*, awaits or expects something that is perhaps something *entirely different*, something *completely other* [*tout autre*]. As such, either one can await oneself in oneself [*s'attendre soi-même à soi-même*] or, from the moment that this waiting or this expectation is turned toward what happens or comes, one can await something else, hence expect some other [*s'attendre à quelque chose d'autre, à quelqu'un d'autre*]. And each of these possibilities, moreover, can have a signal relation to what we call death. But Derrida gives special emphasis to a third possibility contained in this grammatical construction: the possibility of waiting for each other [*attendre l'un l'autre, l'une l'autre*], a possibility in which the *reflexiveness* of the absolute awaiting in question actually echoes rather than contradicts the most heterological reference to the wholly other, doing so, moreover, precisely when it comes to the question of death. Why? Because when this awaiting one another is related to death, the *anachrony of time* or the *contretemps of mourning* are irreducible. We know *a priori* that, when we await one another until death, we are both awaiting a meeting at which we will never arrive *together*. We know *together*, and know at the same time, that we will never reach death together:

death is ultimately the name of impossible simultaneity and of an impossibility that we know simultaneously, at which we await each other, at the same time, *ama* as one says in Greek: at the same time, simultaneously, we are expecting this anachronism and this contretemps.[84]

What we *share* in time, because this is certainly a matter of sharing, is its irreducible anachrony. The solitude of death is the impossibility of our ever reaching it together. Need it be said that this line of argument inflects the Heideggerian logic of the possibility of death in a wholly different direction? For Heidegger, it is with death that Dasein is brought before itself, before its ownmost potentiality for being, before the truth of itself, since death, as he writes, also needs to be understood as the unveiling of the self. There would be, therefore, a truth of death echoed in the untruth (*Unwahrheit*) of the flight in the face of death that characterizes everyday existence. With death, Dasein would stand before or await itself at the limit [*s'attendrait lui-même à la limite*], which is the truth, the unveiling of the self. For Heidegger, therefore, death stands at the point that marks the limits of truth and untruth.[85] And it is at precisely this juncture in his commentary that Derrida turns to the possibility of the impossible, to that other series of statements that form an aporetic supplement to the first.

As the ownmost possibility of Dasein, death is also the possibility of an *impossibility*. The first occurrence of this second series of statements immediately follows the passage that leads Derrida to address the notion of impendence, the *bevorstehen* through which Dasein awaits [*s'attend à*] its death as its ownmost possibility. It is announced in the following way:

"This is a possibility in which," Heidegger abruptly adds, "the issue is nothing less than Dasein's Being-in-the-world [*in-der-Welt-Sein*]. Its death is the possibility of no-longer-being-able-to-be-there [*die Höglichkeit des Nicht-mehr-Dasein-Kön-nens*]."[86]

In his ensuing commentary, Derrida will want to insist on the fact that Heidegger speaks here of the possibility of not-being-able or of the possibility of no-longer-being-able, and *not* of the impossibility of being-able; if this is but a nuance, it nonetheless has a very real importance. For Heidegger the possibility of not being able is not an *in*ability; despite their negative or privative character, each of the formulations being used here belongs essentially within a *horizon of a potentiality-for-being*. As Dasein's ownmost possibility, death, therefore, is the possibility of a being-able-no-longer-to-be-there or of a no-longer-being-able-to-be-there as Dasein:

As Heidegger adds: "As potentiality-for-Being, Dasein cannot outstrip the possibility of death. Death is the possibility of the absolute impossibility of Dasein."[87]

Derrida remarks, next, that Heidegger can in no sense be said to thematize the logical form of the contradiction contained in this statement; indeed, he appears, on the contrary, to see in the persistence of this contradiction (ownmost possibility as possibility of an impossibility) the very condition of truth, of a truth that can no longer be measured in terms of the formal logic of judgment.[88] Death, Dasein's ownmost possibility, is also what is closest to it. And yet, whilst the imminence of being-toward-death is indeed an absolute proximity, the fact that death is nothing actual, that its absolute proximity is what is furthest from any actual reality, means that it is an absolute proximity that is also as far from it as possible. Death is the possibility of the impossible, of a *nonreal as impossible*. Now, Derrida shifts the entire burden of his argument onto the status of this possibility of the impossible, onto the status of this unveiling—of this truth, therefore— given in the guise of the possibility of the impossible:

"The more unveiledly this possibility gets understood [*Je unverhüllter diese Möglichkeit verstanden wird*], the more purely [*um so reiner*] does the understanding penetrate it [advances into, *dringt vor*] as the possibility of the impossibility of any existence at all [underlined by Heidegger: *als die der Unmöglichkeit der Existenz überhaupt*]."[89]

It is the syntax of this sentence, the syntax of the *als*, of the *as*, that Derrida wants to address here. Certainly the *als* means that the possibility is unveiled *as* impossibility, something that, for Derrida, implies that it cannot be a simple matter of the *paradoxical* possibility of an impossibility, but it also means that the possibility is to be understood *as* impossibility. Death is at once the most proper possibility and this most proper possibility *as* impossibility. And, as Derrida points out, therefore, it is the *least proper* possibility, even if Heidegger never actually says as much. If the *als*, the *as*, holds what is unthinkable in reserve, it is only because it is not yet the *als solche*, the "*as such*," since—and one might well have suspected that this is actually where Derrida was going—the ownmost possibility as impossibility cannot appear *as such* without immediately disappearing. And the essential disappearance of the "as such" *as such* entails the *loss* of everything that distinguishes Dasein from other modes of being—both from other forms of beings and, above all, from living beings in general. The loss in question, therefore, is also the loss of its own death; properly dying would be originarily contaminated by perishing and by deceasing.[90] Now, according to Heidegger, *impossibility* as death, the impossibility of death or the impossibility of that mode of existence we call "death," can *appear* as such and announce itself *as possible* and *as such* for Dasein, and for Dasein alone. Dasein, and Dasein alone, would be capable of such an *aporia*, of maintaining a relation to death as such, a relation that is indissociable from its ability to speak—the two possibilities of which the animal is deprived. Dasein's most proper possibility, its essence and its freedom, its ability to question, its opening onto the meaning of being: all this would be announced in the *aporia as such* of death, in the possibility of the act of authentic, resolute assumption by which Dasein would take upon itself the possibility of this impossibility. Derrida's objection to this is straightforward enough: "What difference is there between the possibility of appearing as such of the possibility of an impossibility and the impossibility of appearing *as such* of the same possibility?"[91] Again, the nuance is slight; again, however, the conclusions that Derrida will want to draw from it are no less decisive. The impossibility of existing of which Heidegger speaks under the name "death" becomes thus the disappearance, the end, of the *as such*. And consequently becomes the disappearance, the end, of any phenomenology. Let me try to follow Derrida's logic here: the impossibility that is possible and proper to Dasein, is that there is not, or there is no longer, Dasein. Up to this point, the argument is Heidegger's own. It is the impossibility of the "as such" that, *as such*, would be possible for Dasein whilst being denied to any other form of being or living being. And yet—

and here Derrida's voice cuts in—if the impossibility of the "as such" is indeed the impossibility of the "as such," it is also what *cannot* appear *as such*. Now, and this is the decisive point that needs to be made, this relation to the disappearance as such of the "as such," of the "as such" that Heidegger wants to make the ownmost ability of Dasein and Dasein alone, is also a trait common not merely to both the authentic and inauthentic forms of Dasein's existence, to all experiences of death (whether as dying, perishing or deceasing) but also, beyond Dasein, to all living beings in general. Derrida emphasizes that this sense of a common trait of course entails no sense of homogeneity; rather, it entails the impossibility of an absolutely pure and uncrossable limit between the existential analytic of death on the one hand and all anthropological and animal cultures of death on the other. Since *animals, too, can die*, they themselves have a very significant relation to death, even though or even if they have neither a relation to *death* nor to the *name* "death" *as such* nor, consequently, to the *other as such*, to the purity as such of the alterity of the other. But neither, indeed, does man, not even man as Dasein, always assuming, of course, as Derrida does not, that we could ever rigorously say "man as Dasein."[92] And it is here, moreover, that we rediscover the relation of death to language:

Who will guarantee that the name, the ability to name death (like that of naming the other, and it is the same) does not participate as much in the dissimulation of the "as such" of death as in its revelation, and that language is not precisely the origin of the nontruth of death, and of the other?[93]

For, conversely, if death is indeed the possibility of impossibility and so the possibility of the appearance as such of the impossibility of appearing as such, then man *qua* Dasein has never had a relation to death as death, to pure death itself, but only to perishing, to deceasing, to the death of the other who, likewise, is no longer *the other as such*. If the death of the other is indeed "first," it cannot be a matter of the death of the other as other, but only of this experience of originary mourning that alone constitutes self-relation:

The death of the other again becomes "first," always first. It is like the experience of mourning that institutes my relations to myself and constitutes the egoity of the *ego* as well as every *Jemeinigkeit* in the *différance*—neither internal nor external—that structures this experience. The death of the other, this death of the other in "me," is fundamentally the only death that is named in the syntagme "my death," with all the consequences that one can draw from this. This is another dimension of awaiting [*s'attendre*] as awaiting one another [*s'attendre l'un l'autre*], awaiting oneself at death and expecting death [*s'attendre soi-même à la mort*] by awaiting one another [*s'attendant l'un l'autre*], up to the most advanced longevity in a life that will have been so short, no matter what.[94]

Death, the ownmost possibility of Dasein, as the possibility of its impossibility, becomes thus its most improper and most expropriating possibility. As such, the proper of Dasein is contaminated, within its most originary interior, by what is most improper. Derrida points out that Heidegger is careful to say that inauthenticity is not an exterior accident that befalls authentic existence. According to Derrida, however, Heidegger still has an *essential need* for this distinction between the authentic and the inauthentic, as well as for the distinction between properly dying and all the other forms of ending. Yet all these distinctions become impracticable as soon as one grants that an ultimate possibility is nothing other than the possibility of an impossibility.[95]

We have already glimpsed the conclusions that Derrida will want to draw from this; let me briefly address them once more, before turning to my own. The resources deployed in the existential analytic of Dasein are the very ones that also call possibility into question from within, the very ones that compromise the phenomenological principle of the "as such," the hierarchical difference between the various spheres of knowledge, the conceptual limits that Heidegger sets up between Dasein and other beings, whether these are *vorhanden* or *zuhanden* or other living beings;[96] the very ones that also call into question the distinction between awaiting *oneself* at death, awaiting death and expecting *that* death will come and, finally, awaiting or expecting *one another* at or from death as at the limits of truth. What, in short, is being called into question, as always in Derrida, is the *pure* possibility of tracing *pure* limits. It is not a matter of questioning the Heideggerian axiomatic in the name of a more radical, originary or fundamental thinking of death, but a matter, instead, of showing that *the dimension of the originary* is *unsustainable*, and is so in two different senses. No "anthropo-thanatology," however rich and informed it may be, is ever going to be able to be founded on anything other than presuppositions that lie beyond its knowledge or its competence and that refer thus to the sort of questioning undertaken by Heidegger, for example.[97] But in turn, this type of questioning can never be safe from the biological, anthropological and theological sciences, etc. Not because of a—perhaps inevitable but nonetheless contingent—failure on its part, not because of a failure to take the necessary precautions, but for essential reasons.[98] No method will ever give access to things themselves, for the simple reason that things themselves do not exist outside of the contamination of the empirical and the transcendental that produced them. The conditions of possibility of experience do not actually precede it. What we are doing is *the repetition of nothing*, of nothing that would have preceded it (not even in a non-chronological anteriority). What we are doing does not have a law of possibility that lies elsewhere: neither in the system of transcendental conditions of possibility, nor in the *pure opening* onto being that constitutes Heideggerian Dasein. No pure opening precedes that onto which it opens. And this is why, despite the extreme rigor of Heidegger's repetition, despite the force of his project of repeating the history of metaphysics in order to tunnel down to the very originarity of its ontological foundations, he fails to do so. Whether with *Verfallen*, with the fall into inauthenticity, with *cura* or with care (*Sorge*), with originary being-guilty (*Schuldigsein*), or with anxiety, Heidegger wants to repeat the tradition in order to bring to light the ontological foundations that rendered it possible and that can thus be said to precede it as its (ontological) condition of possibility, as the very origin of all the metaphysics, all the religions, all the theologies of our history. Yet no part of his discourse, writes Derrida, no part at all, neither his language nor his path of thinking, would have been possible without the Christian, even Judeo-Christiano-Islamic experience to which his work testifies—and so without the *event* and the *irreducible historicity* to which it testifies.[99] If one can never really protect the limits, however uncrossable one may wish them to be, between the originary and the derivative or between the empirical and the transcendental, it is because *historicity is irreducible* and because historicity can accommodate no origin: nothing precedes it and, if repetition is not merely possible but also constituting, it is because it is never pure repetition, never repetition of the same. *Which is another way of saying that repetition repeats nothing.* It clears a path that did not precede it, and thus a path that it opens always anew. And yet, the very opening of the new is not inaugural, if by inaugural we understand pure emergence. Just as there is no origin, so there is no pure emergence; the paths that we clear are new, when they are new, only to the extent that they stem from the forgetting that alone carries memory. Which is another way of saying that there is no past without passivity, no time without past and so without future.

All of which seems to me to confirm our initial hypothesis regarding the determining role played in Derrida's thinking by Husserl's phenomenology. A transcendental phenomenology, to be sure, but a transcendental that is obliged to take account of time in order to be, as Husserl maintained, the constitutive origin of experience and not simply the prior and always already written scene of the conditions of possibility of thought. A transcendental haunted by its genesis, then. And just as there is no genesis without passivity, so the transcendental is itself always confronted anew by this empirical that it can constitute only if, in turn, it allows itself to be constituted by it, allows itself to be contaminated by it. A transcendental, then, that, because it wanted to think the essence of temporality, was obliged to strike up against the temporality of essence.

Conclusions

I.

What sort of passage is there from genesis to trace? Between them, there exists a relation that is neither a straightforward continuity nor a simple break; a relation caught in the *tension* that the young Derrida sees at work in the concept of genesis; a tension between two apparently contradictory—yet necessary—demands; a tension, then, that there can be no question of resolving or neutralizing, still less of "sublating," a tension whose non-linear path would have to be followed. The tension that first introduces the concept of genesis, its "aporia," as Derrida would probably say today, is the one between the transcendence of origin and the immanence of becoming. The concept of origin, of absolute emergence from out of nothing that would exist prior to that emergence, allows for the possibility of there being something new, for the possibility that something can tear apart the closed continuity of a history in such a way as to allow for the emergence of what would be irreducible to a foreseeable and long-awaited possibility, to a future as a present still to come. The concept of becoming, on the other hand, demands to be read as a development inscribed within a continuity; a development borne by a past and oriented by a future; a development, then, in which every event takes on sense in relation to the context that surrounds it. If origin marks the radical discontinuity of a transcendence, becoming marks the continuity of an immanence. Do we, however, have to conclude from this that origin is placed thus under the sign of alterity and becoming under that of identity? Hardly, for it is here that the concept of genesis intervenes. As origin, genesis is indeed productive of the new; in marked contrast to origin, however, it is not self-generative, makes no claims to being an origin from out of nothing (else), since genesis, like becoming, is always borne by something other than itself. Genesis is shot through by alterity, denoting birth rather than origin. Already for the young Derrida, therefore, the production of the new is unthinkable outside of the contamination of an alterity.[1] What interests him as regards the concept of genesis, therefore, is its complication of origin and becoming, its introduction of the possibility of an event that is neither a continuous progress "in the series of nature or in the series of essences"[2] nor an emergence from out of nothing. Genesis is a "becoming" shielded from any of the unsurprising linkages of cause and effect, a fractured becoming that complicates the opposition between immanence and transcendence, between identity and alterity, between continuity and break.

Now, if one still wants to credit the concept of genesis with sustaining this aporetic tension, then the relation of genesis to trace is a "genetic" one. And let us not forget that passive genesis, like the trace, is what, for Derrida, calls the discontinuity of phenomenological and worldly time into question, what, in a "dialectic without synthesis," draws together the constitutive origin of time and a time constituted within a passivity that overflows the transcendental sphere in order to communicate with an objective time imposed beyond any activity on the part of the subject.[3] Worldly time and empirical time, the non-transcendental passivity that is a figure of alterity: the contamination of *Weltzeit* and phenomenological temporality signals thereby a break with the idea of temporality as auto-affection. The "outside" of the (empirical) world already inhabits the "intimacy" of the subject, and already inscribed within the movement of temporality are the alterity of space, of the other and, ultimately, the alterity of the subject to itself. The "passivity" of time aims to uncouple temporality from the present. As a form of time, the present is in effect indissociable from the self-presence of the subject, from the mastery of a consciousness that has lived everything as experience [*qui a tout vécu*] since everything has always taken place in a present. In this sense, then, the privilege of the present amounts to an effacement of time; if the present is all that there is (along with the past or future present), then nothing is going to escape anticipation and reactivation, nothing, at least in principle, can either be lost or unforeseeable. By contrast, passive genesis introduces a temporality that escapes all auto-affection, a temporality stemming from a past that has never been present, a past sheltered from the all-powerful reactivation not because of the finite character of memory but because it has never been lived in the synchrony of a present. An absolute past, therefore, that connects with a future that itself resists anticipation for all the same reasons. If the new is ever possible—and what else would the future be?—it comes to us from the passivity, the passivity of the past as necessary as retention to the very appearing of the present. The possibility of there being something new, of an unforeseeable event being able to break the continuity of a linear and anticipated future, is rooted in the alterity of time, in the alterity of the other; like genesis, the "new" is always borne by something other than itself. And there can be no inside, no within, without this contamination by a multiple outside.

The notion of trace, also elaborated in terms of a reflection on the movement of phenomenological temporalization, inherits much from the question of genesis. Once again, it is a matter of what, from the outset, "from the origin," as it were, contaminates temporality as auto-affection, of what contaminates temporality "from the origin" which is thus no longer an origin. The *Ur-impression*, the absolute origin of the Living Present as self-generation, ought not to be affected by anything other than itself, by the pure emergence of a new living now in which it becomes a past now. An originary impression can only be affected by another originary impression; the origin can only originate another origin—from out of nothing. And yet, the necessity of the retentional trace to the very appearance of the present opens the intimacy of time to exteriority, to spacing, to the im- or non-proper and thus to every form of alterity.[4] The trace as *différance* or delay is the delay of the present to itself that causes a rift in it before any distinction between inside and outside. The trace marks the impossibility of the origin and, by the same token, the impossibility of any pure opening; if there is no purely phenomenological origin of time, so, too, there is no originarily finite temporality.[5] The notion of the trace establishes a relation (according to a necessity to which we will turn shortly) between temporalization as spacing and the irreducibility of signification. The trace or arche-writing draws together the question of the sign with that of time:

The general structure of the unmotivated trace connects within the same possibility, and they cannot be separated except by abstraction, the structure of the relationship with the other, the movement of temporalization, and language as writing.[6]

Although the initial problem of genesis was indeed a problem of the orig-inary temporality of sense, it was one that remained deaf to the question of writing. Nonetheless, from genesis to trace, there is a sure passage. Of course, it can always be objected that it is only possible to read *The Prob-lem of Genesis* in the way that I have wished because of what Derrida him-self has developed in his later work. But is this really an objection? With the movement from genesis to trace, are we not confronted by an altered repetition that defies the very opposition between continuity and break?

2.

This altered repetition that leads from genesis to trace seems to me to indicate a profound dissymmetry in Derrida's relation to Husserl on the one hand and Heidegger on the other. Derrida's thinking has often been seen, and legitimately so, as taking as its point of departure the opening provided by Heidegger's own questions. The early works that Derrida de-votes to Husserl—*Introduction to the Origin of Geometry* and especially *Speech and Phenomena*—can be situated in this opening; and if they do signal an originality as regards Heidegger in the way that they draw support from the question of the sign rather than from the question of the sense of being, the very project of a deconstruction of the "metaphysics of presence" would nonetheless remain indebted to the thought of the ontological dif-ference. From this perspective, then, Husserl would be no more than de-construction's initial "object," a preliminary stage before the more arduous task of confronting Heidegger's thinking itself. Indeed, all the evidence would seem to point toward just such an evaluation of the relative places of Heideggerian and Husserlian phenomenology on Derrida's path: after the initial texts—and so very early on along that path: *Speech and Phe-nomena* dates from 1967—Husserl disappears, or very nearly so, as a proper name in Derrida's work. Heidegger, by contrast, has always been present as an explicit reference point, and has become ever more so; it is rare indeed among Derrida's more recent texts for him not to engage with Heidegger, to say nothing of those that are devoted entirely to his work. Now, the point here can hardly be to deny that Derrida's thinking owes much to Heidegger; instead, I want to suggest that the evidence mentioned here is misleading when it underestimates the role that Husserl's work plays in guiding Derrida's path and the singular place that it occupies along it. To consider Husserl as little more than a first stage, as an initial "object" of a deconstructive approach that would itself be prior to and exterior to Husserl, as it were, is to run a double risk: on the one hand, the risk of failing to recognize the importance of Husserlian questions for Derrida, on the other the risk of turning deconstruction into a formal and empty structure, a method that one might indifferently apply to all sorts of texts in order to investigate their undecidability. The two risks, moreover, are fundamentally related.

Now, although it is true that an impulse toward just such a formalism, far from being simply the product of a certain "Derrida-ism," can also be found in the work of Derrida himself, who also falls prey on occasion to the allure of method, this is far from being of a piece with Derrida's project as a whole or from corresponding to his most fundamental insights (at least insofar as one can speak in such terms regarding a thinking of contamination).[7] The undecidable, the double bind, the aporia, etc., are names for an irreducible contamination that resists any and all attempt to reduce it to an atemporal metastructure, to a sort of philosophical Gödel's theorem that might be used in order to demonstrate the undecidability of any axiomatic whatsoever.[8] The contamination of the empirical and the transcendental points toward a double demand and a double fidelity that run throughout the whole of Derrida's work, a demand and a fidelity forged in the interpretation of Husserl that constitutes the "internal" and avowed point of departure for his thinking as a whole. It is this work on Husserlian phenomenology that informs and motivates the question of contamination, a question that is accordingly very different from any abstract formalism. Deconstruction, then, is born in Derrida's work on Husserl; more than this, however, it is born in the work that Derrida has done *with* Husserl, *thanks to* him and, ultimately, *against* him, something that cannot be said of any of the other authors with whom Derrida has concerned himself. Not even Heidegger.

It is in the Husserlian problem of a genetic and non-static form of the transcendental, of a temporality of truth itself of which omnitemporality is but one form, that Derrida finds the possibility of a passivity that overflows the sphere of the transcendental, of a depth or profundity of genesis that complicates any purely phenomenological origin, of an alterity that cuts through all constitution. The empirical is a figure, a name for this alterity, the name of an "already constituted" before any constitution (whether active or passive). The contamination of the empirical and the transcendental, this "point" at which the two levels can no longer be separated into their pure component parts, not even by way of the insubstantial difference, the "supplementary nothing" that Husserl incessantly seeks in the face of all ontological doubling, points toward a double necessity. It justifies the transcendental demand of sense and of truth—of *justice*, even, if one shares Derrida's fear that the horizon of truth in our Western history is rather too epistemological to allow any scope for an ethics.[9] It is a "transcendental" demand because it is not immanent, identifiable or locatable, never present if the present is taken to refer to the synchrony of a manifestation or a recognition.[10] It is the demand to *make* sense and to *make* truth, as Derrida himself has it,[11] a sense and a truth neither of which is destined to disappear from the moment of their emergence but, as Celan writes of the poem, to forge a path toward eternity *through* time and not *beyond* it. Through a time that is always also a place, if all sense, all truth, is an event and not an essence, if one day they were born (and they could have not been born), born at a particular time and place, like the *eidos* of Europe. Yet there can be no guarantee, no assurance that they will not one day disappear, like a trace, since a *trace*, remember, is also and above all precisely what can always be effaced. This "transcendental" demand is already worked by the "empirical"; the empirical already inscribes within the transcendental the singularity, the contingency, the fragility of every event, a contingency that does not merely signal resignation in the face of the chaos and chance of the world (and what would be the merit in that?), but points toward the ethical tension of a temporality no longer centered on the present. The inscription of the empirical in the transcendental opens the latter to a constitutive alterity that can no longer function as an illusion or a protective strategy against anxiety. Why? Because there is also something of this in the attempt of all thought of the transcendental to situate the coming of what happens within the whole of its conditions of possibility. To want to determine what it is that renders an event possible in the first place, what preceded it, even if one does not try to think of it as a chronological anteriority, is to buy into the illusion of an original arche-scene that would dictate the law of everything that we do or think, as if the laws and conditions of possibility for everything that happens lay elsewhere, caught in the web of a destiny. This is one way of neutralizing what is irreducibly temporal about time, held between "the irreparability of the past" and "the imprevidibility of the future" that always make it something other than the movement of a pure auto-affection.[12] The contamination of the empirical and the transcendental reminds us that in what happens "there is always something more or other than its possibility."[13] It reminds us that what comes comes from beyond the horizon of expectation, that something or someone else can happen to us, that "the analysis of conditions of possibility will never suffice in giving an account of the act or the event."[14]

Now, *this* thinking of the contamination of the empirical and the transcendental is not something that Derrida "applies" to Husserl; rather, it is through Husserl's phenomenology, its preoccupations and its concerns, that he elaborates such a thinking by focusing on the tension between origin and becoming introduced by the notion of genesis.[15] The fact that this thinking also calls into question the phenomenological project as a whole does not prevent it from being constituted within that very project, according to a relation between inside and outside that has nothing to do with the exteriority of method as regards the objects to which it is applied. Derrida has continued to elaborate this thought of contamination, to repeat it, in his understanding of repetition as not being such without altering what it repeats. The disappearance of Husserl as a proper name, therefore, does not indicate a deconstruction of phenomenology without remainder, but a deep, profound lineage, as the never abandoned categories of ideality and the contamination of the empirical and the transcendental suggest. Even in the confrontation with Heidegger. If Derrida continues to work with the notions of the empirical and the transcendental, therefore, rather than with the distinction between the ontic and the ontological, it is certainly not by chance. True, Derrida has always refused to credit concepts themselves with being either "good" or "bad," insisting more on the syntax that puts concepts to work than on their isolated semiotic charge. Yet he still entrusts such a work of syntax to certain determined concepts.

Why the preference, therefore? Because Heidegger's thought of ontological difference, whilst certainly not reaffirming the distinction between empirical and transcendental, nonetheless plays out in the articulation of the ontic and the ontological a trait that is wholly unacceptable to Derrida,[16] without for all that allowing for the tension of genesis on which Derrida will never cease to draw. We have already seen why Derrida wants to separate his own thinking from Heidegger's epochal considerations of the progressive concealment and forgetting of being, as well as from the initial position of the question of being from the horizon of an originarily finite temporality. Without going back over ground already covered, let me again draw attention to the hierarchizing tendency of Heidegger's thinking, a tendency that comes into play when it becomes a matter of subordinating the positive sciences to regional ontology, or even to general ontology: to the question of being, itself the only question worthy of thinking. In the works following *Being and Time*, this hierarchizing tendency takes on a rather different modulation without ever contradicting itself, whether it is a matter of difference between (the) thinking (of being) and science, "which does not think," or a matter of the primacy of *Dichten* over "literature" as a whole. In the articulation of the ontic and the ontological, Derrida espies the power and desire of a philosophical discourse that wants to think itself and that, in order to do so, has also to think its other as *its* other, a process of reappropriation that protects it from any outside and from any exteriority such that "its *outside*, never surprises it, such that the logic of its heteronomy still resounds from within the vault of its autism."[17] We are not a long way from the Lévinasian allergy: the question of being, principally because of the force with which Heidegger endows it, remains of a piece with question of the proper,[18] all the way to the thought of proper death. For Derrida, Heidegger's question of being and time, his powerful attempt to think the temporality and historicity of being itself, insufficiently disrupts this horizon of the originary and the proper that is the first target of any thought of the trace as temporalization, as spacing, as alteration. While there is room for the origin in Heidegger's thinking, there is none for the question of becoming, unless it be under the flattened form of a connection between causes and effects.[19] If Husserl correctly identifies the transcendental dimension of genesis, Heidegger sees only the ontological dimension of the origin, every genetic dimension being referred back to a scientific causality that can only foreclose any access to the whole question about being. It should be said, however, my concern here is not to sever Husserl "from metaphysics" or to refer Heidegger back to it—any such exercise being *a priori* derisory—but to understand the articulation of Derrida's relation to Husserl and to Heidegger.

Given that Derrida's opening question is that of an irreducible contamination, his project has never been the Heideggerian project of originary finitude (the originary finitude either of Dasein or being itself), from *The Problem of Genesis* on. What is at stake in the move from genesis to trace is a thought of contamination in which borders *are* always being crossed. Not even finitude is unsurpassable. Nor is, primarily, the border, apparently the most secure of all, that separates life from death. Derrida's thinking is neither a thinking of the infinite (whether as an actual infinite or as an infinite under the guise of a teleological idea[20]) nor a thought of finitude. If Derrida does call into question Husserl's own recourse to the horizon of a teleological idea in contrast to the contamination brought to light by the very phenomena that he describes, he certainly does not do so in the name of an originary finitude. Why? Because originary finitude itself tries to avoid *any and all* contamination. The transcendental sense [*sens*] of death that Derrida evokes in the face of Husserlian phenomenology as a philosophy of life in no way coincides with the ontological sense [*sens*] of death captured in Heidegger's notion of Dasein. The transcendental sense of death is evoked in order to recall that there can be no pure life, no life ignorant of death, no "true life," no absolutely living and victorious life. And yet, turning to a Dasein originarily doomed to die, Derrida reminds us that, just as there is no "true" life, so there is no "true" death. No purely ontological death that in its sense could do without the impure life of living beings, the life, in any case, that ought never to define Dasein in its essence—and that is also to say, in its existence. The immemorial separation of true and false life, of true and false death, is common to both Husserl and Heidegger. It should be possible to know whether the shared destiny of human being is played out under the sign of an infinite Living Present or under that of originary finitude. It would have to be as possible to distinguish death proper from any biological sense of end, from all cultural and ritual forms of deceasing and, above all, from all mute and animal life that could never define Dasein *qua* Dasein, as it would to distinguish the absolute of transcendental life from any empirical figure of death. Whether on the side of finitude or infinitude, the dividing line would have to be clear. Also how are we to think the contamination of the finite and the infinite when everything seems to separate life from death, when the passage from one to the other seems to be a one-way street? However, it is perhaps that contamination is *primarily* the contamination of life and death, each one always crossing over and intersecting with the other. Perhaps it is *precisely life and death* that tolerate no sense of purity, neither pure life nor pure death. Of what, exactly, are they supposed to be pure? How could there be a life that was never defined in relation to death, or a death that was never defined in relation to life?

The contamination of the finite and the infinite, of life and death, is both what is imposed *by* the Derridean notion of writing and what imposes writing, as a paradigm of the contamination of the empirical and the transcendental, on Derrida. Indeed, if the stakes of such a contamination were all that united temporalization and spacing, this "place" where time and the world can no longer be separated, then one might well be confronted with a thought of finitude, and paradigms other than the one of writing would impose themselves. The body, for example, might well be this "place" where time and the world, the other, even, would intersect. Others have taken this path, indeed starting from Husserl. Not Derrida, however. Not Derrida because, to his way of thinking, *inscription in a place is inseparable from a notion of temporality as survival.* Now, a thought of the body can only be a thought of radical finitude or a thought of the infinite, if the body is envisaged as matter rather than as the body proper (*corps propre*). The same cannot be said of writing; consigned to or inscribed within a body (whatever body that may be), necessarily traced, writing will never be able to dispense with a world or a place. Threatened from the very moment of its inception, nothing can promise writing an eternal life; writing will never be able to survive the destruction of all worldly archives. It is always a trace, essentially effaceable. And yet, writing cannot be a body proper; its very fragility does not prevent it surviving if not beyond time then at least through time, at least through a certain time. Writing is not a body but what always leaves the body, what can only separate itself from the body.[21] Although arche-writing, the trace, *différance*, whatever other name one likes, are not equivalent to writing in the accepted sense of the term, since they refer to a field that "encompasses the field of beings as a whole," and above all to the movement of temporalization as spacing, it is still the case that writing in the strict sense of the term is an exemplary paradigm of this, and the singularity of this paradigm should not be effaced. Now, in Derrida's work, the notion of writing is inseparable from that of ideality. It is this bond that allows contamination to be thought as survival. The apparent symmetry in the relation to Husserl and Heidegger, each one questioned as to life and death, is broken anew. Once again, it is Husserl's notion of ideality—doubtless skewed in a rather different direction—that will allow Derrida to think the contamination of life and death.

3.

It is precisely this contamination of the finite and the infinite, of life and death, that Derrida's notion of writing allows us to think. It undoes the classical opposition between living speech and the dead sign, between outside and inside, between absence and presence, doing so insofar as it is wholly ideal, according to a notion of ideality without presence (a notion that reveals thereby both its Husserlian provenance and its displacement of that provenance). For Husserl, as for Derrida, it is this faculty of idealization that opens the possibility of sense and its transmission, the possibility of a historicity unable to take place without repetition and return. Repetition and return of what, precisely? Of the "first time" of a sense that draws from historicity not only the possibility of its transmission but also the very possibility of its birth. If sense is indeed radically temporal, if, that is, it needs time even in order to do without it, in order to become omnitemporal, then ideality can open memory only as a faculty for repetition. From the necessity of the first time and of its return, however, Derrida does not draw the same consequences as Husserl: the essence-of-the-first-time (*Erstmaligkeit*) is inscribed in ideality and modifies it. Repetition and return would be the repetition and return of what was once a *first time*, and so of what will never return *as such*. If repetition and return open memory—open ideality as memory—they do so only insofar as they inscribe within it a forgetting. This "forgetting," however, is one that "precedes" all loss; if ideality can never restore to us the first time as such, it is not because of some limit to its repetitive structure that prevents the restoration of the thing itself, "in the flesh." Rather, the first time is itself shot through, constituted, by a repetition that not only allows it to survive, to be reproduced in memory long after it has taken place, but also allows it to appear in the unicity of its first time. The possibility of repetition is not something added to the presence of the first time, but renders it possible, just as retention renders the present itself possible.

We can understand this modification only once we consider that although, for Husserl, sense and truth need the possibility of history in order for there to be any possibility of their being born, for Derrida, this possibility is no longer a pure possibility but the necessity of an event, of an always singular event that, like everything that happens [*arrive*], carries with it something more and something other than its pure possibility: the ideality of a singularity, like the *eidos* of Europe. The ideality that opens the possibility of history is, according to Derrida, an ideality that will never be free of history. It is a *dated* ideality. And it strikes me as being far from coincidental that Derrida's early considerations of the ineffaceable singularity of the time and place of the birth of the *eidos* of Europe find themselves reformulated much later on in terms of the ideal structure of every date.[22] The singular event does not destroy ideality but modifies it, contaminates it, if you will. No ideality is ever completely free of the empirical circumstances of its birth. The ideality of every date reminds us that every ideality is dated. Much as the question "What is a date?" by taking the form of a question as to the essence of the date in general, refers us to the determined and singular history of what is called Western philosophy. A date is something imposed from without in order to allocate an event its conventional numerical place on a calendar; it is something external, contingent and empirical that does not even seem to touch on what is essential to the event. Like the dates with which Celan marked his poems, for example, before erasing them for publication. Like these external dates that recall the moment of the poems' writing, and that seem to have nothing in common with the dates commemorated by the poems themselves, with the intimate and necessary dates that each poem "blesses." But can one really separate the external, "empirical" date of the poem from the internal date of its very genealogy? Certainly not so far as Derrida is concerned, once the genealogy of the poem is seen as being no less dated, no less temporal, than its actual writing. The limit between the external and internal date of the poem, just like that between the empirical and the essential, is blurred; the dates all share the same destiny, all sharing an ideality in which memory and forgetting are the conditions, the very truth, of one another:

A date marks itself and becomes readable only in freeing itself from the singularity which it nonetheless recalls. It is readable in its ideality; its body becomes an ideal object: always the same, traversing the different experiences which point to or constitute it, objective, guaranteed by codes. *This ideality carries forgetting into memory, but it is the memory of forgetting itself, the truth of forgetting.*[23]

The date, then, confronts us with the fate of any ideality. It is there to commemorate, to recall to memory, to save what has happened once, for a first time, from being forgotten. But it is only able to work as memory by "becoming legible," by being ideal, only by functioning as a date within an always conventional calendar that is, in principle, comprehensible and accessible to all. A date can commemorate only in the return of ideality, a return that will never restore to us the very event that the date commemorates in its first time, an event that will never be restored to us "in the flesh." Whatever a date commemorates, it also exposes to forgetting, to a forgetting that does not strike at memory by chance but, on the contrary, runs throughout the very "legibility" of the date, there where its return is the return of what does not return. Legibility and illegibility become inseparable in the movement of return. A date would not be a date without this essential possibility of becoming "no one's and nothing's date."[24] Nothing can sever a date from either legibility or illegibility. And it is at this point that all hermeticism, every strategy of appealing to the hidden secret, as well as all hermeneutics encounter their limit. The legibility and illegibility of the date stem from its ideality and render illusory the alternative between hermeticism and transparency. Granted, one can always entrust to a date a solitary or a shared secret. Yet an encrypted date is no less exposed to the possibility of its one day becoming a date that no longer signifies anything, and that day is not merely waiting for the death of those who would seek to protect the secret of a particular date; we are all mortal, and our dates are always exposed to the mourning of "lost singularity."[25] In the same way, a date that hides nothing, that is open and absolutely legible to all, also confronts us with the originary mourning of what will never return through the return of the date: the singularity of the other. Since, for Derrida, a date is not confined to commemorating a past event, it is always also a point of departure; it separates itself from the singularity that it designates in order to address itself to the other.[26] Like all ideality, the ideality of the date testifies to what cannot return, to what is lost in every return. Only thus can the date address, an address that, for Derrida as for others, exists only in separation. The ideality of the date is the originary mourning of an unassignable singularity and the possibility of an address that can only take place at a distance.

Ideality without presence, repetition that is never a repetition of the same, simultaneously memory and forgetting, because of its being the return of what will never return, Derrida's ideality is the "site" or the "place" of the contamination of life and death, neither an opening onto the infinite presence of transcendental life, nor the originary finitude of being-toward-death. Derrida's ideality is ideality as survival or as originary mourning, as the opening of experience for the mortals that we are, of this experience of the "return of what will never return" that needs neither the anticipation of death proper nor the projection of a present that comes "before and after" my death:

Spectral errancy of words. This spectral return does not befall words by accident, following a death which would come to some or spare others. The spectral return is partaken of by *all* words, from their first emergence. They will always have been phantoms, and this law governs the relationship in them between body and soul. One cannot say that we know this *because* we have experience of death and of mourning. That experience comes to us from our relation to this spectral return of the mark, then of language, then of the word, then of the name. What one calls poetry or literature, art itself (let us not distinguish them for the moment), in other words a certain experience of language, of the mark or of the trait *as such*, is nothing perhaps but an intense familiarity with the ineluctable originarity of the spectre. One can naturally translate it into the ineluctable loss of the origin. Mourning, the experience of mourning, the *crossing* of its limit too, so that it would be hard to see here a law governing a theme or a genre. It is experience, and as such, for poetry, for literature, for art itself.[27]

It is writing that quickly becomes for Derrida the paradigm of this sort of deflected ideality. For Derrida, and this despite Husserl's insistence on the necessity for freeing ideality from any dependence on an empirical community because of its capacity to function as empty, writing comes to mark the contamination of the empirical and the transcendental that can be seen in the necessity of a worldly inscription at that point where intentional sense can no longer be separated from the body of the sign. Yet the body that belongs to writing is not a body proper; it is an ideal body constituted by repetition, and as such it renders its survival possible. Because writing's ability to outlive the writer means that it testifies to his or her always possible death, its testamentary value testifies both to "originary mourning" and to survival, always assuming that these are not actually the same thing. Always exposed to the possibility of its own effacement, writing does not promise eternal life, but remains for a time; it survives for a while. It does so as an address: like every testament, writing is addressed to those who remain. It is the "return of what will never return," and begins accordingly by separating itself: from the body of the writer, certainly, but also from his or her soul, from his or her intentions and meanings. If writing fails to return, then it does so principally for the subject who writes. And for Derrida, it is here that writing's ethical dimension is opened up, a dimension on which I want to conclude this study.

4.

In fact, "that which does not return" is also the definition of another concept that has become steadily more important in Derrida's work: that of the gift. Many of the themes that we have already encountered intersect around the question of the gift; yet they do so with an explicitly ethical bearing that entails a singularly thetic move on Derrida's part. This move is imposed from the very position of the question of the gift onwards, a question that points to the necessity of an absolute break with an entire

tradition. With what tradition? The tradition, shared by metaphysics, anthropology, even psychoanalysis, that thinks the gift within an economy,
that thinks the gift as the law (*nomos*) of the home (*oikos*), of the proper or
property [*propriété*], as the law of the within that requires all exchange to
take the circular form of a return. Like Ulysses, who only moves away in
order to come back to himself. The gift, thought within the circle of an
economy, introduces a debt calling for restitution, whether real or symbolic, and becomes a gift that always returns to the giver.[28] Derrida affirms
the necessity of another thought of the gift that separates itself "in a sharp
and forthright manner," from this tradition, from tradition as such. This is
an affirmation, one will agree, that is rather unusual in his work:

> We will take our point of departure in the dissociation, in the blinding evidence of
> this other axiom: There is gift, if there is any, only in what interrupts the system as
> well as the symbol, in a partition without return and without division [*répartition*],
> without the being-with-self of the gift-counter-gift.[29]

A gift that calls for restitution is an exchange, a debt or a calculation, the
return that it commands annulling its value as a gift. A gift ought to be
gratuitous, but can only be so if there is no restitution, if there is no return.
Now, the non-return of the gift, rigorously thought, implies the suspension
of all appearing. According to Derrida, there can be no phenomenology of
the gift since, from the moment that the gift appears as such, as a gift, the
circle of economy is engaged; consciously or not, therefore, restitution annuls the gift in the return. The gift, paid back, effaces itself as a gift. The
"departure" that would be imposed by another thought of the gift as regards the tradition is also a departure from phenomenology and ontology,
therefore, from manifestation and appearance, from the as such of phenomena as the site of truth. If the mere appearance of the gift is enough to
transform it into a demand or an exchange, if a gift recognized as such can
only ever institute a debt, the "place" of the gift is no longer truth. Truth is
too much of a piece with manifestation, with being, with intentional or
unconscious signification, to suspend this return. Between the gift and
truth, therefore, there is no possible reconciliation: "The truth of the gift is
equivalent to the non-gift or to the non-truth of the gift."[30] The gift ought
not to appear as a gift: neither to the giver nor to the recipient, in accordance with a modality of non-appearance that has nothing to do with the
still phenomenological or ontological modality of concealment or veiling.
And if the gift has to be severed from all phenomena, it has thus also to be
severed from phenomenological temporality, whether retentional, proten-

tional or ecstatic, all such modes of temporality necessarily engaging a reappropriation.[31] As such, the gift demands a *time* without return, the time of a forgetting (and of a memory) sheltered from any horizon of awaiting or remuneration. Thus defined, the gift is placed under the sign of the *impossible*. How are we to think a gift if every intention to give, if every manifestation immediately annuls it in debt? How are we to think a gift without volition and without signification? How are we to think a gift that is not held in an impossible *double-bind*?

On the one hand, there is no gift without bond, without bind, without obligation or ligature; but on the other hand, there is no gift that does not have to untie itself from obligation, from debt, contract, exchange, and thus from the bind.[32]

The recourse to the impossible in the form of the double-bind is a response, it seems to me, to two specific demands. On the one hand, the need to sever the gift from ontology, on the other, the need to bear in mind that what is severed thus from ontology or from economy does not unfold in the outside of a pure exteriority but in an internal overflowing. Although the gift overflows the circle of economy, it does not thereby oppose it. The impossibility of the gift, the gift as the impossible, is not of the order of the ineffable or the unthinkable but is, on the contrary, the excess and the immeasurability [*démesure*] without which there could be no thinking as such. The impossibility of the gift indicates that although the gift is severed from the present of manifestation, this is not to say that it takes place in some sort of absence that would be merely the inverse of the phenomena. The impossibility of the gift is not an impossibility *tout court* but the limit of a thinking subjected to the present as the form of all mastery. Derrida's insistence that the gift, "if there ever is one," *s'il y en a*, as he says, is itself the impossible, needs to be read in this sense. The phrase "if there ever is one" separates the gift from the space of the possible as hypothesis or supposition. It separates it from a possibility that, without being an actual certainty, still refers to future verification. It marks the difference between what is today uncertain but that might be certain tomorrow, on a day that is far or near, and that which, in principle, cannot belong to the domain of certitude. The "if there ever is one" opens the gap between the possible as a modality of time anchored in the present, the possible as what will (or will not, it hardly matters which) be certain in a future present, and a modality of time severed from all form of presence and manifestation. The gap between ontology and an *otherwise* than being that is in no sense a *being* otherwise, as Lévinas would say. The difference between the "if there ever is one" and an "is" or an "exists" leaves open the possibility of a thinking that can renounce any claim to theoretical certainty, to the assurances of knowledge and judgment. Yet this renunciation is not the effect of frailty or weakness on the part of that thinking but of the recognition that there is a space beyond certainty that is the "place" of ethics. A gift, if there is ever a gift [*s'il y en à*], *is* not necessarily: *perhaps* it doesn't exist, *perhaps* it never will; the dimension of the gift is irreducible to all objectivizing observation, to all subjective mastery.[33] The "perhaps," like the "if there ever is one," introduces not a hypothetical doubt that could be alleviated but another dimension of time. For Derrida, the "perhaps" is the "most just category" for thinking the *future* [*avenir*], something for which the category of the possible is ultimately insufficient; if what comes were only the possible, there would still be a future present understood from out of the horizon of awaiting, in principle always foreseeable and calculable. For the future [*avenir*], there has to be a notion of the impossible that is not an impossible in itself but the excess of a time that is no longer auto-affection or ecstatic departure from the self. The impossible, the time of the impossible, always escapes prediction, mastery or calculation. It is not opposed to the possible, but frees it for the future [*avenir*]:

A possible that would only be possible (non-impossible), a possible surely and certainly possible, accessible in advance, would be a poor possible, a futureless possible, a possible already *set aside*, so to speak, life-assured. This would be a programme or a causality, a development, a process without an event.[34]

The impossible as a category of an unassured possible is the most just category for thinking the future [*avenir*], the gift, the event or the other. For thinking everything that overflows the circle of economy, of reappropriation, of calculation or of projection. Yet this overflowing is precisely what sets the circle in motion; remaining faithful to his thinking of contamination, Derrida seeks an outside that runs through the inside or an inside always already open to outside. The gap between knowledge, philosophy, science and the order of presence on the one hand and thought, language and desire on the other, a gap that Derrida summarizes in terms of the figures of economy and the gift, does not fall under the rubric of exteriority. Against the circle of what returns there is the excess of what does not return. Yet it is precisely this excess marked by the figure of the gift that sets the circle in motion. Inseparable from reappropriation (or from any one of its many figures), the gift always exceeds it. For Derrida, one never has as one's starting point the origin—this archetype of the law of economy—but always the excess of the impossible:

> Perhaps there is nomination, language, thought, desire or intention only there where there is this movement still for thinking, desiring, naming that which gives itself neither to be known, experienced, nor lived—in the sense in which presence, existence and determination regulate the economy of knowing, experiencing and living. In this sense, one can think, desire and say only the impossible, according to the measureless measure [*mesure* sans *mesure*] of the impossible.[35]

This excess is all the less ineffable when it calls reason to account, the principle of reason in the strictest and most classical sense of the term. There has to be reason, but there also has to be anxiety over what exceeds the *principium reddendae rationis.* Whence the reason why Derrida recalls, on precisely this point, the Kant of the Transcendental Dialectic. The Gift is a sort of transcendental illusion, reason as such demands that we think it. Reason itself is not content with the theoretical order of the calculable and the foreseeable, a reason that can no longer be divided into "theoretical" and "practical reason" since, wherever we do philosophy or science, wherever we do economics or politics, wherever we calculate—and, for Derrida, there has always to be calculation—we do so in fidelity to, out of anxiety and in the desire for what cannot be calculated, "in the memory (which is also always a promise) of the impossible." One could say, even if Derrida himself doesn't put it in quite these terms, that reason, when faithful to itself, is always arche-ethical.

Now, this thought of the gift, of the impossible, of the measureless gap that sets in motion thought in all its forms, that continually calls out to an elsewhere, again finds its privileged paradigm in writing. The gift, never present as such but not ineffable, can be read in writing, in writing as the time and space of the non-return. Allow me to recall here the "blinding evidence" of the other axiom that Derrida took as his point of departure, the fact that there is a gift, if there ever is one, only if it does not return. The gift, like writing, is what does not return. For Derrida, the non-return of the gift is unthinkable in terms of ontology and phenomenology, in terms of a metaphysics of the present or the sign, of the signifier or the signified, even, all such metaphysics being founded on the opposition of absence and presence, of manifestation and concealment. For Derrida, the non-return of the gift is only thinkable in terms of a problematic of the trace: the non-return of the gift coincides with this structure of ideality without presence, of ideality as the memory-forgetting that writing allows us to think. The forgetting of the gift, although never memorable in a present, is not nothing; it is no more reducible to a sort of non-experience than to an ineffable experience. As the possibility of the return of what does not return, it is a forgetting before all loss. The circle of economy and the excess of the gift intersect in this return without return that is unthinkable as the simple opposition of absence and presence, of memory and forgetting. Both gift and forgetting can be thought in relation to the other and both in terms of a problematic of the trace. The time and space of the without-return, if neither is ever present as such, take place (if one can actually say that) in writing:

> . . . we always set out from texts for the elaboration of this problematic, texts in the ordinary and traditional sense of written letters, or even of literature, or texts in the sense of differential traces according to a concept we have elaborated elsewhere. And we are unable to do otherwise than *take our departure in texts insofar as they depart* (they separate from themselves and their origin, from us) *at the departure* [*dès le départ*].[36]

Writing, as what separates itself from the start, from the outset, is the "place" of the without-return. It necessarily escapes—and not here or there, from without or by chance—the circle of reappropriation. It escapes it insofar as it is essentially testimonial, insofar as the death of the writer is inscribed in the very act of writing. This death that waits for no actual death and that is precisely the necessity that destines the non-return (to the giving subject). Granted, one can always write in order to assure an eternal life, along the lines of a calculation, conscious or not, of a reappropriation. Perhaps just such a desire lies behind all writing. The subject that writes, the "giving" subject, is no more generous than any other subject (the subject as such being, according to Derrida, incapable of a gift; there is no subject that constitutes itself without a view to a possible reappropriation). But through the circle of production and reappropriation, through the work of the subject, wherever there is a trace, a gift can take place. Because writing always overflows the intentional aim of the one who writes as much as it does the hermeneutic horizon of sense. Differential trace, ideality without presence, inappropriable writing is the condition for a gift at precisely that point where forgetting always relates to memory, death always relates to life:

The death of the giver (and here we are calling death the fatality that destines a gift *not to return* to the giver) is not a natural accident external to the giver; the giver can only be thought in terms of the gift. This does not simply mean that death alone or the dead can give. No, only a "life" can give, but a life in which this economy of death is presented and lets itself be exceeded. Neither death nor immortal life can ever give anything, only a singular *surviving* can give.[37]

The testimonial essence of writing does not open onto an ownmost being-toward-death, but onto a *survival*, a contamination of the finite and the infinite, in which the inappropriable, as the necessity of what does not return, gives ethics a chance (with no guarantees). The chance of the possibility—beyond calculation—that something else might happen (to us).

    Derrida's thought of writing, a thought that provides his work with its most recognizable, most overtly original trait, as well as its most well-known themes, gradually takes over from the initial question of genesis. It does so by retaining from the question of genesis the concern for an irreducible contamination that, far from being a threat to thinking is, on the contrary, the disquiet and the excess that sets it in motion. And so, too, through its harboring of the—deflected—inheritance of Husserl: as ideality without presence, writing marks the limit at which the empirical and the transcendental no longer can be separated. The "ambiguity" that is always at work in Derrida's notion of writing, the "ambiguity" between writing in the strict sense of the term and writing as arche-writing, as the differential trace that encompasses "the whole field of beings," does not strike me as a weakness on Derrida's part or as the slippage due to a certain kind of chance (or a certain necessity). Rather, it seems to me to indicate the impossibility of dividing an "empirical paradigm" from a "transcendental necessity." In writing, the (worldly) body and the (ideal) soul no longer can be distinguished; neither finite nor infinite, it is the place of this *originary mourning* that structures experience for the mortals that we are. Promised to no eternity, without being bound to an originary finitude that could still provide us with the illusion that we may one day be able to appropriate the inappropriable. Exposed to the irreversibility of time through the very form of its return, to the alterity of others, to the distance that separates us and forces us to address one another, in the inappropriable return of what never returns as such. From the deconstruction of the "metaphysics of presence" and of the sign right up to the thought of the gift, from genesis to trace, Derrida's reflections are sustained by the question of an originary contamination of which writing is the exemplary figure. A contamination of the finite and the infinite, of life and death, that no longer has any place either in a phenomenology—of the visible or of the invisible, it scarcely matters which—or in a thought of ontological difference. Neither trace nor *différance* can be gathered.

Notes

1. Jacques Derrida, *Le Problème de la genèse dans la philosophie de Husserl* (Paris: PUF, 1990). Translated by Marian Hobson as *The Problem of Genesis in Husserl's Philosophy* (Chicago and London: The University of Chicago Press, 2003). Henceforward *PGH*. Where two page references are given, the first refers to the text in the original language, the second to the translation.

2. One might legitimately wonder whether this is not simply indicative of the role played by phenomenology in the French philosophical debates of the time. To my mind, however, the opposition between "historical" and "internal" reasons—in other words, between *structure* and *genesis*—is ultimately insufficient for reading a work that, from *The Problem of Genesis* on, constitutes an attempt to reconsider all such categories.

3. The unity of the philosophical or metaphysical project, the very possibility of identifying it as such, is clearly not straightforward, but because this question is dealt with at length in chapter 2.1, it will not be addressed directly in these preliminary remarks.

4. This tension between Husserl's intentions and his descriptions will be the principle of reading followed by Derrida in *La voix et le phénomene* (Paris: PUF, 1967), translated by David Allison as *Speech and Phenomena* (Evanston: Northwestern University Press, 1973). Henceforward *Speech*.

5. One must perhaps abandon the word "radicality," which implies that one is *always going further*, although it is simply a question of going *elsewhere*. The same can be said of the notion of finitude, except that in this case the stakes are even higher. In what follows, we will continue to see how, according to Derrida, the relationship of the finite to the infinite cannot be thought in terms of a pure opposition. "Radicalizing Heidegger's thought of finitude" is thus a provisional and insufficient formulation.

6. *PGH* 7; xxi.

7. When it comes to dealing with Heidegger's notion of death, Derrida will call into question the value of *Eigentlichkeit*, a gesture that runs throughout his work on

Heidegger, up to and including the most recent texts. Cf., most notably, "Apories. Mourir—s'attendre aux limites de la vérité" in *Le passage des frontiers. Autour du travail de Jacques Derrida* (Paris: Galilée, 1994), translated by Thomas Dutoit as *Aporias* (Stanford: Stanford University Press, 1993). See also Ch. 2.3, below.

8. Even if, as is well known, Heidegger's thought cannot be entirely subsumed under the heading of an "ontology," there is perhaps a certain continuity on this point that I shall want to try to explain.

9. Ch. 2.3, below.

10. *PGH* 194; 115.

11. *PGH* 160; 91.

12. *PGH* 53; 14.

13. *PGH* 46; 10.

14. Kant's idea of the subject, the *I* as "empty form," as pure logical necessity that "accompanies my representations," allows for no substantial presentation principally because time as a "form of internal sense" is itself an empty form. Whereas the Cartesian *cogito* would allow for the presentation of the self under the form of an intellectual consciousness, the Kantian *cogito* is pure form. On this point, see Philippe Lacoue-Labarthe and Jean-Luc Nancy, *The Literary Absolute*, translated by Philip Barnard and Cheryl Lester (Albany: SUNY Press, 1981), 35ff. Husserl is well aware of the purely formal character of the Kantian subject; rather than subscribing to this gesture of exhaustion, however, renouncing thereby the very project of a transcendental subjectivity, as did most subsequent philosophers, he tries to think a subject that would be properly transcendental—and not worldly, as is the case for Descartes' *cogito*, on his reading—without being an empty form.

15. *PGH* 47 note 2; 10 note 5.

16. E. Husserl, *Philosophie der Arithmetik. Psychologische und logische Untersuchungen.*

17. On this point, Husserl follows Weierstrass' suggestion that arithmetic presupposes nothing more than the concept of number.

18. *PGH* 60ff; 19ff.

19. *PGH* 159; 108.

20. E. Husserl, *Logische Untersuchungen*, translated by J. N. Findlay as *Logical Investigations* (New York: Humanities Press, 1970). Henceforward *LI*.

21. *PGH* 108ff; 54.

22. E. Husserl, *Erfahrung und Urteil*, written up and edited by L. Landgrebe in 1939, based on manuscripts that date, by and large, from 1919; English translation by James Churchill and Karl Ameriks, *Experience and Judgment* (Evanston: Northwestern University Press, 1973).

23. E. Husserl, *Vorlesungen zur Phänomenologie des inneren Zeitbewusstsein* (1905), edited by Martin Heidegger, *Jahrbuch für Philosophie und Phänomenologie*, IX, 1928, 367–496; republished in *Husserliana*, v.X: *Zur Phänomenologie des in-*

neren Zeitbewusstsein, translated into English by James S. Churchill in *The Phenomenology of Internal Time-Consciousness* (Bloomington: Indiana University Press, 1964). Henceforward *Lectures*. The manuscripts that form this text (courses of 1905, texts from 1908–1909, and 1911) were reworked by Husserl in 1917.

24. While writing *The Problem of Genesis*, Derrida was able to consult a number of Husserl's unpublished manuscripts in the Husserl Archives at Louvain: Group D: 'Primordial Constitution,' Group B: 'The Reduction' and Group C: 'Constitution of Time' (*PGH* 241–243; 149–150). For an analysis of the historical evolution of Husserl's research on time, see Gerd Brand, *Welt, Ich, Zeit. Nach unveröffentlichten Manuscripten Edmund Husserls* (The Hague: Martinus Nijhoff, 1955), devoted to Group C, Rudolf Bernet's Introduction to the *Texte zur Phänomenologie des inneren Zeitbewusstseins (1893–1917)* (xi–lxvii) and N. Depraz, A. Montavont, S. Nagaï, "Trois lectures phénoménologiques de la temporalité: R. Bernet, G. Brand, K. Held," *Alter*, no. 2, 437–474.

25. "What we accept, however, is not the existence of a world-time, the existence of a concrete duration, and the like, but time and duration appearing as such. These, however, are absolute data which it would be senseless to call into question. To be sure, we also assume an existing time; this, however, is not the time of the world of experience but the *immanent time* of the flow of consciousness" *Lectures* 23.

26. *Lectures* 28–9.

27. Brentano, with whom Husserl studied, did not publish his analyses of time in his lifetime. Expositions of these analyses can be found in Husserl's *Lectures* and in the works of Marty and Stumpf. See also the posthumously published *Grundzüge der Ästhetik* (Bern: Francke, 1959) and *Philosophische Untersuchungen zu Raum, Zeit und Kontinuum* (Hamburg: Felix Meiner, 1976).

28. This holds equally for each isolated sound, absolute punctuality being only an ideal limit. *Lectures* 29ff.

29. *Lectures* 29–30.

30. *PGH* 116; 58.

31. *Lectures* 30 and §6.

32. Gerard Granel points out that, by confining the unity of the present and the past in the melody to the imagination, Brentano forecloses on any possibility of understanding the difference between the past that forms part of the present of the melody that I am actually hearing and the memorial past that I can only imagine because I can no longer *give* it to myself. "The *Imago* is always phenomenologically what it is etymologically: the image of the dead"; *Le sens du temps et de la perception chez Husserl* (Paris: Gallimard, 1968), 42. When, in *Speech and Phenomena*, Derrida discusses the difference between primary and secondary memory, he will take this aspect of imagination into account. See Ch. 1.3, below.

33. Husserl actually writes, regarding Brentano: "These lived experiences are psychical, they are objectified, they themselves have their time, and the point at is-

sue is their generation and development. Such matters belong in the sphere of psychology and do not interest us here" (*Lectures* 35).

34. *PGH* 117ff; 60 ff.

35. *PGH* 117; 60.

36. *Lectures* 43ff.

37. *Lectures* 50ff.

38. The value of the present as a source-point is never denied by Husserl, co-existing as it does with the idea of temporal density. I will come back to the difference, marked in the analyses of *Speech and Phenomena*, between primary and secondary memory in Ch. 1.3, below.

39. The simultaneously active and passive character of intentionality raises the problem of the status of *phenomenological passivity*. In his introduction to the French translation of *Ideas* (*Idées directrices pour une phenomenologie*, Paris: Gallimard-Tel, 1985), Paul Ricoeur claims that the activity and passivity of intentional consciousness have nothing to do with real (*real*) activity and passivity. According to Derrida, however, this only sets the problem back. If, as Husserl suggests, phenomenological evidence is founded on "an originary donating act," an act in which the object comes to be given "in person," one would have thus to admit of a fundamental passivity prior to noetic activity and to the formation of noematic sense. Derrida wonders whether the object that intentionality originally "receives" ought not, insofar as it is passive, to be necessarily "real" (*real*) and prenoematic. The question is one of knowing whether perception, the originary act of giving, does not in fact shatter the closed world of pure lived experience; in other words, whether one cannot deepen intentionality in the sense of activity and passivity, the generation of sense and originary "seeing" (see *PGH* 148; 82). Derrida's line of argument involves a detailed consideration, one that I cannot here follow in detail, of the status of the sensual *hylé* that is the *real* (*reell*) and not the intentional component of lived experience. According to Husserl, the *hylé* is constituting of all perception, the question being thus one of knowing how it can be lived before being animated by the *morphé*. According to Derrida, however, the choice here is between a worldly reality and a phenomenological one, and Husserl's decision remains unclear. We cannot know if the *hylé* begins by soliciting intentionality or if it is latent intentionality that animates encountered matter. Husserl raises but does not solve the problem in §85 of *Ideas: General Introduction to Pure Phenomenology*, trans. W. R. Boyce Gibson (London: Collier Books, 1962); henceforward *Ideas*. For Derrida, the reason why Husserl fails to elucidate the constitution of sense on the basis of a noetic-hyletic duality lies in the fact that he situates his analyses on the level of an already accomplished constitution. From the moment the analysis begins, the genetic synthesis is already complete (see *PGH* 157; 89).

40. *PGH* 121; 63. The claim that the question of the *hylé* is central in the *Lectures* is also maintained by Gérard Granel in *Le Sens du temps*. According to Granel, in *Ideas* Husserl is still working on the Kantian level of the problem. There

is a hyletic phenomenology that concerns material elements and a more important noetic phenomenology that concerns noetic moments (see *Ideas* §86). The primal unity of the "sensual" and the intentional is postulated ad infinitum. But there one remains at a constituted level where the hyletic and the transcendental, matter and form, are juxtaposed. What is called upon is the return to a deeper origin; one must abandon constituted time for the constitution of time. And this is what Husserl does in the *Lectures*, where he seeks the primal unity of the sensual and the intentional in the very constitution of the *hylé*, beneath their factual unity in perception. If in *Ideas* intentionality prescribes ad infinitum the unity of itself and its opposite, in the *Lectures* it is the *hylé* that plays the same role. The difficulty is thus, for Granel as well, that of managing simultaneously to avoid time as content (psychologism) and time as form (Kantianism). The fact that unity is always prescribed ad infinitum indeed signals that Husserl has not fully resolved this difficulty. This problematic, as is clear, is rather close to Derrida's. But it is not without interest to note that Granel's conclusions are nonetheless quite different. For Granel, it is a question of showing that the *Urimpression* is Husserl's name for ontological difference. What he is aiming for is thus an interpretation of Husserl that gives phenomenology the scope of a thought of being. Yet another interpretation of Husserl, or rather another problematic direction, opened on the basis of the problems emerging from the question of the temporal *hylé* is proposed by Didier Franck in *Chair et corps. Sur la phenomenology de Husserl* (Paris: Minuit, 1974). According to Franck, the impossibility of any constitution of an absolutely originary temporality is due to the fact that no *hylé* in general is thinkable without reference to flesh: it is through the flesh that worldly consciousness *and* transcendental consciousness are linked to their hyletic infrastructure. This implies that *it is flesh that constitutes time* and since flesh always refers back to another flesh, it is difference and carnal relation that temporalize time. At least two consequences follow from this: first, since my flesh is always affected in itself by another flesh, auto-affection is immediately hetero-affection; next, it is flesh that constitutes temporality and not the inverse, and there could be no place for flesh in an analytic of Dasein entirely oriented by temporality. If I make reference to Franck's thesis without being able to discuss it in itself, it is because it develops a thought of flesh and incarnation from the same problematic point as Derrida, which the latter would never envision for essential reasons that I will address in the *Conclusions*.

41. Jean-Luc Marion, in *Réduction et donation* (Paris: PUF, 1989), translated by Thomas A. Carlson as *Reduction and Givenness* (Evanston: Northwestern University Press, 1998) underlines the character of givenness in Husserl's thinking. According to Marion, the concerns of the *Logical Investigations* lie not in categorial intuition, as Heidegger would have it, or in the autonomy of signification, as Derrida maintains in *Speech and Phenomena*, but in the fact that Husserl considers the two as the originary phenomena of givenness (*Gegebenheit*). It is this idea of originary givenness that allows Marion to identify the possibility of developing a new perspective for phenomenology. This is hardly the place to discuss such a project,

and if I make reference to Marion's work it is only in order to underline the importance of the question of givenness in Husserl's own work and in the work of the tradition of thinking that has developed out of phenomenology.

42. From *Experience and Judgment* until the end of his life, Husserl makes transcendental genesis the centre of his reflections. The thematization of genesis, of *Lebenswelt*, of historicity, has often been presented as an abandonment of the project of transcendental phenomenology. According to Derrida, however, such an abandonment was never an issue for Husserl. Given that the rigorous division between the worldly and the transcendental cannot be supported by a static phenomenology, genetic phenomenology constitutes an attempt to give it a more secure foundation. And yet, still according to Derrida's argument, the fact that genetic becoming is no longer constituted, in its signification, through the activity of the transcendental subject but is, on the contrary, constituting of the *ego* itself, only renders the difficulty more acute. The sphere of phenomenology is no longer immediately transparent to a theoretical spectator of essences, the immanence of lived experience no longer ruled by noetico-noematic structures. The question, therefore, is whether a transcendental "I" can be generated within a history by maintaining a purely "phenomenologizing" attitude. I cannot here follow Derrida's analyses in *PGH* of *Experience and Judgment* and *Formal and Transcendental Logic*, and shall limit myself accordingly to the theme of transcendental historicity.

43. *PGH* 111–12; 56.

44. *PGH* 112; 56.

45. It should be pointed out that, according to Derrida, the movement in the *Idee der Phänomenologie*, ed. W. Biemel (The Hague: Martinus Nijhoff, 1958), *Hua* II, trans. W. P. Alston and G. Nakhnikian, *The Idea of Phenomenology* (The Hague: Martinus Nijhoff, 1964) from the eidetic reduction to the transcendental reduction does not alter the problem. If the eidetic reduction ought to allow one to move from the "fact" to the essence, the essence is, in turn, constituted by the *act* of a consciousness. And it is precisely this activity of transcendental consciousness that the phenomenological reduction ought to unveil. Yet as long as constitution is thematized only as static, one cannot really account for this transcendental activity that necessarily implies time. *PGH* 133ff; 71ff.

46. *PGH* 117; 60.

47. *PGH* 124; 64–65. Emphasis added.

48. The dimension of the irreducible passivity of time is closed off from the moment that one turns the past into nothing more than a past *present*. It is to this passivity that the idea of a "past that was never present," an idea found in Lévinas and incorporated into Derrida's own account with somewhat different intentions, is directed. See Ch. 2.2, below.

49. See "Force et signification" in *L'Ecriture et la différence* (Paris: Seuil, 1967), translated as "Force and Signification" by Alan Bass in *Writing and Difference* (Chicago: University of Chicago Press, 1978), 23; 12.

50. *PGH* 126–7; 66.

51. Husserl will later attempt to unify these in the texts of Group C where it is a question of the absolutely originary synthesis that unites absolute subjectivity and absolute temporality.

52. See *Ideas* §83.

53. *PGH* 169 note 89; 98 note 89.

54. See *PGH* 118; 61.

55. *PGH* 223; 136. Emphasis added.

56. See Ch. 2.3, below.

57. On the necessity of a transcendental *trajectory* in order to prevent the critique of the transcendental from falling back into a form of objectivism, see *De la grammatologie* (Paris: Editions de Minuit, 1976), translated by Gayatri Spivak as *Of Grammatology* (Baltimore: Johns Hopkins University Press, 1976), 90ff; 61ff. On the irreducibility of contamination to a formal and empty structure, see Ch. 1.3. and Conclusions, below.

58. Derrida clearly intends for the notion of a dialectic without synthesis to point in the direction of the essential complication of the origin: the dialectical duality is *a priori* incompatible with the simplicity of origin. To appeal to a dialectical origin is already to appeal to the non-originarity of the origin.

59. See *PGH* 123; 64.

60. *Speech* 114; 102. In *Speech and Phenomena*, this observation will also be played off against the Hegelian dialectic. See 1.3, below.

61. See *PGH* 172–3; 100.

62. E. Husserl, *Cartesianische Meditationen und Pariser Vorträge*, translated by Dorion Cairns as *Cartesian Meditations: An Introduction to Phenomenology* (The Hague: Martinus Nijhoff, 1960).

63. See *PGH* 228; 139–140.

64. *PGH* 160; 91.

65. See *PGH* 251; 154.

66. E. Husserl, *Die Krisis der europäischen Wissenschaften und die transzendantale Phänomenologie*, translated by David Carr as *The Crisis of European Sciences and Transcendental Phenomenology* (Evanston: Northwestern University Press, 1970). Henceforward *Crisis*.

67. *PGH* 249; 154.

68. The reference is to Husserl's Vienna lecture, "Philosophy and the Crisis of European Humanity," *Crisis* 276.

69. See *PGH* 254; 158.

70. *PGH* 251; 156.

71. According to Derrida's *Introduction* to *The Origin of Geometry*, the theoretical consciousness in itself is, for Husserl, nothing other than an ethical consciousness. See *L'origine de la géométrie* (Paris: PUF, 1962), translated by John P. Leavey, Jr. as *Edmund Husserl's Origin of Geometry: An Introduction* (Lincoln: University of Nebraska Press, 1989). Henceforward *IOG*. From which it follows that there will be no privilege in Husserl of the theoretical over the ethical, as suggested by

Emmanuel Lévinas; see *La théorie de l'intuition dans la phénoménologie de Husserl* (Paris: Vrin, 1978), translated by André Orianne as *The Theory of Intuition in Husserl's Phenomenology* (Evanston: Northwestern University Press, 1995).

72. The reference is to §5 of the *Crisis*, "The Ideal of Universal Philosophy and the Process of its Inner Dissolution." See *Crisis* 11.

73. These are terms that Derrida adopts from Husserl himself.

74. Exemplary in this sense is the figure of Galileo; see *IOG* 16–17; 35–7, and Ch. 1.2, below.

75. On Husserl's strategy for leaving transcendental consciousness unaffected by any danger, see Chs. 1.2 and 1.3, below.

76. This is the sort of question fundamental in Derrida, one that will be found throughout his work.

77. See *PGH* 274; 172.

78. See *PGH* 274; 171–172.

79. *PGH* 275; 172.

80. *PGH* 257, note 8; 211 note 8.

81. In fact, I think that it is *not*, at least in the sense that the resolute decision is, for Heidegger, evidently not an act or a state in which one could be settled once and for all. Still, the notion of *Eigentlichkeit* will be at the centre of Derrida's pre-occupations and will motivate the majority of his reservations concerning Heidegger, most notably those concerning the question of an originarily finite temporality (see Ch. 2.2, below). For a very different interpretation of Heidegger's notion of resoluteness, see Jean-Luc Nancy, "La décision d'existence" in *Une pensée finie* (Paris: Galilée, 1990), translated by Brian Holmes as "The Decision of Existence," in *The Birth to Presence* (Stanford: Stanford University Press, 1993), 82–109.

82. On the role of the concept of genesis and its relation to the concept of trace, see Ch. 2.2, below.

83. It should be clear by now that this study is not an attempt to situate Derrida's thought within the categories of continuity and/or rupture, which always strikes me as having only a limited relevance. I believe, and on this specific point I follow Derrida himself, that there is no repetition without alteration. Such an approach seems to me more competent to account for a trajectory of thought.

CHAPTER 1.2

1. Appendix 3 to paragraph 9a of *Crisis*.

2. *Crisis* 276. For Husserl, the openings of philosophy, science and history are one and the same.

3. *Crisis* 276.

4. *Crisis* 278.

5. *IOG* 54; 64. Emphasis added.

6. At the time, this sort of Platonism was not uncommon in the field of research on mathematics and its foundations, Hilbert, Russell and Gödel being only a few of the better-known examples.

7. See *Speech* 4–5; 6. I will come back to this in Ch. 1.3., below.

8. As, for example, Gödel's discovery in 1931 of the possibility of undecidable propositions. This discovery seems to challenge the Husserlian demand for a system of axioms on the basis of which every proposition is determinable as being either an analytic consequence or an analytic contradiction. As Derrida notes, however, from Husserl's own perspective it is only *from within the unity of a geometrico-mathematical horizon* that preoccupations as to decidability can themselves arise. The notion of undecidability is unintelligible outside something like *the* geometrical or *the* mathematical sciences, "whose unity is still *to come* on the basis of what is announced in its origin" (*IOG* 38–40; 53).

9. See *IOG* 32; 48.

10. See *IOG* 53; 64.

11. In *The Problem of Genesis*, Derrida had translated *Rückfrage* first by *régression* (*PGH* 260; 161) and then by *réflexion* (*PGH* 261; 162). The choice of *question en retour* has thus a very precise theoretical intention. [While Husserl's Rückfrage is generally rendered as "inquiring back," Leavy's choice of "return inquiry" captures both Husserl's meaning and Derrida's own translation (see the English version of *IOG*, 50)—Trans.]

12. *IOG* 36; 50. The citation is from *The Origin of Geometry, Crisis* Appendix VI: 354.

13. See in particular "Envois" in *La carte postale. De socrate à Freud et au-delà* (Paris: Flammarion, 1980), translated by Alan Bass as *The Post Card: From Socrates to Freud and Beyond* (Chicago: The University of Chicago Press, 1987).

14. Derrida's thinking cannot properly be addressed if one dispenses with the strictly philosophical side of his work. His reflections are underpinned by a rigorous line of inquiry, even if this appears to be hidden behind the veritable explosion of texts, themes and styles of writing. The calling into question of "metaphysics" is worked out from within, according to an overtly avowed strategy whose motives we have begun to glimpse. This has all too often been forgotten, whether in the "literary" accounts of Derrida's work, which continue to multiply, or in the contempt for his apparently "loose" style shown by those committed to a "rigorous" (and often unquestioned) philosophical thinking.

15. See *Grammatology* 90; 61.

16. *Crisis* §9 l, 57–9.

17. See *IOG* 56; 65.

18. "No theory we can conceive can mislead us in regard to the *principle of all principles:* that e*very primordial dator Intuition is a source of authority (Rechtsquelle) for knowledge,* that *whatever presents itself in "intuition" in primordial form* (as it were in its bodily reality), *is simply to be accepted as it gives itself out to be,* though *only within the limits in which it then presents itself*" (*Ideas* §24 83).

19. On this point, see *"La forme et le vouloir-dire,"* in *Marges de la philosophie* (Paris: Minuit, 1972) 185–207; translated by Alan Bass as "Form and Meaning" in *Margins of Philosophy* (Chicago: The University of Chicago Press, 1982) 155–73.

20. *IOG* 72; 78. If language is the site of ideality, three different levels of ideality need to be distinguished. First and foremost, there is the ideality of expression (of the signifier, in Saussure's terminology), free as regards its sensible, phonetic or graphic incarnations, but tied to a historical use of language. Then there is the ideality of the unity of sense, of the "intentional content" (of the signified, in other words): the "same" intentional content can be intended through several different languages. But the object itself is neither the expression nor the content of sense and, in the case of the empirical object, its contingency is going to reverberate in the ideality of its expression and its sense. It is only with the geometrical object that one reaches a level of absolutely free ideality, one that is no longer simply that of the expression or the content of sense, but that of the object itself. See *IOG* 60–4; 70–72.

21. *IOG* 87; 90. The connection between life and survival will be continually taken up and developed by Derrida. Among the many other texts one could cite, see, in particular, *Parages* (Paris: Galilée, 1986).

22. See *IOG* 72; 78.

23. *IOG* 82; 86.

24. See *IOG* 84; 87–8.

25. See "The Origin of Geometry" in *IOG* 164, and *Crisis* 361.

26. *IOG* 85; 88. Emphasis added.

27. See Ch. 1.3. below.

28. *IOG* 98; 98.

29. For Husserl, forgetting, seen as intentional modification of the *ego*, is, or ought to be, always reversible. In "La Présence du passé," Rudolph Bernet draws attention to this problem in a text devoted to the much more general question of the fundamental tension in Husserlian phenomenology between the absence and presence of what appears. In Husserl, absence always has the figure of a *temporal* absence arising at the very heart of the presence of the transcendental subject itself. Husserl considers the fundamental mode of this presence of absence to be the presence of the *past*. Given the importance that Husserl accords to remembrance in the constitution of an objective act of knowing, Bernet draws attention to his constant preoccupations and worries as regards the possibility of memory being able to restore exactly something that took place elsewhere: "With an honesty that verges on the masochistic, Husserl itemises the causes of error as *confusion* (*Vermengung*) between past and present experiences, *repression* (*Verdrängung*), *compression* (*Verdichtung*), *fabrication* (*Ausmalung*), *painting over* (*Übermalung*) and *covering over* (*Verdeckung*) (see *Analysen zur passiven Synthesis, Hua* XI). For, far from being constituting of memory, such pitfalls can and should be avoided by repeating a memory, by explicating the temporal horizon of the lived experience that is being remembered, and by moving from the present to the past with *prudence and caution* (ibid.). Hence, so long as one proceeds with precaution, it should be possible for an act of re-membrance not to be mistaken about a past lived experience"; *La vie du sujet: recherches sur l'interpretation de Husserl dans la phénoménologie* (Paris: PUF, 1994), 240.

30. All of which confirms the importance of Derrida's remarks, cited above, concerning intersubjectivity as a non-empirical relation that I have with myself.

31. See Ch. 1.3, below.
32. See *IOG* 17 note 1; 36 note 21.
33. *Crisis* §9 h, 49ff.
34. *IOG* 17; 36.
35. *IOG* 17 note 1; 36 note 21.
36. Whether it is a matter of Husserl, as we are seeing here, or of Hegel or Heidegger, Derrida never calls the arche-teleological concept of history into question in the name of an end of history or an *ahistoricity*, but always in the name of another thinking of history (and of time). See Chs. 2.1 and 2.2, below.
37. See "Origin" in *IOG*, 166 and *Crisis* 363.
38. See *IOG* 108; 105; see also "Origin" in *IOG* 168, and *Crisis* 365.
39. See *IOG* 107; 105.
40. See *IOG* 109; 106.
41. *IOG* 108; 105. We will see that originary finitude will not continue to be—if indeed it ever was—the best concept for thinking the historicity of which it is question. See Ch. 1.3 and especially Chs. 2.2 and 2.3, below.
42. See *IOG* 162ff; 146ff.
43. *IOG* 164; 147–8.
44. *IOG* 164; 148. Translation slightly modified.
45. *IOG* 165; 149.
46. On the enigma of this "life," see Ch. 1.3, below.
47. See *Schibboleth. Pour Paul Celan* (Paris: Galilée, 1986) 80, translated by Joshua Wilner as "Shibboleth: For Paul Celan" in *Word Traces: Readings of Paul Celan,* ed. Aris Fioretos (Baltimore: The Johns Hopkins University Press, 1994) 48.

CHAPTER 1.3

1. What is at issue here is the possibility of there *being something new*, a possibility that is not incompatible with—indeed, that is fundamentally related to—the possibility of the irreducibility of the past, a "past that was never present." On this sense of the past, see also Derrida's analyses of Freud's notion of *Nachträglichkeit* in "Freud and the Scene of Writing" (*Writing and Difference* 293–430; 196–231).
2. James Joyce, *Ulysses* (Harmondsworth: Penguin, 1986), 571.
3. See *IOG* 98; 97.
4. For Rudolphe Gasché, the strategy of deconstruction is centred on the construction of "quasi-synthetical concepts" that account for the conditions of possibility and impossibility of the fundamental concepts of philosophy. For these quasi-concepts, Gasché proposes the name "infrastructure." See *The Tain of the Mirror* (Cambridge: Harvard University Press, 1986), 7. On one level, this aspect of Derrida's work is undeniable, but I am equally convinced of the need to resist the lure of a certain formalization of the analysis if one wants to bring out what is, to my mind, at stake in the problematic of the quasi-transcendental and the undecidable. On this point, see Conclusions, below.
5. See Ch. 1.2, above.

6. See *IOG* 70 note 1; 77 note 75.

7. "This determination of being as ideality is properly a *valuation*, an ethico-theoretical act that revives the decision that founded philosophy in its Platonic form" (*Speech* 59; 53).

8. *Speech* 11; 12, citing the *Phänomenologische Psychologie* (*H* IX: 343).

9. "Let us suppose that . . . the whole of nature—and the physical in the first instance—has been 'annulled,' there would then be no more bodies and therefore no men. As a man I should no longer be. . . . But my consciousness, however its states of experience might vary, would remain an absolute stream of experience with its own distinctive essence. . . . Certainly an incorporeal and, paradoxical as it may sound, even an inanimate [*seelenloses*] and non-personal [*nicht personales*] consciousness is conceivable, i.e., a stream of experience in which the intentional empirical unities, body, soul, empirical ego-subject do not take shape, in which all these empirical concepts, and therefore also that of *experience in the psychological sense* (as experience of a person, an animal ego), have nothing to support them" (*Ideas* §54 151–2).

10. *Speech* 12–13; 13.

11. *Speech* 13; 14.

12. Derrida refers here to a difficulty that has been often been pointed out by Eugen Fink. See *IOG* 60 note 1; 69 note 66, and E. Fink, "La philosophie phénoménologique face à la critique contemporaine" in *De la phenomenologie* (Paris: Editions de Minuit, 1974), 95–175.

13. See *Speech* 14; 15. One might wonder whether Derrida himself is immune from the practice of quotation marks, visible or not, in his strategy of disruption of philosophical concepts. See, for example, the suggestion of Giorgio Agamben: "But if quotation marks are a summons against language, citing it before the tribunal of thought, to be such—to be able, that is, to refer to something standing outside language—must work itself out entirely within language. A humanity able to talk only within quotation marks would be an unhappy humanity that, by dint of thinking, had lost the capacity to carry thought through to a conclusion." *The Idea of Prose*, translated by Michael Sullivan and Sam Whitsitt (Albany: SUNY, 1995), 104.

14. See *Speech* 14; 15–16. Note that the question being raised here is the same as the one that Derrida had already posed in *The Problem of Genesis* as regards the notion of passivity. See Ch. 1.1., above.

15. "Pure psychology is a *precise parallel* to transcendental phenomenology of consciousness. Nevertheless the two must at first be kept strictly separate, since failure to distinguish them, which is characteristic of *transcendental psychologism*, makes a genuine philosophy impossible. We have here one of those seemingly trivial nuances that make a decisive difference between right and wrong paths of philosophy. (Husserl, *Cartesian Meditations* §14 32).

16. See *Speech* 14; 15.

17. See "Freud and the Scene of Writing" (*Writing and Difference* 301ff; 202ff)

and "To Speculate—On Freud" (*The Post Card* 277–437; 259–409). See also Ch. 2.3. below.

18. Whether it takes the form of Platonic *topos ouranois* or the form of Husserlian ideality, what is at stake here is the possibility of ascribing a value to what is not eternal. The question that needs to be addressed, therefore, is whether or not truth or sense, perhaps even beauty, subjected to time rather than severed from it, lose their respective values. Such, at least, is how Freud raises the question in his admirable essay "On Transience," in *The Standard Edition of the Complete Psychological Works of Sigmund Freud*, translated and edited by James Strachey (London: Hogarth, 1953–74), vol. XIV, 305–307.

19. See *Speech* 14; 15.

20. One could equally say, it amounting to much the same thing, that philosophical empiricism is the dream of the infinite exteriority of the other, the dream of thought purely heterological at its origin, of a *pure* thought of *pure* difference. This is what Derrida writes regarding Lévinas' project, and of all the philosophical gestures that have been called empiricism in the history of philosophy: "But the true name of this inclination of thought to the Other, of this resigned acceptance of incoherent incoherence inspired by a truth more profound than the 'logic' of philosophical discourse, the true name of this *renunciation* of the concept, of the a prioris and transcendental horizons of language, is *empiricism*. For the latter, at bottom, has ever committed but one fault: the fault of presenting itself as a philosophy" (*Writing and Difference* 224ff; 151ff). If Derrida does not himself adopt the name empiricism, it is because he has little faith in the project of a *pure thought* of *pure difference*, this thought being no more than 'a dream' that 'must vanish *at daybreak*, as soon as language awakens' (ibid.). Such is the refusal of *purity* that establishes Derrida's well-known strategy as regards the language of metaphysics and its structures of binary opposition.

21. See also "Survivre" in *Parages*, 135–218, translated as "Living On: Borderlines" by James Hulbert in *Deconstruction and Criticism*, ed. Harold Bloom, et al. (New York: Seabury, 1979), 75–175, and *Donner le temps* (Paris: Galilée, 1991), 132, translated by Peggy Kamuf as *Given Time* (Chicago: The University of Chicago Press, 1992) 101–2, as well as Ch. 2.3, below.

22. *Speech* 1; 3.

23. *Speech* 83–4; 75.

24. Speaking of the results of phenomenology, Husserl writes: "Our monadological results are *metaphysical*, if it be true that ultimate cognitions of being should be called metaphysical. On the other hand, what we have here is *anything but metaphysics in the customary sense*: a historically degenerate metaphysics, which by no means conforms to the sense with which metaphysics, as 'first philosophy,' was instituted originally" (*Cartesian Meditations* 139, §60).

25. See *Speech* 2–3; 4–5.

26. See *Speech* 7; 8.

27. Once again, *eidos* is determined on the basis of *telos*. Indeed, it is when the

normative idea of language as a relation to the object becomes problematic that the question of literature becomes urgent for philosophy—unless, though it would change nothing, it was literature itself that forced the question on philosophy: the question of literature, the question of style. If the philosophical question that, with Heidegger and Wittgenstein, opened and has continued to haunt the twentieth century is the question of language, it is Nietzsche who, more than anyone else, forced this question on an entire epoch. See principally *Of Grammatology's* (31ff; 18ff), *Epérons. Les styles de Nietzsche* (Paris: Champs-Flammarion, 1978), translated by Barbara Harlow as *Spurs* (Chicago: The University of Chicago Press, 1979) and Philippe Lacoue-Labarthe, "La fable (Littérature et philosophie)" in *Le sujet de la philosophie. Typographies I* (Paris: Flammarion, 1979) translated by Hugh J. Silvermann as "The Fable (Literature and Philosophy)," in *The Subject of Philosophy* (Minneapolis: Minnesota University Press, 1993), 1–13.

28. See Ch. 2.1, below.

29. Although it is certainly possible—Heidegger's claims notwithstanding—to raise the question of an ontological dimension of consciousness in Husserl, the constitutive link of consciousness to the object cannot be denied.

30. See *Speech* 83; 75.

31. On this point, see "Form and Meaning" (*Margins* 187–207; 157–73).

32. Not until Wittgenstein—but not his most direct legacy, or at least not the one most often claimed for him—and Heidegger is the question of language separated from the question of how to speak of objects.

33. The link between voice and phenomena that is raised by phenomenology is, for Derrida, merely the most accomplished form of a privilege of *Logos* as the living word, a privilege that constitutes as such something like the history of metaphysics, what Derrida terms *logocentrism*. On this point, see, amongst many other texts, *Of Grammatology* (15ff; 6ff) and "La pharmacie de Platon" in *La dissémination* (Paris: Seuil, 1972) 71–198, translated by Barbara Johnson as "Plato's Pharmacy" in *Dissemination* (Chicago: The University of Chicago Press, 1982), 61–171. Nonetheless, the question of whether logocentrism is an *epoch*, the question of whether there is *a* history of metaphysics, as Derrida occasionally seems to suggest in *Speech and Phenomena*, is far from being cut and dried. On this, one of the more decisive points of confrontation between Derrida and Heidegger, see Ch. 2.1, below.

34. *Speech* 15–16; 16.

35. *Speech* 60; 53.

36. *Speech* 60; 54.

37. Speech 60–1; 54. Derrida is obviously not the first to have tied language to death; the move is made equally by Heidegger. On the relation between them on this question, see Ch. 2.3, below. Long before Heidegger, however, Hegel has some intimation of this. The "Hegel question" lies beyond the scope of this study, but we should briefly recall a passage from Kojève's commentary on the *Phenomenology*, a passage of which Derrida cannot but be aware: " . . . Hegel can call Death

the 'unreality' that is Negativity or the 'negative-or-negating-entity.' But if Man is Action, and if Action is Negativity appearing as Death, Man, in his human or speaking existence, is merely a death, more or less differed and conscious of itself. Thus, to take philosophical account of Discourse, or of Man as a speaking being, is to accept frankly the fact of death and to describe its significance and its import on the three philosophical planes." Alexandre Kojève, *Introduction à la lecture de Hegel* (Paris: Gallimard *tel*, 1992), 548.

38. This double determination of death as *mine* and as *empirical* continues to mark a distance in relation to Heidegger's being-for-death. See Ch. 2.3, below.

39. *Speech* 60; 54.

40. In "Circonfession," commenting on the *Confessions* of St. Augustine, Derrida insists on the dimension of "making *truth*," something that does not belong to the order of *knowledge* of what is, something that is distinct from the classical notion of truth, from any *theory* of truth whatsoever, but is bound to an experience of writing (in *Jacques Derrida* by Geoffrey Bennington [Paris: Seuil, 1991] 48; translated by Bennington as "Circumfession" in *Jacques Derrida* [Chicago: The University of Chicago Press, 1993], 48).

41. At stake here is Celan's notion of eternity, the eternity sought by the poem, the eternity to which the poem aspires, but an eternity that is also one sought through and not beyond time, an eternity that means that the poem is indelibly temporal in its very desire for the eternal: "*Denn das Gedicht ist nicht zeitlos. Gewiss, es erhebt einen Unendlichkeitsanspruch, es sucht, durch die Zeit hindurchzugreifen—durch sie hindurch, nicht über sie hinweg*"; "Ansprache anlässich der Entgegennahme des Literaturpreises der Freien Hanstadt Bremen" in *Der Meridian und andere Prosa* (Frankfurt am Main: Suhrkamp, 1983), 37–8.

42. In a text dedicated to Paul Celan, Derrida writes about the date as a figure of singularity: "A date marks itself and becomes readable only in freeing itself from the singularity which it nonetheless recalls. It is readable in its ideality; its body becomes an ideal object: always the same, traversing the different experiences which point to or constitute it, objective, guaranteed by codes. This ideality carries forgetting into memory, but it is the memory of forgetting itself, the truth of forgetting" (*Shibboleth* 65; 38). Ideality is not that which frees itself of empiricity once and for all; it is the very memory of singularity, but the memory that, in order to be the memory of an irreducibly singular event, should be the memory of a forgetting, the truth of a forgetting. See Conclusions, below.

43. That a singularity can entail the capacity for making an event, the memory of a promise irreducible to all that has taken place, and that this is only possible through and thanks to finitude, without denying either mortality or the animality of humans, is the principle *ethical* stake of Derrida's thought. For an opposing point of view, see Alain Badiou, who claims singularity for the event of truth, but only in the dimension of eternity: humans have an ethical dimension only insofar as they are immortal; nothing based in their "animality" could be related to the

ethical (*L'Éthique: Essais sur le Mal* [Paris: Hatier, 1992], 13ff; translated as *Ethics: An Essay on the Understanding of Evil* [London: Verso, 2001]).

44. Husserl does not accept Frege's distinction between *Sinn* and *Bedeutung* as a distinction between descriptions of the object and the object as referent. See Frege's "On *Sinn* and *Bedeutung*," translated by Max Black in *The Frege Reader*, ed. Michael Beaney (Oxford: Blackwell, 1997), 153.

45. *Speech* 17–18; 18. [Rather than adopt the somewhat ungainly standard of translating *vouloir dire* as "to want to say," I have chosen here to follow Derrida's *own* suggestion. See *Speech* 18 note 1; 18 note 2.—Trans.]

46. "Such a definition excludes facial expression and the various gestures that involuntarily accompany speech without communicative intent . . . such utterances [not being] expressions in the sense in which a case of speech is an expression, they are not phenomenally one with the experiences made manifest in them in the consciousness of the man who manifests them, as is the case with speech. In such manifestations one man communicates nothing to another: their utterance involves no intent to put certain 'thoughts' on record expressively, whether for the man himself, in his solitary state, or for others. Such 'expressions,' in short, have properly speaking, *no meaning* (*Bedeutung*)" (*LI* I:275). For Husserl, everything involuntary is excluded from the essence of language and from the essence of consciousness, which is understood only as explicit will (see *Speech* 37–8; 35).

47. *LI* I:270. Husserl's emphasis.

48. See *LI* I:276–277.

49. Husserl, it should be recalled, will want to distinguish *Hinzeigen* from *Anzeigen*. Both are acts of reference, but whereas the latter denotes an existing sign's referral to a content whose existence is presumed, *Hinzeigen* implies no detour through empiricity. It is rather a referral of expression to sense in solitary mental life in which all contingency is excluded and in which only the act of a wholly certain demonstration (*beweisen*) can be said to intervene. See *LI* I:271 and *Speech* 46–7; 42.

50. *LI* I:279.

51. *LI* I:277.

52. *Speech* 23; 22.

53. *Cartesian Meditations* 108–11, §50.

54. *Speech* 47–8; 43.

55. Bernet, while not contesting the legitimacy of Derrida's analysis of this "essential distinction" between expression and indication, nonetheless argues that making it bear the entire weight of the phenomenological reduction fails to take into account the importance of that reduction. Still, he grants that the impossibility of pure expression, which stems from the impossibility of the speaking subject's ever being purely and immediately present to itself, affects the project of the phenomenological reduction to transcendental consciousness in the specifically *Cartesian* form of the project. Without denying Husserl's fascination with a consciousness that would be transparent to itself, Bernet insists that Derrida's reading (and

to an even greater extent, readings by self-proclaimed Derridians), centered as it is on the interpretation of language, runs the risk of installing a new "linguocentrism," precisely what Husserl himself always opposed. See "La Voix de son maître" in *La vie du sujet*, 267–96. That such a risk does exist is proved by a whole body of literature. Yet it does not seem to me that this would prevent "linguocentrism" from being also one of Derrida's principle targets. See "Philosophie et littérature. Entretien avec Jacques Derrida" (*Moscou Aller-Retour*, 108ff).

56. Derrida points out that, despite the distinction between indicative and expressive signs, it is indications alone that are signs in the true sense of the term for Husserl, who writes: "shall one say that in soliloquy one speaks to oneself, and employs words as signs, i.e. as indications, of one's own inner experiences?" (*LI* 1:279).

57. *LI* 1:279. Derrida points out that Husserl's line of argument here avoids the weakness of a classical psychology of the imagination according to which the image is a picture-sign whose reality, whether psychical or physical, indicates the imagined object. According to Husserl, the image, as intentional sense or noema, is not a reality that duplicates another reality; this is why he insists that the noema is a non-real (*reell*) component of consciousness. Intentionality intends the object itself, not an internal portrait that would be its double. See *Ideas* §90 and *Speech* 49–50; 46–47.

58. See *Speech* 49; 44.

59. See *Speech* 63; 56.

60. Derrida will often come back to this idea, most notably in his commentary on Austin's *How to do Things with Words*, "Signature Event Context." How can there be "normal" and "parasitic" uses of language, successful and unsuccessful uses, unless there is a structure to language that renders both usages possible? And how could such a structure not thus render each one as *normal* as the other? See *Margins* 376–93; 309–30, reprinted, alongside the ensuing polemic with John Searle, in *Limited Inc.* (Paris: Galilée, 1990), translated by Samuel Weber under the same title (Evanston: Northwestern University Press, 1988).

61. *Ideas* §52.

62. *Speech* 65; 58.

63. *Ideas* §43, 123.

64. See *Speech* 68ff; 61ff. For an analysis of the status of the punctual now (*Jetzpunkt*) as ideal limit in Husserl, see Bernet, "La présence du passé" in *La vie du sujet*, 217ff. See also *Being and Time* §82 and "*Ousia* and *grammè*" (*Margins* 33–78; 31–67). I will discuss this Heideggerian interpretation and Derrida's commentary on it in Ch. 2.2, below.

65. See *Lectures* 70.

66. *H* X: 28; *Lectures* 48. Cited in *Speech* 65; 62.

67. *H* X: 28; *Lectures* 49.

68. *H* X: 30; *Lectures* 52 and *Ideas* §81.

69. The principle of identity is not a norm amongst others, but the norm of norms, the principle that regulates classical ontology: "the founding expression of

the metaphysics of presence" (see *Grammatology* 308; 215 and *Writing and Differ-ence* 307; 206). It is the principle of identity that allows the chain of metaphysical oppositions, the principle of oppositional difference itself to be established. There could be no simple opposition between good and evil, true and false, presentation and representation, life and death, etc., if it were not first of all clear that good is good (and not evil), that life is life (and not death), etc. Without the *simple* self-identity of an element, it could not be in a simple opposition to its contrary. See *Dissemination* 117ff; 103ff. On the proximity at a few very precise points—and on the principle of identity in particular—between the Wittgensteinian and Der-ridean critique of Husserl, see Henry Staten, *Wittgenstein and Derrida* (Oxford: Blackwell, 1985).

70. See Ch. 1.1, above.

71. *H* X: 41; *Lectures* 64; cited in *Speech* 72; 64.

72. *H* X: 39–40; *Lectures* 62–63; cited in *Speech* 72–3; 65.

73. *Speech* 73; 65. Emphasis added.

74. *Speech* 75–6; 67.

75. See *LI* I:280.

76. See *Speech* 80; 71 and *Ideas* §§114–127.

77. *Speech* 87; 78.

78. See *Speech* 88; 78.

79. According to Derrida, the concept of *Selbstaffektion* used by Heidegger in the *Kantbuch* is the concept best able to describe the movement of temporalization found in the *Lectures*. See *Speech* 93; 83 and *Kant und das Problem der Metaphysik* (Frankfurt am Main: Klostermann, 1965), translated by Richard Taft as *Kant and the Problem of Metaphysics* (Bloomington: Indiana University Press, 1997), §34.

80. See *H* X: 100; *Lectures* 131.

81. *Speech* 96; 86. Emphasis added.

82. Which explains why, from the moment that one attempts to describe the pure movement of temporalization, one finds that "all names are lacking," and is obliged to turn instead to "ontic metaphors." The word "movement" is one such metaphor: with it, a determinate being is introduced into the description of a tem-poralization that ought to be free of such determination; "movement" should not be the name of pure temporalization, but of what such temporalization makes pos-sible. Yet if the world is originally implicated in temporalization, then one is always already adrift in "ontic metaphor," See *Speech* 95; 85 and "White Mythology" (*Margins* 249–324; 209–71); and "Le retrait de la métaphore" in *Psyché. Inventions de l'autre* (Paris: Galilée, 1987), 63–93, translated by Frieda Gasdner, Biodun Ign-lia, Richard Madden and William West as "The Retreat of Metaphor" in *Enclitic* 2:2 (1978), 5–33.

83. *Speech* 96; 86.

84. *Speech* 92; 81–82.

85. On the notions of *trace* and *différance*, see also Chs. 2.1. and 2.2 below.

86. See *Speech* 98; 88. On the need for a plurality of names, see Ch. 2.2., below.

87. *Speech* 99; 89.

88. "The trace, where the relation with the other is marked, articulates its possibility in the entire field of the entity [*étant*], which metaphysics has defined as the being-present starting from the occulted movement of the trace" (*Grammatology* 69; 47). See Ch. 2.2.

89. See *LI* I §9, 280–282 and §14, 290–291.

90. It is interesting to note both the proximity and distance of Husserl and Wittgenstein on the question of the intentionality of language. Despite the lack of explicit references to Brentano by Wittgenstein, there is every reason to believe that Brentano's distinction between "internal perception" (*innere Wahrnehmung*) and "external perception" (*äussere Wahrnehmung*) played an important role in Wittgenstein's analysis of intentional language acts (see Aldo G. Gargani, *Lo stupore e il caso*). But this was in a direction opposed to that of Husserl. For Wittgenstein, intentionality is an *internal relation*. Recognizing the sense of a proposition does not imply two steps and their confrontation: one recognizes a sentence *as* a sentence, one does not first recognize a scribble and only later identify it as a sentence endowed with sense. In the same way, for Brentano, tasting a white sugar cube does not mean tasting a sugar cube as white (see Brentano, *La psychologie d'un point de vue empirique*). Intentionality has the status of an *intransitivity* of language, that on its own can account for the fulfillment of intentional acts, without requiring a division between comparison and perception. This is why Wittgenstein writes that in language, the wait (*Erwartung*) and fulfillment (*Erfüllung*) touch each other (*sich berühren*). See Ludwig Wittgenstein, *Philosophical Investigations* §445 and *Blue and Brown Notebooks*.

91. "Every expression, in fact, that includes a *personal pronoun* lacks an objective sense. The word 'I' names a different person from case to case, and does so by way of an ever altering meaning. [. . .] If we read the word without knowing who wrote it, it is perhaps not meaningless, but is at least estranged from its normal sense. In solitary speech the meaning of 'I' is essentially realized in the immediate idea of one's own personality, which is also the meaning of the word in communicated speech. Each man has is own I-presentation (and with it his individual notion of I) and this is why the word's meaning differs from person to person." (*LI* I: 315)

92. *Speech* 106; 95.

93. *Speech* 107–8; 96–97. If, logically, one cannot derive the necessity of something based on its possibility, one might think that Derrida has fallen into a logical error regarding the modalities of possibility and necessity. In fact, he takes a different step: if it can potentially be the case that I speak without a full intuition of what I am saying, if it can happen that what I write is readable after my death— and indeed this occurs all the time—then one must account for what it is about language that makes such events possible. And the way language functions so as to allow for such events, its structure as a testament, is not in turn something that happens by chance, but constitutes language. On this point see also "Le facteur de

la vérité" in *The Postcard* (441–524; 411–496) and Silvano Petrosino, *J. Derrida e la legge del possible*, 153ff.

94. See, amongst other texts, "Signature Event Context" (*Margins* 372ff; 309ff).

95. Derrida remarks that this conclusion is reinforced by the supplementary distinctions that Husserl makes between fulfillment by an object and fulfillment by sense (see *Speech* 108; 97). "As said above, relation to an actually given objective correlate, which fulfills the meaning-intention, is *not* essential to an expression. If this last important case is also taken into consideration, we note that there are two things that can be said to be expressed in the realized relation to the object. We have, on the one hand, the *object itself,* and the object as meant in this or that manner. On the other hand, and more properly, we have the object's ideal correlate in the acts of meaning-fulfillment which constitute it, *the fulfilling sense* [*erfüllende Sinn*]." See *LI* I 290.

96. "We shall have to concede that such replacement is not only impracticable, for reasons of complexity, but that it cannot in the vast majority of cases, be carried out at all, will, in fact, never be so capable. Clearly, in fact, to say that each subjective expression could be replaced by an objective expression, is no more than to assert the *unbounded range of objective reason.*" *LI* 321.

97. *Speech* 113; 101.

98. This is one of the reasons why Derrida will have renounced the dialectical vocabulary he had used in *The Problem of Genesis*.

CHAPTER 2.1

1. "Envoi" in *Psyché*, 109–144; trans. Peter and Mary Ann Caws as "Sending: On Representation" in *Transforming the Hermeneutic Context: From Nietzsche to Nancy*, ed. Gayle L. Ormiston and Alan D. Schrift (Albany: SUNY Press, 1990), 107–138.

2. See "Die Zeit des Weltbildes" in *Holzwege* (Frankfurt am Main: Klostermann, 1983), 73–111, trans. William Lovitt as "The Age of the World Picture" in *The Question Concerning Technology and Other Essays* (New York: Harper and Row, 1977), 115–154.

3. For Heidegger, causality, a physical category, cannot be a category of historicality, any more than it can be a category of what is called psychism. To think historicality or Dasein in terms of causality signals a failure to respect the difference of ontological domains (see *Zollikoner Seminare*, ed. Medard Boss [Frankfurt am Main: Klostermann, 1987], 32ff, trans. Franz Mayr and Richard Askay as *Zollikon Seminars*, ed. Medard Boss [Evanston: Northwestern University Press, 2001], 26ff.).

4. *Sein und Zeit* (Tübingen: Niemeyer, 1986), trans. John Macquarrie and Edward Robinson as *Being and Time* (New York: Harper and Row, 1962).

5. From the *Introduction to Metaphysics* onward, Heidegger will renounce the term ontology in order to eliminate any confusion with the discipline called "on-

tology," which does not retain the slightest echo of ontological difference, see *Einführung in die Metaphysik* (Frankfurt am Main: Klostermann, 1983), 44; trans. Gregory Fried and Richard Polt as *Introduction to Metaphysics* (New Haven: Yale University Press, 2000), 57–8.

6. See, in particular, "What Calls for Thinking?" (*Was heisst Denken?*) and *What is Called Thinking? (Was heisst Denken)*, trans. J. Glenn Gray (New York: Harper and Row, 1968).

7. On the notion of *Geschichte*, see also Ch. 2.2, below.

8. See "World Picture" 73–74; 115–117.

9. Far from being a simple "application" of the sciences, technology plays a dominant role in our epoch: the sciences themselves belong to the domain of the *essence* of technology. See *What is Called Thinking*, 14 and "Die Frage nach der Technik" in *Vorträge und Aufsätze* (Pfullingen: Neske, 1985), 9–40; trans. William Lovitt as "The Question Concerning Technology" in *The Question Concerning Technology and Other Essays*, 3–35.

10. "World Picture" 85; 127.

11. On the ontological character of scientific method, see *Zollikon Seminars* 24ff, 30ff, and 147ff.

12. On the history of the notion of the subject, see Jean-Luc Nancy, "Un sujet?" in *Homme et sujet: La subjectivité en question dans les sciences humaines* (Paris: L'Harmattan, 1992), 47–114.

13. "World picture, when understood essentially, does not mean a picture of the world but the world conceived and grasped as picture [*Weltbild, wesentlich verstanden, meint daher nicht ein Bild von der Welt, sondern die Welt als Bild begriffen*]" ("World Picture" 87; 129).

14. "World Picture" 89; 131.

15. "World Picture" 90; 132. What is of concern here is the same capacity for repetition that we have already seen to be operative in the notion of ideality. See Ch. 1.3, above.

16. An ontological bearing, moreover, that takes on a decidedly ambiguous value. In the passage from one language to another, it is the determination of essence that is at stake. How could it be otherwise if, as Heidegger thinks, it is in *Sprache* that being happens? Yet the passage from one language to another is also often marked by loss, by a loss of origin, as in the move from Greek to Latin. The Latin translations of Greek terms are the first step along the path of *Entfremdung*, the alienation of the originary essence (*ursprüngliche Wesen*) of Greek philosophy. See *Introduction to Metaphysics*, 15ff; 19. On the function of Greece—and *a contrario* of Rome—in the constitution of German identity, see the work of Philippe Lacoue-Labarthe on Heidegger and German Romanticism, in particular *L'imitation des moderns, Typographies II* (Paris: Galilée, 1986), trans. as *Typography*, edited by Christopher Fynsk (Stanford: Stanford University Press, 2000) and *La Fiction du politique. Heidegger, l'art et la politique* (Paris: Bourgois, 1987), trans. Chris Turner as *Heidegger Art and Politics* (Oxford: Blackwell, 1992).

17. "Sending" 120–1; 116. Emphasis added.

18. On the difference between Heidegger's notion of epochality and Husserl's notion of transcendental historicity, and so on the difference between *crisis* and *destiny*, see Ch. 2.2, below.

19. In any case, no place for ethics in the sense of a specific discipline that appears at a particular moment in the history of metaphysics and that rests on categories themselves in need of questioning. See "Letter on Humanism" translated by Frank A. Capuzzi with J. Glenn Gray in *Basic Writings* (New York: Harper and Row, 1977), 193–242. For it is far from clear that ethics in a broader sense, as arche-ethics (a term borrowed from Lacoue-Labarthe) has nothing to do with historicality.

20. "World Picture" 88–89; 131.

21. See "Sending" 123; 120.

22. See the lecture courses published as *Nietzsche*, in particular §§5–9.

23. See "Sending" 124–125; 120–121.

24. See *Identity and Difference* 43ff.

25. "It would not be a question simply of subjecting so-called philosophical language to ordinary law and making it answer before this last contextual court of appeal, but of asking whether, in the very interior of what offers itself as the philosophical or merely theoretical usage of the word representation, the unity of some semantic center, which would give order to a whole multiplicity of modifications and derivations, is to be presumed. Is not this eminently philosophical presumption precisely of a presentative type, in the central sense claimed for the term, in that a single self-same presence delegates itself in it, send [*envoie*], assembles, and finally recognizes? This interpretation of representation would presuppose a representational pre-interpretation of representation, it would still be a representation of representation. Is not this presumption (unifying, bringing together, derivationist) at work in Heidegger all the way up to his strongest and most necessary displacements? Do we not find an indication of this in the fact that the epoch of representation or *Vorstellung*, or more generally *Gestell*, appears there as an epoch in the destiny or the *Geschick* of being?" ("Sending" 134; 129–130).

26. "Sending" 135; 131.

27. See Ch. 2.3, below.

28. On the determination of *logos* as gathering (*Versammlung*), see Heidegger's reading of Heraclitus' fragment 50, "Logos" (*Vorträge und Aufsätze*, 199–21), trans. David Farrell Krell and Frank A. Capuzzi in *Early Greek Thinking* (New York: Harper and Row, 1975), 59–78. For Derrida, it is precisely this determination of *logos* as gathering, more than the centrality of *logos* itself, that constitutes logocentrism. "And whether it is a matter of *Versammlung* or of *Sein*, this always passes through the logos and concenters itself around logos. At bottom logocentrism is perhaps not so much the gesture that consists in placing the logos at the center as the interpretation of logos as *Versammlung*, that is, the gathering that precisely concenters what it configures" ("L'oreille de Heidegger. Philopolémologie (*Geschlecht IV*)" in *Politiques de l'amitié* [Paris: Galilée, 1994], 378; trans. John P. Leavy, Jr. as "Philopolemology: Heidegger's Ear" in *Reading Heidegger: Commemorations*, ed. John Sallis [Bloomington: Indiana University Press, 1993], 187).

29. "Sending" 136; 131.

30. See "*Hors livre*" ("Outwork"), in *Dissemination*, 9; 3ff.

31. "Sending" 136; 131.

32. See "Sending" 137; 132. Even if, in Heidegger's text, alongside the gesture of appealing from a stricter determination of presence to a less strict determination of presence, of going back from presence toward a more originary thought of being as presence (*Anwesenheit*), there is another gesture, which consists in questioning this originary determination itself, in thinking a *Wesen* that would not yet even be *Anwesen*. See "Ousia and grammè" (*Margins* 75; 65) and Ch. 2.2, below.

33. "In any case, we are fully aware that if there are marked periods, epochs, even turning points in the history of metaphysics, there is in reality—and for the reason, no doubt, that there is no history but that of the Same—only one *same* history (of metaphysics): this, the historial, presupposing the radical *heterogeneity* of Being within its *own* (un)veiling to be the Same (not the identical), is strictly *homogenous*." (Lacoue-Labarthe, *Typographies*, 179–180; 53). On the difference between the identical (*Gleiche*) and the self-same (*Selbst*), see *Identity and Difference* 45ff.

34. On the notion of *Geschichte* in *Being and Time*, see Ch. 2.2, below.

35. "Zeit und Sein" in *Zur Sache des Denkens* (Tübingen: Niemeyer, 1988), 8–9; trans. Joan Stambaugh as *On Time and Being* (New York: Harper Collins, 1977), 8.

36. "Being—a matter [*Sache*], presumably *the* matter of thinking . . . Time—a matter, presumably *the* matter of thinking . . . To reflect upon this situation is the task of thinking" (*Time and Being* 4; 4).

37. See *Time and Being* 6; 6–7.

38. See *Time and Being* 3–4; 3–4.

39. *Time and Being* 5; 4–5.

40. "*Answesen lassen heisst: Entbergen, ins Offene bringen. Im Entbergen spielt ein Geben, jenes nämlich, das im Answesen-lassen das Anwesen, d.h. Sein gibt*" (*Time and Being* 5; 5).

41. "*Das Geschichtliche der Geschichte des Seins bestimmt sich aus dem Geschick-haften eines Schickens, nicht aus einen unbestimmt gemeinten Geschehen*" (*Time and Being* 8–9; 8–9).

42. If either is possible, it should nonetheless be noted that if its translation by *envoi*, sending, maintains the possibility of divisibility, the same cannot be said for its translation by *destin*, destiny.

43. See *Time and Being* 9; 8.

44. See *Time and Being* 9; 9. If this notion of *epoch* refers to a sort of suspension it is clearly not that of the attitude or natural belief that Husserl will call by the same name.

45. The history of metaphysics, as history of being, is completely identified, according to Heidegger, with being itself: being is *nothing other* than the history of being. See *Nietzsche* I: 281ff.

46. And it is for this reason that if one can still, as I maintain, describe Heidegger's thinking as a phenomenology, it is a "phenomenology of the inapparent" (*Vier Seminare* [Frankfurt am Main: Vittorio Klostermann, 1954], 138). On the

link between Heidegger's thinking and a certain idea of phenomenology, if not the form that it takes in Husserl's work, see Jean-François Courtine, "La cause de la phénoménologie" in *Heidegger et la phénoménologie* (Paris: Vrin, 1990), 161ff.

47. See *Identity and Difference* 49ff.

48. See "Spéculer sur Freud" in *La carte postale. De Socrate à Freud et au-delà* (Paris: Flammarion, 1977), 277ff; trans. Alan Bass as "To Speculate—on 'Freud'" in *The Post Card* (Chicago: University of Chicago Press, 1987), 259ff.

49. This is not an isolated text in Derrida's output, moreover. The positions advanced in "Envois" are continuous with remarks in both earlier and later texts. I will make reference to these wherever necessary.

50. On the questionable opposition between serious and non-serious, see, for example, the remarks of *Dissemination* (72; 81) and *Limited Inc* (63ff). For an interpretation of Derrida that locates the originality of his work in the demand for a "creative" writing free from all argumentative constraint, an interpretation clearly opposed to the one that I want to put forward here, see Richard Rorty, *Contingency, Irony, Solidarity* (Cambridge: Cambridge University Press, 1989).

51. A thinking, moreover, that is not simply reducible to philosophy. Between thinking and philosophy there is a marked gap, which means both that a non-philosophical thinking is possible and that philosophy is not the only "thoughtful" path. Thinking, in other words, is not the exclusive domain of philosophy. See *Given Time* (45ff; 29ff), where this break is referred more to Kant's transcendental dialectic than to Heidegger's meditation on (the) thinking (of being).

52. See "Envois," in *The Post Card*, 106; 96.

53. Indeed, the German prefix *ge* has the value of gathering. Hence ge-shick would be a gathered destiny.

54. See "Envois" 72; 64.

55. See "White Mythology" (*Margins* 247ff; 207ff) and "Le retrait de la métaphore" in *Psyché* 63–93, translated by Frieda Gasdner, Biodun Iginla, Richard Madden, and William West as "The Retreat of Metaphor" in *Enclitic* 2: 2 (1978), 5–33.

56. "Envois" 72–3; 64–65.

57. See "Letter on Humanism" 189ff and "Building Dwelling Thinking" in *Basic Writings,* 319–340.

58. One could ask the same question of Gilles Deleuze's "Un précurseur méconnu de Heidegger, Alfred Jarray," *Critique et clinique* (Paris: Minuit, 1993), 115–25 [trans. Daniel W. Smith and Michael A. Greco as Essays Critical and Clinical (Minneapolis: University of Minnesota Press, 1977), 91–98], or even of Thomas Bernhard's *Alte Meister* (Frakfurt am Main: Suhrkamp, 1985), in which it is clear that parody is directed at something in thinking, something that is far from negligible.

59. "Envois" 73; 65.

60. With the difference that in the *Geschick* of being, there is precisely not the possibility of diversion, and that the forgetting in question is not the same.

61. "Envois" 73; 65.

62. [*Arriver* in French has the double value of "to arrive" and "to happen," an ambiguity that Derrida consistently exploits. Because of the emphasis in this argument on the post and on sending, it is most often translated simply as "arrive," but the double resonance should be kept in mind.—Trans.]

63. "Envois" 206–207; 192.

64. See "Envois" 73–74; 66.

65. Derrida himself recognizes that this is not the only possible interpretation of the unconscious. See "Freud and the Scene of Writing" in *Writing and Difference* 293–340; 196–231.

66. The divisibility of the letter, its absence from its proper place, is also what Derrida opposes to the transcendental topology that he sees in Lacan, for whom the *phallus*, like the letter that takes its place, would, by contrast, always remain in its place. See "Le facteur de la vérité" in *The Post Card* 469ff; 441ff.

67. "Envois" 133; 121. Although the word "tragic" does appear in these remarks, I nonetheless think that what is at stake here amounts to an essentially *non-tragic* thought, the tragic being indissociable from the idea of destiny and the idea of destiny being incompatible with the indivisibility of sending. The time in which a destiny unfolds, whether the destiny of a life or the destiny of a history, appears to me to be an essentially fictive one in which nothing happens since everything that does happen is only the unfolding of a scene already written elsewhere. As Denis Guénoun writes in "Qu'est-ce qu'une tragédie contemporaine?" in *Théâtre et démocratie* (March 1995), 18: "We are caught within a tragedy about whose structuring myth we know nothing. If we say that our existence is tragic, we presuppose that it indeed exists. We grant that something is completed in our lives that has its form or its necessity elsewhere. If our freedom is tragic, it is nothing other than the ineluctable completion of this necessity. Is this a good schema for thinking the world today?"

68. See *Shibboleth* 16; 6–7.

69. "Envois" 206; 191–2.

70. And a difference, too, as to language; but the two questions are indissociable. See Chs. 1.3 and 2.3.

71. See Ch. 2.2. below.

72. See Giani Vattimo, *Essere, storia e linguaggio in Heidegger* (Torino: Edizioni di Filosofia, 1963) and *Le avventure della differenza* (Milan: Garzanti, 1980; trans. Cyprian Blamires as *The Adventure of Difference* [Baltimore: Johns Hopkins UniversityPress, 1993].

73. See *Zollikon Seminars* 9.

74. The narrative of history, its story [*récit*], if you like, will always be secondary to what makes an event in and as history. Narrative, even as a work of language, will never constitute an epoch, will never have the dignity of the poetic *Dichten* or the philosophical word. Heidegger's contemptuous treatment of Thucydides in *Being and Time* would be emblematic in this regard (see *Being and Time* 39; 63). This passage has been commented on at length by Jacques Tamini-

aux, but from another point of view; for Taminiaux, it would be a question of Heidegger's disdain for the affairs of men, for the specifically *public* dimension of life; see *Arendt et Heidegger: La fille de Thrace et le penseur professionnel* (Paris: Payot, 1992), 65. According to Derrida, however, *story*, with its *narrative* and *dative* dimensions, is not simply external to the possibility of the event: "Let us note in passing: In every situation where the possibility of narration is the condition of the story, of history [*de l'histoire*], of the historical event, one ought to be able to say that the condition of knowing or the desire to know (*episteme, historia rerum gestarum, Historie*) gives rise to history itself (*res gestae, Geschehen, Geschichte*), which could complicate, if not contradict, many argumentations of the Hegelian or Heideggerian type that always seem to require the inverse order of things (no *Historie* without *Geschichte*), although it is true they do so only after having first integrated the possibility of narration or of the relation to knowing into that of the event" (*Given Time* 155–6; 122). The disavowal of the narrative dimension is not unrelated to a hidden teleology: "The *fourth thread*, finally, leads, through the thinking of *epochality*, in itself and in the way it is put to work, into what I shall call, a little provocatively, the hidden teleology or the narrative order" (*On Spirit* 29; 12). On the necessity of the narrative dimension in history, see also Jacques Rancière, *Les Noms de l'histoire: Essai de poétique de savoir* (Paris: Seuil, 1992). On the originary dependence of historical and philosophical questioning, see Massimo Cacciari, *Geo-filosofia dell'Europa* (Milan: Adelphi, 1994), 12ff.

75. "Sending" 141; 136. The refusal of beginning or origin does not equate to the refusal of genesis or becoming. On the difference between genesis and origin, see Ch. 2.2, below.

76. See "Envois" 74; 66 and "Sending" 142; 136.

77. See "Envois" 74; 66.

78. "La différance" ("Différance") in *Margins* 28; 26.

79. In the strictest sense, however, difference *means nothing*, if meaning [*vouloir-dire*] is understood from within the horizon of the intentionality of the subject (see "Différance" 15ff; 13ff).

80. Precisely what is at the centre of Derrida's objections to Foucault's *History of Madness*: "The attempt to write the history of the decision, division, difference runs the risk of construing the division as an event or a structure subsequent to the unity of an original presence, thereby confirming metaphysics in its fundamental operation" ("Cogito et histoire de la folie" ["Cogito and the History of Madness"] in *Writing and Difference* 65; 40).

81. "If the word 'history' did not in and of itself convey the motif of a final repression of difference, one could say that only differences can be "historical" from the outset and in each of their aspects" ("Différance" 13; 11).

82. "Différance" 13; 11.

83. See "Différance" 28; 26.

84. For a critique of deconstruction as a non- or anti-historical way of proceeding, see Michel Foucault, "My Body, This Paper, This Fire," *Oxford Literary Review* 4: 1 (1979), 5–28. For a consideration of some of the critiques of Derridean decon-

struction made on behalf of the historical dimension and of Marxism, see Peter Zima, *La Déconstruction. Une Critique* (Paris: *puf*, 1994), 112ff. Even if such critiques rest on what is, to my mind, an equivocation, this equivocation is still rooted in a temptation to which even Derrida himself has on occasion submitted: the temptation of a somewhat risky *formalization* of the practice of deconstruction.

85. This is exactly what Derrida had pointed out with the problem of genesis in Husserl (see Ch. 1.1, above, and Conclusions, below).

86. *Time and Being* 9; 9.

87. And, by the same token, has no end. The deconstruction of the concept of history is precisely the deconstruction of *a certain* concept of history that destroys historicity. As Derrida writes: "Permit me to recall very briefly that a certain deconstructive procedure, at least one in which I thought I had to engage, consisted *from the outset* in putting into question the onto-theo- but also archeo-teleological concept of history—in Hegel, Marx or *even in the epochal thinking of Heidegger*. Not in order to oppose it with an end of history or an anhistoricity, but, on the contrary, in order to show that this onto-theo-archeo-telology locks up, neutralises and finally cancels historicity. It was then a matter of thinking another historicity—not a new history or still less a "*New Historicism*," but another opening of event-ness as historicity." (*Spectres de Marx* [Paris: Galilée, 1983], 125–126, translated by Peggy Kamuf as *Specters of Marx* [London: Routledge, 1996], 74–75). Emphasis added.

88. *Introduction to Metaphysics* 29; 39–41.

89. On this point, Heidegger is unfailingly constant. *Being and Time* (§6) and "Time and Being" (*Time and Being,* 97) might be taken as suitable points of reference here.

90. On the link between *Andenken* and *Vordenken*, see Marlène Zarader, *Heidegger et les paroles de l'origine* (Paris: Vrin, 1994), 27ff.

91. *Identity and Difference*, 34.

92. On the structure of Dasein's temporality (*Zeitlichkeit*) see Ch. 2.2., below.

93. On the impossibility of repeating a beginning (*Anfang*) that would not be a new beginning, see Françoise Dastur, "La fin de la philosophie et l'autre commencement de la pensée" in *Heidegger: Questions ouvertes, Cahiers du Collège International de Philosophie* (Paris: Osiris, 1988), 129ff.

94. On the paradoxical character of the imitation of the Greeks in Hölderlin and Heidegger, where it is a matter of imitating something that has never taken place, see Philippe Lacoue-Labarthe, *Typography*, 71ff; 236ff and 113ff.

95. *Being and Time* §6.

96. *Introduction to Metaphysics* 29–30; 41.

97. *Introduction to Metaphysics* 111; 154–5. It should be recalled that it is in saying (*Spruch*), in language, in *Sprache*, that the possibility of the inception (*Anfang*) and of origin, of essence (*Wesen*) and non-essence (*Umwesen*), comes to be played out. See "Hölderlins Hymnen "Germanien" und "Der Rhein" (Frankfurt am Main: Klostermann, 1980) §7, 59ff.

98. See *Being and Time* §1.

99. The dividing line is clear-cut, even if the movement of distanciation is

punctuated by stages. Plato represents the great end of a great beginning, and it is only with the Latin translations of Greek terms that the true *Bodenlosigkeit* of Western thought begins. See *Introduction to Metaphysics* 28; 37.

100. "Logos," 77–8. Emphasis added.

101. Paul Friedlander's claim that *aletheia* meant for the Greeks nothing more than *orthotes*, exactness of representation and precision of articulation, probably pressed Heidegger to modify his position. See Paul Friedländer, *Plato: An Introduction* (Princeton: Princeton University Press, 1985).

102. See "The End of Philosophy and the Task of Thinking" in *Basic Writings* 390ff. Heidegger abandons thus the thesis of a change in the essence of truth; see also "Platons Lehre von der Wahrheit" in *Wegmarken* (Frankfurt am Main: Klostermann, 1978), 203–238, trans. Thomas Sheehan as "Plato's Doctrine of Truth" in *Pathmarks*, ed. William McNeill (Cambridge: Cambridge University Press, 1998), 155–182.

103. Derrida himself has commented on what he calls the "supplement of originarity" in Heidegger's thought of epocality, especially in regards to Heidegger's reading of Trakl in *Unterwegs zur Spache*, see *De l'esprit* (Paris: Galilée, 1987), 131ff; trans. Geoffrey Bennington and Rechel Bowlby as *Of Spirit* (Chicago: University of Chicago Press, 1989), 83ff. The movement toward the more than early *Frühe* would be in fact a returning before the beginning itself. And for this reason what comes "later" would in fact be what comes before the "earliest." Derrida summarizes this complicated movement in the following way: "What is most matutinal in the *Frühe*, in its best promise, would in truth be of an *other* birth and an *other* essence, origin-heterogeneous [*hétérogène à l'origine*] to all the testaments, all the promises, all the events, all the laws and assignments which are our very memory. *Origin-heterogeneous*: this is to be understood at once, all at once, in three senses: (1) heterogeneous from the origin, originarily heterogeneous; (2) heterogeneous with respect to what is called the origin, other than the origin and irreducible to it; (3) heterogeneous *and* or *insofar as* at the origin, origin-heterogeneous because at the origin of the origin. "*Because*" and "*although*" *at the same time*, that's the logical form of the tension which makes all this thinking hum" (*Of Spirit* 177; 107). Although these remarks would appear to grant more to Heidegger than what I have granted him here, it does not seem to contradict what I have just said, especially if one remembers, as Derrida does, that this arche-origin is inseparable from the *originary essence of time*: only this originary essence of time would have been kept in the arche-origin. *Of Spirit* 143–144; 91–92.

104. If classical ontology is ultimately insufficient, it is precisely because it is unable to take account of the historical (*geschichtlich*) character of factical life, a character that Heidegger sees articulated in the Christian experience of faith as well as in Dilthey's philosophy of history; see Otto Pöggeler, *Der Denkweg Martin Heideggers* (Pfullingen: Neske, 1983), 25ff.

105. See *Being and Time* §9.

106. It is not without interest to note that the total absence of this genetic and

thus dynamic dimension in Heidegger's thought is the reason that lead Ludwig Binswanger never distanced himself from Husserl: "The result is that I can increasingly appreciate Heidegger's ontology in its purely philosophical signification, but that I always separate it from its "application" to science, in particular to psychiatric science. From this perspective, Husserl's doctrine of transcendental consciousness, rather than that of Heidegger's ontology, appeared to me always more in the foreground. . . . This point of view is maintained in the principal sections BI and BII of this work, which are in large part consecrated to the phenomenology of experience and, based on this, the experience of delirium" (*Délire* 9). Binswanger's affirmation becomes clear at the very beginning of section BI in question: "With the term of (phenomenological) *description*, I want to express that what concerns us here is no longer the "*model*" of delirious "*experience*," which is to be understood not phenomenologically but only in the manner of an analytic of Dasein, meaning that it is based on the Dasein-analytical hermeneutic of the *illness* of "delirium" and the realization of Dasein specific to the delirious *patient* (See *Schizophrenie*, 430–432); but what concerns us, rather, is the description of structures and phenomenological structural sequences in the *constitution* and *genesis* of delirious 'experience'" (ibid. 33; see Ch. 2.2, below).

107. On the question of Dasein and animality, see *Of Spirit* 27ff; 11ff, and "La main de Heidegger" in *Psyché* 427ff. See also Ch. 2.3, below.

108. Let me make clear that the concern of the following analyses is not a direct confrontation of the respective phenomenologies of Husserl and Heidegger but a consideration of the role that Husserl's phenomenology plays in Derrida's thinking in general, and in its relation to Heidegger in particular. On the vexed question—still far from being satisfactorily answered—of the relation between Husserl and Heidegger, there are numerous studies. Allow me just to refer to the following texts: Jean-François Courtine, *Heidegger et la phénoménologie* (Paris: Vrin, 1990); Gerard Granel, *Traditionis traditio* (Paris: Gallimard, 1972), 93–113; Jean-Luc Marion, *Réduction et donation: Recherches sur Husserl, Heidegger et la phénoménologie* (Paris: PUF, 1989); Pöggeler, *Der Denkweg Martin Heideggers*; and Jacques Taminiaux, *Lectures de l'ontologie fondamentale: Essais sur Heidegger* (Grenoble: Jérôme Millon, 1989).

CHAPTER 2.2

1. Although the second part of *Being and Time* never saw the light of day, one can nonetheless find in other texts by Heidegger the principle lines of a destruction of ontology centered on the question of time; see, in particular, *The Basic Problems of Phenomenology* and *Kant and the Problem of Metaphysics*. For a full list of Heidegger's works on this question, see Jean Greisch, *Ontologie et temporalité: Esquisse d'une interprétation intégrale de Sein und Zeit* (Paris: PUF, 1994), 101.

2. See Paul Ricoeur, *Time and Narrative* (Chicago: University of Chicago Press, 1987), III: 62.

3. Heidegger distinguishes a third, even more derivative sense: phenomenon in the sense of *Erscheinung*, appearance. With this third sense it is a matter of everything that comes under the order of the indicative, of the symptom, of a reality that does not manifest itself. Jacques Taminaux suggests that the Heideggerian description of *Erscheinung* is a terminological transposition of the Husserlian description of *Anzeichen*. The consequence of which is that if Husserl's phenomenology is from the outset supported by a distinction between the register of the intuitive and that of the symbolic, the same goes for phenomenology in Heidegger's sense of the term. The phenomenon as "what shows (or hides) itself from out of itself" is distinct from the level of mediacy and of the symbolic; see *La fille de Thrace et le penseur professionnel*, 80ff.

4. The structure of manifestation-concealment has to be understood in the sense that allows manifestation itself to be a mode of concealment. Being, phenomena in the its highest sense, never gives itself as pure manifestation but is, on the contrary, progressively more withdrawn (see Ch. 2.1, above). It is interesting to note that such a definition of phenomena is indebted not only to Heraclitus' "*physis* likes to hide itself" but also to the ecclesiastical tradition according to which the divine shows itself as what conceals itself. One finds the formula "it is in showing itself that it hides itself (*phainomenos kryptetai*)" in Denys, *Lettre 3* (PG, 3, 1069b) and then in Maxim the Confessor, *Ambigua* (PG, 91, 1048d-1094a) and in John Scot Erigena, *De divisione naturare*, III (PG, 122, 633c), cited in R. Brague, *Europe. La voie romaine* (Paris: Criterion, 1992), 144.

5. See *Being and Time* 35–6; 59–61.

6. In *Being and Time* Heidegger distinguishes *Zeitlichkeit* from *Temporalität*: the temporality of Dasein and the temporality of being itself. Reference will be made to the German wherever an ambiguity is possible. As to the term *Geschichte* and its derivatives, in *Being and Time* they concern Dasein alone and never being itself.

7. *Being and Time* 274–278, §45.

8. It is imperative that *Ganzsein* is not interpreted in terms of a simple totality. Dasein is not a whole of which one could distinguish parts; rather, it can be whole only in the sense that it always sustains a relation with its beginning and its end. On this, see Françoise Dastur, *La Mort: Essai sur la finitude* (Paris: Hatier, 1994), 60ff.

9. See F. Dastur, *Heidegger et la question du temps* 56ff and Paul Ricoeur, *Time and Narrative* III 119.

10. The "beyond" Heidegger is referring to is very probably Husserl. Such is, at least, the claim made by Heidegger in the last of the Marburg lecture courses, *Metaphysical Foundations of Logic*: "Concerning the problem of time (in Husserl) everything remains in principle much as it was" (GA 26: 263–4), cited in R. Bernet, *La vie du sujet*, 201.

11. See Paul Ricoeur, *Time and Narrative* III 63ff.

12. *Being and Time* §65.

13. [Future here renders the French *avenir* which, like the German *Zukunft*, could be literally translated as what is yet to come or coming toward.—Trans]

14. *Being and Time* 325; 373.

15. *Being and Time* 325–6; 372–4.

16. "Temporality as unity of future, past, and present does not carry Dasein away just at times and occasionally; instead, as temporality, it is the original outside itself, the ekstatikon. For this character of carrying-away we employ the expression the ecstatic character of time. . . . Original time is outside itself. . . . Within its own self, intrinsically, it is nothing but the outside-itself pure and simple" *Basic Problems of Phenomenology* (Bloomington: Indiana University Press, 1982). One should nonetheless note that the originary outside-itself of time is an *auto*-affection: the alteration or the alterity that lies at the heart of temporality does not come from another, but from Dasein's relation to itself; see Courtine, "La voix (étrangère) de l'ami" in *Heidegger et la phenomenologie* (Paris: Vrin, 1990), 343 n26. Derrida makes an analogous remark regarding spirit, something that is not without its link to time: "What is proper to spirit is this auto-affective spontaneity which has need of no exteriority to catch fire or set fire, *to pass ecstatically outside itself*" (*Of Spirit* 158; 98). Emphasis added.

17. *Being and Time* 329; 378.

18. *Being and Time* 326; 373. Heidegger's emphasis.

19. The belated appearance of birth in the analyses of *Being and Time* is due, according to Ricoeur, to the necessity of having first introduced the notion of original temporality, without which the ex-tension of Dasein would not be thinkable except as an interval between two inexistent extremes; see Ricoeur, *Time and Narrative* III: 89. It should nonetheless be pointed out that the privilege of the future and of anticipatory resoluteness hardly chimes with a thought of birth that is obliged to take account of a certain passivity scarcely reducible to simple *Geworfenheit*. For Heidegger, in fact, after the analyses of *Geworfenheit*, there remains little left to say about birth; it can be reduced to the bare fact that Dasein is *thrown*. See Ch. 2.3., below.

20. See *Being and Time* 374; 426–427.

21. *Being and Time* 380; 432.

22. *Being and Time* 380; 432.

23. *Being and Time* §74.

24. *Being and Time* 383–4; 435.

25. *Being and Time* 386; 437. Emphasis added.

26. This is the same logic that we saw to be operative when it was a matter of the repetition of the origin; see Ch. 2.1, above.

27. *Being and Time* 385–6; 437–438.

28. I will come back to this point, but it should be noted that if, in Husserl, finitude renders the reactivation of the past problematic if not downright impossible, for Heidegger it is *originary finitude* that allows for the "*reactivation*" of the past. The whole question is one of knowing in what sense the notion of originary

finitude needs to be read: can originary *finitude* contest the value of the origin or does this value make an origin of finitude itself? If finitude is the *impossibility of origin and end*, can it be thought as *originary*? (I owe this formulation to Francis Fischer, during an informal discussion, one of the many we continue to have. I do not know if he would want to lay claim to it, and I only mention it to thank him for everything he has given me to think about, through his friendship). Unless the very term "finitude," whether originary or not, is profoundly inadequate to what is trying to be thought here. See Ch. 2.3 below.

29. *Being and Time* 386; 438.

30. On the "existential solipsism" of Dasein, that being for which the alterity that affects its *Selbstbestimmung* is always that of being or of the nothing, but never that of the other, see Courtine, "La voix (étrangère) de l'ami. Appel et/ou dialogue" in *Heidegger et la phénoménologie*, 327–353. Clearly, Heidegger never speaks of Dasein in terms of solipsism; the term he uses is *Vereinzelung* (see *Being and Time* §40). Still, the exclusion of any sense of the other from the determination of the alterity that affects Dasein seems to me to justify Courtine's interpretation.

31. It is because being-in-the-world necessarily implies being-with that the becoming-historical (*Geschehen*) of Dasein is a *Mitgeschehen*, which is itself determined as destiny (*Geschick*). It is significant, moreover, that the horizon of *Mitgeschehen* is that of community (*Gemeinschaft*) as a people (*Volk*) (see *Being and Time* 384; 436). The difficulty that one encounters here is inseparable from the question of the relation of temporality (whether originary or not) to alterity. I address this in this chapter, but see also Greisch, *Ontologie et temporalité*, 399–402.

32. See *Specters of Marx* 125–6; 74–5.

33. Even in the theme of the *specter*, of that which returns in a form that can be thought as neither presence nor as absence.

34. Rudolphe Bernet, in "Origine du temps et temps originaire," confronts Heidegger and Husserl's respective positions as to the phenomenological origin of time from a point of view entirely different from my own. According to Bernet, the point of departure "in the origin," shared by both Husserl and Heidegger, leads both to distinguish different levels in the experience of time and to establish a link of foundation and derivation between these levels. The difference between their respective positions is played out in the determination of world-time (*Weltzeit*). If, for Husserl, this latter signifies the objective time of natural reality, for Heidegger it denotes the unity of the ekstatic horizons of temporality. Now, according to Bernet, it is through these different elaborations of the notion of world-time that Heidegger distances himself from Husserl's originary, subjective and constituting temporality. And this is because Heidegger links world-time to historicity. In *Being and Time* the relation of foundation between Dasein's ekstatic temporality and intratemporality is mediated by way of the analysis of *Geschichtlichkeit*, a mediation that is conspicuously lacking in Husserl. For Heidegger, world-time would announce thus a new thought of time and of being that would allow him to take leave of the question of the origin of time, of Dasein's

originary temporality and, finally, of the temporal foundation of the understanding of the meaning of being on the basis of Dasein.

35. *Grammatology* 69; 47. The reasons why Derrida will have abandoned the notion of genesis in favour of that of the trace seem to me obvious. First and foremost, the notion of the trace refers directly to the question of writing. Equally, the notion of genesis was, in the context of the 1960s, difficult to dissociate from that of *origin*. (And let me point out that, to the best of my knowledge, Derrida's last text that treats of the question of genesis dates from 1959, "'Genesis and Structure' and Phenomenology" in *Writing and Difference*, 154–168). Even though, in *The Problem of Genesis*, Derrida distinguishes (passive) genesis from origin, he could have maintained this reference to genesis only at the cost of an extraordinarily complicated work of reelaboration which, in the event, must have seemed to him to be pointless. It is important, I think, to recall here two letters from Louis Althusser, dating from 1966, two letters which ought, if it were possible, to be cited in their entirety. In these letters, Althusser develops a rigorous critique of the concept of genesis in relation to the possibility of a genesis of the *unconscious*: "Whoever says genesis is thus implementing, with necessary organic unity, the following concepts: the process of *engendering*, the *origin* of the process, the *end* or term of the process (phenomenon A), and the *identity* of the *subject* of the process of engendering (. . .) The continuity of the process of engendering and development founds the continuity of the process of knowledge: one can follow, in knowledge, *the very trace* of the process of genesis in reality and reproduce it in the form of a genesis within thought. To follow the very trace signifies something quite important: one can follow the trace only of an *individual* that possesses an identity, that is, an *identifiable* being that is always the same individual, that *always* possesses *the same identity through all its transformations* (. . .) That implication, which may appear to be excessive in my crude presentation of it, no doubt haunts, without its 'practitioners' realizing it, *every use* of the concept of genesis. One can express it still more compactly by saying that the structure of every genesis is necessarily teleological: if the end is already, in itself, in germ, virtually, etc., present from the beginning-origin, it is because every process is *governed by its end*, tends toward its end (. . .) It would be extremely interesting to see the source of the retrospective illusion that projects onto the *order* of the process of engendering in reality the very order of the process of knowledge (. . .) Through that *obligatory* confusion (the ideology of genesis doesn't leave us a choice: it *obliges* us to think every irruption *as a birth*) however, through that misconstruction, the concept of genesis does indeed *designate a reality* that can be thought only on the condition of rejecting the concepts of its miscognition. That reality is (. . .) the *irruption* of phenomenon A, which is radically new in relation to all that has preceded its own irruption. Whence the imperative of a *logic* different from that of a *genesis*, but precisely to *think* [*penser*] that reality and not to *dispense* [*dispenser*] with thinking that reality" (*Ecrits sur la psychanalyse. Freud et Lacan* [Paris: Stock-Imec, 1993], 84–89, trans. Jeffrey Mehlman in *Writings on Psychoanalysis* [New York: Columbia University

Press, 1996], 55–59. For the full text of the letters, see 57–110; 33–77). If the concept of genesis is thus unsalvagable, it nonetheless points to a reality that needs to be thought. Although there is no indication that Derrida could have known of these letters, which were not published until 1993, it seems to me that the demands that drove him to move from his work on genesis to his work on the trace are very close to those expressed here by Althusser. My thanks to Denis Guénoun for having drawn my attention to this text.

36. If the question of genesis is defined in *The Problem of Genesis* as a question "of the originary sense of temporality or of the originary temporality of sense" (*The Problem of Genesis* 160; 91), the question of writing is also indissociable from the question of temporality. What conception of temporality would allow us to think the experience of writing as *surviving*, in the very precise sense that Derrida gives to this term in *Parages* (Paris: Galilée, 1986), 119–218 and in *Given Time* (132; 101–2).

37. The calling into question of the origin is in fact the point of departure of the problematic of the trace and writing: "For the same reason there is nowhere to *begin* to trace the sheaf or the graphics of *différance*. For what is put into question is precisely the quest for a rightful beginning, an absolute point of departure, a principal responsibility. *The problematic of writing is opened by putting into question the value* of arkhè" "Différance" 6; 6. Emphasis added.

38. See *Speech* 75–6; 67–68.

39. *Grammatology* 97; 66.

40. *Grammatology* 97–8; 67. On the other hand, however, the Freudian concept of *Nachträglichkeit*, of belatedness, points toward the idea of an experience that, in its very "present," would be determined by a past that is radically anterior to it since it has never been lived as experience [*vécu*] in the form of the present. As, too, does Lévinas' work on the trace. See "Freud and the Scene of Writing" and Lévinas' "La trace de l'autre" and "Enigme et phénomène" in *En découvrant l'existence avec Husserl et Heidegger* 186–202 and 203–216, trans. Richard A. Cohen, Michael B. Smith and Michael A. Smith as *Discovering Existence with Husserl* (Evanston: Northwestern University Press, 1998).

41. *Grammatology* 97; 66. It is around the question of the passivity of time that Derrida's work would need to be confronted, to my mind, with that of Lévinas. Any such confrontation would need to consider what unites them—principally a certain critique of phenomenology—as well as allowing for the fundamental differences that separate them. Here, let me merely draw attention to the contrast between Lévinas' referral of the passivity of time to sensibility as exposition and proximity (see *Otherwise than Being, or Beyond Essence* 33ff; 21ff), and Derrida's referral of it to the question of writing. Any such confrontation lying outside the scope of the present problematic, permit me to refer to my "Derrida et Lévinas: éthique, écriture, historicité," *Les Cahiers Philosophiques de Strasbourg*, v. 6 (1997), 257–278.

42. See "L'invention de l'autre" in *Psyché* 53ff.

43. See *Specters of Marx* 48ff; 22ff.

44. If the trace is indeed finite: it should be remembered, however, that *infinite différance* is *finite* (see *Speech* 114; 102).

45. See *Grammatology* 97; 66.

46. See *Specters of Marx* 52; 25.

47. If one cannot entirely separate the categories of the originary and the derivative from those of the authentic and the inauthentic, and if finitude, as Heidegger will continually point out, is originary, it is thus also "authentic," that is, a little too "proper" and a little too "pure" for a thought of contamination like that of Derrida's. See Ch. 2.3, below.

48. It seems to me that the question of the hero and of heroism in Heidegger—with all its political consequences—is directly tied to this conception of temporality: of the relation to the past, to resolution, to repetition, etc. Without being able to develop it in this context, I would want nonetheless to point out that it is difficult to think a destiny without heroes (however negative or "everyday" these may be, as a large part of contemporary literature suggests). Destiny exists only for a hero ready to take it over, or to submit to it—but is there any real difference between the two? To my mind, such would be another reason for abandoning any—tragic—notion of destiny.

49. It is in the name of such a questioning that Derrida will recognize his debt to Heidegger: "I sometimes have the feeling that the Heideggerean problematic is the most "profound" and "powerful" defence of what I attempt to put into question under the rubric of the *thought of presence*" (*Pos* 75; 55). What I am trying to do here is, amongst other things, to account for these sorts of apparently contradictory declarations on Derrida's part.

50. See *Being and Time* §68.

51. *Being and Time* 326; 374.

52. As is well known, the theme of the proper in Heidegger is complicated by that of depropriation. It seems to me, however, that, despite the complication to which Heidegger will want to subject the logic of the proper, which is thus always a logic of the improper, this logic remains trapped within the horizon of a possible appropriation, however abysmal that may be.

53. Finitude is the impossibility of the origin, first in the obvious sense that Dasein is not at the origin of its being (see Dastur, *La Mort* 64). Which, moreover, might well lead one to think that the notion of originary finitude only accentuates the unsurpassable character of this non-being at the origin of oneself. Nonetheless, it seems to me that Heidegger's insistence on the originary is not reducible to this first sense, and that the origin—and the originary—retains all its connotations of an autonomous and absolute emergence, absolutely independent of everything to which it gives rise and that would have preceded it. In short, it seems to me to limit, if not contest, *the impossibility of the originary*. See Ch. 2.3, below.

54. See *Specters of Marx* 48ff; 22ff.

55. "Der Spruch des Anaximander" in *Holzwege* 352; translated as "The Anaximander Fragment" in *Early Greek Thinking* 43, cited in *Specters of Marx* 49 note 2; 23 note 19.

56. See *Specters of Marx*, and also "L'oreille de Heidegger. Philopolémologie (*Geschlecht IV*)" in *Politiques de l'amitié*, 374 ff trans. John P. Leavey, Jr. as "Philopolemologies: Heidegger's Ear" in John Sallis, ed., *Reading Heidegger: Commemorations* (Bloomington: Indiana University Press, 1993).

57. *Specters of Marx* 55; 27.

58. *Being and Time* §81.

59. See Dastur, *Heidegger et la question du temps* 93ff.

60. Cited in "Ousia and Grammè" in *Margins* 40; 36.

61. See *Physics* IV 217 b.

62. "Ousia and Grammè" 44; 40. So far as the privilege of the third person present indicative is concerned, Derrida is clearly referring to the considerations of "The Grammar of the Word 'Being'" made by Heidegger in the *Introduction to Metaphysics* (42ff; 54ff).

63. "Ousia and Grammè" 46; 42.

64. "Ousia and Grammè" 46; 42.

65. "Ousia and Grammè" 48; 43.

66. Hegel, *Encylopedia* §258, cited in "Ousia and Grammè" 48; 44.

67. "Time, like space, is a *pure form* of sense or of *intuition*, the nonsensuous sensuous" (*Encylopedia* §258, cited in "Ousia and Grammè" 49; 44).

68. See *Kant and the Problem of Metaphysics* §34.

69. *Encylopedia* §258, cited in "Ousia and Grammè" 49; 45.

70. See "Ousia and Grammè" 53; 47.

71. "In effect, *as Aristotle says*, it is because time does not belong to beings, is no more a part of them than it is a determination of them, and because time is not of (phenomenal or noumenal) being in general, that it must be made into a *pure* form of sensibility (the nonsensuous sensuous). This profound metaphysical fidelity *is organized and arranged* along with the break that recognizes time as the condition for the possibility of the appearance of beings in (finite) experience, *i.e. also along with that in Kant which will be repeated by Heidegger*" ("Ousia and Grammè" 54; 48).

72. *Physics* 219a; cited in "Ousia and Grammè" 54; 49.

73. "Ousia and Grammè" 56; 49. Emphasis added.

74. See "Ousia and Grammè" 57; 50.

75. This is deconstruction's celebrated theme that metaphysical thought is regulated by an oppositional structure. As such, it would be impossible to escape metaphysics by merely reversing the hierarchy of concepts (substituting for the privilege of presence that of absence, etc.). On the double strategy of deconstruction, see, amongst other texts, *Positions* (Paris: Minuit, 1972), 56; trans. Alan Bass as *Positions* (Chicago: University of Chicago Press, 1984), 41. It is not a matter of substituting one concept for another, everything depending on the *syntax* regulating the concepts. But if precisely what is in question is a syntax and not a concept, why would it be thus impossible to make the concept of time function otherwise, to inscribe it in another syntax? If it is as impossible to create "new

concepts" as it is to create a new language that would be "non-metaphysical" from the outset, it is perhaps not impossible to make concepts and languages function *otherwise*, without being caught between the alternative of silence and infinite precautions.

76. See "Letter on Humanism" 231.

77. See "Ousia and Grammè" 73–4; 63.

78. See *Being and Time* 436; 486, §82.

79. To say nothing of a certain theological connotation. See "Ousia and Grammç" 73ff; 65ff, and *On Spirit* 47ff; 26ff.

80. "Ousia and Grammè" 76; 65.

81. 50; cited in "Ousia and Grammè" 76; 66.

82. "Ousia and Grammè" 77; 66. What is in question in the production of the trace as its own effacement is the limit of the phenomenological (or perhaps simply philosophical) structure of the *as such*. And it is precisely here, moreover, that Derrida's thinking breaks with every possible project of phenomenology. See Ch. 2.3, below.

83. "Ousia and Grammè" 77; 66–7.

84. Or as "infinitely finite," see "Aporias. Mourir—aux 'limites de la vérité' in *Le passage des frontiers* 338, and as a book under the essay's title (Paris: Galilée, 1996), trans. Tom Dutoit as *Aporias* (Stanford University Press, 1993). See also Ch. 2.3, below.

85. If claiming the "inaugural ambiguity" of metaphysics is a useful strategy as regards a thought of the tradition as concealment, which necessarily implies a "lost" origin, it is not without its attendant dangers. The danger, principally, of turning any text whatsoever into an aporetic structure that one can always "deconstruct" according to the same method. See Conclusions, below.

86. It is only because philosophy has an essence that it can be gathered and arrive at its end: "The old meaning of the word 'end' means the same as 'place': "from one end to the other' (*von einem Ende zum anderen*) means: from one place to another. The end of philosophy is the place, that place in which the whole of philosophy's history is gathered into its most extreme possibility. End as completion means this gathering" ("The End of Philosophy and the Task of Thinking" in *Basic Writings* 375).

87. A forgetting that is not a *destiny* but a *crisis*. We have already seen that the two terms are not quite interchangeable.

88. On what makes ideality as an effect of iterability a logic of spectrality, see principally *Specters of Marx* (24 note 1 and 30ff; 178 note 3 and 9ff).

89. "Even if the future is its provenance, it must be, like any provenance, absolutely and irreversibly past. 'Experience' of the past as to come, the one and the other absolutely absolute, beyond all modification of any present whatever" (*Specters of Marx* 16; xix–xx).

90. On the connection between the anachrony of time and the relation to the other—and so to justice—see *Specters of Marx* (48ff; 22ff). As to the definition of

justice as a relation to the other, Derrida is evidently referring to Lévinas. See *To-tality and Infinity* 62; 89–90.

91. See *Of Spirit* 178ff; 109 and "Conversazione con Jacques Derrida" in *Ritorno da Mosca. Omaggio a J. Derrida* (Milan: Guerini, 1993), 190.

CHAPTER 2.3

1. Recall Heidegger's own definition: "*Zukunft meint hier . . . die Kunft, in der das Dasein in seinem eigensten Seinkönnen auf sich zukommt*" ["By the term 'futural' . . . we have in view the coming in which Dasein, in its ownmost potentiality-for-Being, comes toward itself"] (*Being and Time* 325; 373).

2. Whether as a matter of mourning in the strict sense of the term (whose psychoanalytic conceptuality Derrida tries to problematize) or as the more general matter of *survival* or *living on*, Derrida himself has made reference to the occurrence of this theme in his work (see *Specters of Marx* 24 note 2; 178 note 3).

3. "Furthermore, in each case Dasein is mine to be in one way or another. . . . And because Dasein is in each case essentially its own possibility, it *can*, in its very Being, 'choose' itself and win itself; it can also lose itself and never win itself; or only 'seem' to do so. But only in so far as it is essentially something which can be *authentic*—that is, something of its own—can it have lost itself and not yet won itself. As modes of Being, *authenticity* [*Eigentlichkeit*] and *inauthenticity* [*Uneigentlichkeit*] (these expressions have been chosen terminologically in a strict sense) are both grounded in the fact that any Dasein whatsoever is characterized by mineness" (*Being and Time* 42–43; 68).

4. See *Being and Time* 236; 279–280.

5. For an excellent commentary on §48, "What is Outstanding, End and Totality," see Françoise Dastur, *La Mort* 59ff.

6. See *Being and Time* 53; 79.

7. See *Being and Time* 238; 282.

8. "The greater the phenomenal appropriateness with which we take the no-longer-Dasein [*das Nichtmehrdasein*] of the deceased, the more plainly it is shown that in such Being-with the dead, the authentic Being-come-to-an-end [*Zuendegekommensein*] of the deceased is precisely the sort of thing which we do *not* experience. Death does indeed reveal itself as a loss [*Verlust*], but a loss such as is experienced by those who remain [*die Verbleibenden erfahren*]. In suffering this loss, however, we have no way of access to the loss-of-Being as such which the dying man 'suffers' [*Im Erleiden des Verlustes wird jedoch nicht der Seinsverlust als solcher zugänglich, den der Sterbende 'erleidet'*]. The dying [*sterben*] of Others is not something which we experience [*erfahren*] in a genuine sense; at most we are always just 'there alongside' [*Wir erfahren nicht im genuinen Sinn das Sterben des Anderen, sondern sind höchstens immer nur 'dabei'*]" (*Being and Time* 238–239; 282).

9. *Being and Time* 239; 283. In the phrase immediately preceding this one, Heidegger suggests that any "psychological" representation of the death of others,

even if such were to be possible, would have no real relevance here; psychology, and psychoanalysis even more, with all its work on the role of mourning in the formation of the *psychè*, has nothing to add to the existential analytic. The functioning of the *psychè* is of little interest to Heidegger, who considers it dependent on metaphysical and scientific concepts unable to match the questions posed by fundamental ontology. Nonetheless, I would want to suggest another reason for Heidegger's failure to take into account the body of work done on the functioning of the *psychè*: all such work implies the hypothesis, which is unimaginable for Heidegger, of a constitution and so of a becoming of psychism; by contrast, the existentials that constitute the opening of Dasein are immediately given conditions of possibility. Dasein does not *become*. See *Zollikon Seminar* 266ff.

10. *Being and Time* 240; 284.

11. *Being and Time* 263–4; 308.

12. It should be pointed out that the theme of *Vereinzelung* returns in §64, "Care and Selfhood," where we find the following: "Dasein *is authentically itself* in the primordial individualization of the reticent resoluteness which exacts anxiety of itself" (*Das Dasein* is eigentlich selbst *in der urspünglichen Vereinzelung der verschwiegenen, sich Angst zumutenden Entscholssenheit*). (*Being and Time* 322; 369). Without this originary isolation, selfhood would be impossible, therefore.

13. *Being and Time* 250; 294. Emphasis added.

14. Since the first appearance of *Being and Time*, more than one commentator has remarked, on the basis of very different perspectives, a certain insufficiency as regards Heidegger's analyses of being-with. For a brief but informative description, see the remarks of Jean Greisch, *Ontologie et temporalité* 168–72. Regarding our immediate concern here, Jean-Luc Nancy has sought to read this insufficient development of *mit-sein*, which Heidegger describes as an originary mode of Dasein, in terms of the absence from *Being and Time* of any consideration of mourning (see "Un sujet?" 104–5). This absence, moreover, might well be related to another missing analytic: that of love. I owe this suggestion to Jean-Philippe Schlick. For an analytic of love, one must of course consult the work of Ludwig Binswanger, *Grundformen und Erkenntnis menschlichen Daseins*; as I cannot address this here, allow me simply to refer to a fine overview of the question, Michèlle Gennart and Raphaël Célis, "Amour et souci: les deux formes fondamentales de la nostrité humaine dans l'analytique existentiale de Ludwig Binswanger" in Jean-François Courtine, ed., *Figures de la subjectivité* (Paris: CNRS, 1992), 71–89.

15. It would also be necessary to consider the link between the essential individuation that allows Dasein to attain its *Selbst* and the two forms of authentic *mit-sein* discussed in *Being and Time*: on the one hand, the reference of the other to its own care (namely to its solitary confrontation with death; see *Being and Time* §26, esp. 122; 158–159) and, on the other, the *mit-geschehen* of the *Volk* (§74). As if a "proper" *mit-sein*, (in Heidegger's sense, but also in the sense of any kind of sharing, since it is difficult to see sharing in the pure reference of the other to his solitary care) could only take the form of a community constituted by a people. To

my mind, this link stems from the character of originary temporalization devoid of all passivity, as we have already seen.

16. *"Dieses Seiende, das wir selbst je sind und das unter anderem sie Seinsmöglichkeit des Fragens hat, fassen wir terminologisch als Dasein"* (*Being and Time* 7; 27). See *Being and Time* §§4–6.

17. *Being and Time* 49–50; 75. True, Heidegger takes the precaution of suspending judgment on the positive work undertaken by these disciplines, but he does so only in order to stress once again that there can be no question of hypothetically deducing ontological grounds from already gathered empirical data, such grounds being always-already-there as regards empirical research. Ontology, in other words, has no need for the sciences.

18. Heidegger merely reinforces the hierarchical order between the positive sciences and ontology and, within ontology itself, between regional and general ontology. See *Being and Time* §4.

19. Marking the absolute limit between living beings and Dasein responds to Heidegger's exigence, doubtless justified, to distance himself from any biologism or vitalism. On this, at least, one might well credit him with an irrefutable degree of foresight (see *Nietzsche* II: 402 and 438ff—III: "The Will to Power as Knowledge"). Nonetheless, this distance as regards all biologism did not stop his well-known compromises with regard to National Socialism, compromises, moreover, that maintain a strange connection with the question of the animal (and with spirit) (see *Of Spirit* 75ff; 47ff). I will come back to this question of life in due course; so far as the question of politics is concerned, however, as important as it is, it is beyond the scope of this inquiry. On the political in Heidegger, see Lacoue-Labarthe, *Heidegger Art and Politics* and, with Jean-Luc Nancy, "The Nazi Myth," *Critical Inquiry* 16: 2 (1990).

20. See *Being and Time* §49.

21. *Being and Time* 247; 291.

22. *Being and Time* 247; 291.

23. The point is clearly not to reproach Heidegger for having wanted to free himself from all more or less biologizing evolutionism and from the teleology that this necessarily implies. As we shall see, the question of becoming, possibly that of *becoming Dasein*, is a rather different one.

24. It is Dasein's relation to being that makes existence its concern, and death is already inscribed in this relation to being, as Lévinas shows in a lucid and dense passage that is worthy of citation: "Heidegger is not interested in the signification of human existence for itself. The human emerges in his reflection only as the being that is in question in the epic of being. *Sein* is in question in man and man is necessary because being is in question (. . .). *Dasein* is the very fact that being is in question. Heidegger's manner of going toward death is wholly directed by ontological preoccupations. . . . From this point on, for Heidegger, one must be sure that the analysis of being-there, conducted as an analysis of the question in which being is in question, develops the *esse*—being in its proper sense—according to

its proper sense and not according to any derivative deformation whatsoever (proper, which is translated by 'authentic,' a word that conceals what is in proper: *eigentlich*). Where can the criteria of this originarity, this authenticity, be found, if not in the very appropriation of the question of being by the being-there? In the proper sense in the appropriation, in what Heidegger later calls *Ereignis*; there where the concern of being is imposed on being-there to the point that it makes it its own—to the point that someone says, in the first person, this concern is mine. (The *Ereignis* of *Zeit und Sein* is already in *Sein und Zeit*). Heidegger's later analysis will be that the assumption of the question of being entails its end, that death is thus the occurrence that is most properly mine. *Death is already announced in the emergence of the proper.*" Lévinas, *La mort et le temps* (Paris: L'Herne, Biblio-Essais, 1991), 37–38; trans. Bettina Bergo as *God, Death, and Time* (Stanford: Stanford University Press, 2000), 33–34. Translation modified, emphasis added.

25. Or, more accurately: Being-at-an-end, from an existential point of view, is a Being-toward-the-end. See *Being and Time* 305; 353.

26. On the attitude of the They as fleeing in the face of death, see *Being and Time* 254; 298. What interests me here is the question of the *certainty* of death. Heidegger opposes the *existential* certainty of death to its *epistemological* counterpart: everyday being-toward-death is protected through the *critical prudence* evidenced on the part of the They (such, at least, is the claim made by Heidegger): "So far as one knows, all men "die." Death is probably in the highest degree for every man, yet it is not "unconditionally" certain. Taken strictly, a certainty which is "only" *empirical* may be attributed to death. Such certainly necessarily falls short of the highest certainty, the apodictic, which we reach in certain domains of theoretical knowledge." (*Being and Time* 257; 301). The opposition of existential and theoretical certainty has to be read in terms of Heidegger's discussion of Descartes' *cogito* (see below). What I want to bring to light here is that this passage also confirms that *mit-sein*, however originary it may be, is not constitutive of the *eigentlich* relation to death. Dasein, in its being originarily doomed to death is *alone, alone* in the existential certainty of death.

27. Lévinas, too, brings out the indissociable character of *Ganzsein* and *Eigentlichkeit*: "If death completes Dasein, *Eigentlichkeit* and totality go together. By ridding ourselves of any thing-oriented notion, we see here the coincidence of the total and the proper. Death is a mode of being and it is on the basis of this mode of being that the not-yet arises." *La Mort et le temps* 46; 41. The not-yet is, clearly, the having-to-be of originary temporality, as Lévinas points out in the previous paragraph.

28. Descartes' *ego cogito, ego sum* is insufficient not only because of its failure to inquire as to the *sum* but also, and more fundamentally, because of the fact that the ontological kernel of the *sum*, and so of (temporal) being, has to be clarified in relation to originary mortality. The *sum* is always *sum moribundus*; the *ego* only reaches the level of subject insofar as it is mortal. The future is the going-to-die (*Sterbenwerden*). On this, see Courtine, *Heidegger et la phénoménologie* 307ff. Al-

though Courtine comments on the relation between Descartes and the Heidegger of *Being and Time*, the remarks of the Marburg lecture course of 1925 reveal an affinity between his reading and a passage from Lévinas in which, interestingly enough, it is not a matter of Heidegger's engagement with Descartes but, more simply, of originary temporality as such: "Having to be is having to die. Death is not something in time; rather, time is originarily *zu sein*, that is, *zu sterben*" (*La Mort et le temps* 46; 41).

29. *Being and Time* 262–3; 307. Heidegger's emphasis.

30. See *Being and Time* 263; 307–308.

31. See *Being and Time* 301–2; 348–350.

32. By means of the analysis of the call to conscience that cannot be summarized here, see *Being and Time* §§54–9.

33. See *Being and Time* 297; 343. See also §44, "Dasein, Disclosedness and Truth," in which Heidegger develops his thesis concerning Dasein as the originary phenomenon of truth. The resemblance between the German terms *Entschlossenheit* and *Erschlossenheit* marks still more the link between the authenticity of existence and its truth. Heidegger's confirmation of the co-originarity of truth and non-truth intersects—and accords perfectly—with the co-originary of the authentic and inauthentic modes of existence (see *Being and Time* §60, "The Existential Structure of the Authentic Potentiality-for-Being which is Attested in the Conscience").

34. See *Being and Time* 302; 349.

35. "*Temporality gets experienced* [wird erfahren] *in a phenomenally primordial way in Dasein's authentic Being-a-whole* [eigentlichen Ganzein]*, in the phenomenon of anticipatory resoluteness* [vorlaufenden Entschlossenheit]" (*Being and Time* 304; 351).

36. See Ch. 2.2, above.

37. In commenting on the *Rectoral Address*, Derrida remarks its continuity with the analyses of *Being and Time*, principally as regards the theme of *Entschlossenheit* as opening onto *Eigentlichkeit*: " . . . in essential and internal continuity with *Sein und Zeit*, there is *Entschlossenheit*: *resolution*, determination, the decision which gives its possibility of opening to *Eigentlichkeit*, the authentic property of Dasein." (*Of Spirit* 59; 35).

38. And it cannot be otherwise if death first opens the future, as is the case in Heidegger. But death is always inscribed in the past, in what one has been and is no longer, in all the others that have always inhabited us, in this *Vergänglichkeit*, this transience [*passagèreté*], that is, indeed, the experience of the *passage*—a passage in the sense of that which is irrevocably past, of that which has disappeared for ever, but also in the sense of a traversing, and thus of an experience in which something passes: from one place to another, from one time to another, from one to another. On passage as what passes from one to the other, see Denis Guénoun, *Hypothèses sur l'Europe* (Paris: Circée, 2000).

39. One can clearly argue that *Geworfenheit* is neither active nor passive; if Dasein is *geworfen* before any project on its part, to interpret this in terms of passiv-

ity might well be viewed as reintroducing categories that have far too much in common with a philosophy of subjectivity (see *Psyché* 409, "Difference sexuelle, difference ontologique"). Despite all these necessary precautions, however, it seems to me that if birth does indeed have so little place in *Being and Time*, it is precisely because it is so difficult to reappropriate, at least more so than death. Neither *mit-sein* nor passivity, in the sense that I am using the term, can be suspended in the act of birth.

40. If being is *nothing* outside its difference from beings, if being is not a "supreme being," if ontological difference excludes any substantialization of being, this does not preclude but rather produces the distinction between the ontological and ontic levels, as well as that between the existentiell and the existential.

41. *Of Spirit* 88–9 note 2; 120 note 3.

42. See Ch. 1.3, above, where we considered Derrida's remarks on the *Bedeutung* of the "I" in Husserl's pure logical grammar. This initial sketch by Derrida introduces a thread that will run the whole way through *Aporias*: that of the relation between language and death, for sure, but also that of the relation between language and phenomenology (Heideggerian this time).

43. See *Aporias* 317; 22. In "Donner la mort" (In *L'ethique du don. Jacques Derrida et la pensée du don*, ed. J.-M. Rabaté and M. Wetzel [Colloque de Royaumont, Dec. 1990: Métailié, 1992], 76ff; trans. David Wills as *The Gift of Death* [Chicago: University of Chicago Press, 1995]), Derrida gives a long explanation on this formula regarding the possibility of a distinction between ethics and religion in a debate around Patocka, Lévinas and Kierkegaard. Although I am obliged to leave this debate aside, I must still specify Derrida's interpretation of the formula "*tout autre est tout autre.*" It is also at the heart of his reading of Heidegger. "*Tout autre est tout autre*" may be a simple *tautology*, the simple reproduction of the subject in the attribute. But it may also express the most radical *heterology*: if the first "*tout*" is read as an indefinite pronominal adjective (any other whatsoever) and the second as an adverb of quality (radically and infinitely other), thus giving two different senses to the term "autre." The first becomes a noun, the second, probably, an adjective. The singularity of this formula and the displacement it undergoes according to the function one gives to the two words that compose it bears the weight of a radical distinction. "We would only play slight and bemused attention to this particular formula and to the form of this key if, in the discreet displacement that affects the functions of the two words there didn't appear, as if on the same musical scale, two alarmingly different themes [*partitions*, (musical) scores] that, through their disturbing likeness, emerge as incompatible. One of them keeps in reserve the possibility of reserving the quality of the wholly other, in other words, the *infinite other*, for God alone, or in any case for a single other. The other attributes to or recognizes in this infinite alterity of the wholly other, every other, in other words each, each one, for example each man and woman." *The Gift of Death* 80; 83.

44. For Lévinas, as is well known, the infinitely other as God refers to the infi-

nitely other as an other man. But what is more important for our discussion here is that the—ethical—questioning of self comes from the Other, the infinitely other (*Autrui*). The question thus comes from what is infinitely prior and exterior to the ego. Singularity, the unicity of the self, is constituted by the responsibility for the Other (*Autrui*), by the very fact of bearing the fault of another (see *Autrement qu'être ou au-delà de l'essence* [The Hague: M. Nijhoff, 1986], 143ff, trans. Alphonso Lingis as *Otherwise Than Being Or Beyond Essence* [The Hague: Martinus Nijhoff Publishers, 1981], 112ff). The subject is unique and irreplaceable only insofar as it is hostage: "Responsibility for another is not an accident that happens to a subject, but precedes essence in it, has not awaited freedom, in which a commitment to another would have been made. I have not done anything and I have always been under accusation—persecuted. It ipseity, in the passivity without archè characteristic of identity, is a hostage" (145; 114). Derrida distances himself from Heidegger but also from Lévinas because of what their two logics share: the rooting of responsibility, as an experience of singularity, in what he calls "an apprehensive approach of death." This is never far from another question, that of the possibility of sacrifice in its foundational value (see *The Gift of Death* 46ff; 42ff).

45. " . . . the entire project of the analysis of *Dasein*, in its essential conceptuality, would be, if not discredited, granted another status than the one generally attributed to it. I am thus increasingly inclined to read ultimately this great, inexhaustible book in the following way: as an event that, at least in the final analysis, would no longer simply stem from ontological necessity or demonstration. It would never submit to logic, phenomenology, or ontology, which it nonetheless invokes. Nor would it ever submit to a 'rigorous science,' (in the sense that Husserl intended it), nor even to thought (*Denken*) as that which parallels the path of the poem (*Dichten*), and, finally, not even to an incredible poem—which I would nevertheless be inclined to believe, without, however, stopping on this point for obvious reasons. The event of this interrupted book would be irreducible to these categories, indeed to the categories that Heidegger himself never stopped articulating. In order to welcome into thought and into history such a 'work,' the event has to be thought otherwise. *Being and Time* would belong neither to science, nor to philosophy, nor to poetics. Such is perhaps the case for every work worthy of its name" (*Aporias* 321; 31–2).

46. Heidegger comes back to the question of an ontology of life in the Freiburg lecture course of 1929–30, *The Fundamental Concepts of Metaphysics: World-Finitude-Solitude*, trans. William McNeill and Nicholas Walker (Bloomington: Indiana University Press, 2001), Part II, esp. §42ff. In this course, the question of an ontology of life is strictly tied to the question "What is the world?" In *Of Spirit*, Derrida comments at length on the three theses elaborated there by Heidegger. Here are the theses: 1. The stone is worldless (*weltlos*). 2. The animal is poor in world (*weltarm*). 3. Man is world-forming (*weltbildend*). Now, according to Derrida, if the question of the world is also the question of life, it is around pre-

cisely this latter that all the difficulties are going to be gathered. That the stone is worldless poses relatively few problems. The difficulty comes, however, in the determination of the animal's poverty (*Armut*) in world. It is because the animal is a *living being* that it cannot be said to be simply *worldless*. Now, Heidegger cannot think this relation of the animal to the world (and so to beings) in terms of a simple quantitative difference as regards Dasein's relation to the world. The poverty in question does not signal a difference of degree, an indigence, if you like, in contrast to the fecundity of Dasein's access to the world. Rather, it is a matter of a *qualitative* and *structural* difference, of *another* and not simply less developed relation to the world. Of another sort of relation that has its motive in the fact that the animal does indeed grasp beings, but not beings as beings, not *beings as such*. The chasm that separates the *living animal* (which can have a world because it attains being, even if it is deprived of a world because it does not attain being as such in its being) from *speaking man* is far wider than that the one that separates the animal from the lifeless stone. So far as Derrida is concerned, what is decisive here is that the animal's inability to name is, for Heidegger, not a *linguistic* inability, but stems from the *properly phenomenological* impossibility of its grasping phenomena as such; what the animal lacks is phenomenality as such, which means that it can never unveil the being of beings. The difficulty of this determination of "poorness in world" will disappear with the *Introduction to Metaphysics*, in which Heidegger declares, quite simply, that the animal has no world: at least the formal difficulty, since the basic problem remains unchanged (see *Introduction to Metaphysics* 34; 45). Although Derrida comments at some length on this shift, the problematic lies outside our present context. See *Of Spirit* 75–90; 47–57.

47. *Aporias* 318; 23.

48. The rapid allusion to *sexual* boundaries is in fact of great importance (see *The Gift of Death* 49; 45). Not only for the question of sexual difference of which I have no intention of speaking here (but allow me, nonetheless, to refer to my "Le Rêve et le danger" in *L'Éthique du don. Jacques Derrida et la pensée du don*, but also for the question of Dasein. If Dasein is *neutral* in its selfhood, neutral as regards any sense of "being-I" or "being-you" and, *a fortiori*, as regards sexuality, it is because the analytic of Dasein is situated on the level of ontology, on the level, then, of purely existential structures, before any ontic determination. All the same, however, it is far from clear that such a distinction can be sustained. Da-sein's *Geschlechtlosigkeit* is only one difficulty amongst others (see also *Psyché* 395ff).

49. See *Aporias* 319; 28.

50. *Aporias* 320; 29. Subordinated to the ontology of Dasein, the analytic of death is nonetheless a *founding moment*: as we have continually seen, the whole possibility of originary temporality is played out around it.

51. *Aporias* 320; 29–30.

52. Although I myself do not have much of a taste for etymologies and wordplay, and can therefore not follow Derrida very far in this regard, let me nonetheless point out—indeed, it seems to me necessary to do so—that Derrida under-

lines, and announces thus his problematic, that the Latin *finis* means, amongst
other things, *boundary* or *border* (*Aporias* 310ff; 3ff). And it should also be noted,
moreover, that Derrida prefers to translate *verenden* by *périr*, "perishing," and not
by any of the other alternatives, it is because this word still retains a trace of the
per, of the passage to the limit, of the journey marked in Latin by *pereo, perire*,
meaning "to leave," to disappear," "to pass-on the other side of life" (see *Aporias*
320; 31). Each time, what is at stake is a *passage*, in every possible sense of the term,
and so also in the sense of *experience*; see also Philippe Lacoue-Labarthe, *La poésie
comme experience*, 30–31, trans. Andrea Tarnowski as *Poetry as Experience* (Stanford:
Stanford University Press, 2000), 18–19.

53. See *Aporias* 321; 32.

54. Heidegger writes: "*Die Sterblichen sind jene, die den Tod als Tod erfahren
können. Das Tier vermag dies nicht. Das Tier kann aber auch nicht sprechen. Das We-
sensverhältnis zwischen Tod und Sprache blitzt auf, ist aber noch ungedacht*" ["Mortals are they who can experience death as death. Animals cannot do so. But animals cannot speak either. The essential relation between death and language
flashes up before us, but remains still unthought"] (*On the Way to Language*, trans.
Peter Hertz [New York: Harper Collins, 1979] 107). For a commentary on this passage from an altogether different point of view, see Giorgio Agamben, *Language
and Death*, trans. Karen Pinkus and Michael Hardt (Minneapolis: Minnesota
University Press, 1994).

55. *Aporias* 322; 35. Translation slightly modified.

56. Commenting on a line from George's poem "Das Wort," "Kein ding sei
wo das wort gebricht," Heidegger adds: "thinking within the neighbourhood of
the poetic word, we may say, as a supposition: "An 'is' arises where the word breaks
up"" (*On the Way to Language* 108). Clearly I cannot hope to reconstitute here the
extremely intriguing context of this interpretation by Heidegger. On Heidegger's
relation to *Dichten*, see Philippe Lacoue-Labarthe, "Poetry's Courage" in *The Solid
Letter: Readings of Friedrich Hölderlin*, ed. Aris Fioretos (Stanford: Stanford University Press, 1999), 74–93.

57. See ibid., but there is another essential continuity, this time with *Being and
Time*; see *Being and Time* §34, "Being-There and Discourse," in which silence is
defined as a mode of language: "Keeping silent authentically is possible only in
genuine discoursing" (165; 208). See also §60 in which silence is the mode of the
articulation of discourse proper to Dasein's wanting-to-have-a-conscience (*Gewis-
sen-haben-wollen*) (*Being and Time* 296; 343).

58. What Derrida is aiming for is clearly not an unspeakable experience of
death, but a *phenomenological conception of language*. While this is clear in relation
to Husserl (see Ch. 1.3, above), it is perhaps not as evident in relation to Heidegger. For this reason I take the liberty of offering another citation: "As for the animal, it has access to entities, but, and this is what distinguishes it from man, it has
no access to entities *as such*. This privation (*Entbehrung*) is not that (*Privation*)
which Heidegger situates in *Sein und Zeit* (§32, 149) within the structure of the

'as,' of 'something as something' (*die Struktur des Etwas als Etwas*). This structure of the 'understanding of the world' (*Weltverstehen*) can or must give rise to an anti-predicative and preverbal clarification (*Auslegung*). It is not to be confused with the 'as' of the statement." *Of Spirit* 81; 51.

59. See *Aporias* 322–3; 37–8.

60. [Macquarrie and Robinson's choice of "demise" is, as they note, "an arbitrary one." "Decease," which comes from *decedere*, to depart or to leave, and which, as the *OED* notes, is "the common term where the mere legal or civil incidence of death is in question," seems to me preferable in this instance.—Trans.]

61. *Being and Time* 247; 291. Cited in *Aporias* 323; 38. Translation slightly modified.

62. See *Aporias* 323; 39. But, adds Derrida, there is a further possibility, one that, moreover, orients his own work: "One can also . . . take into account a sort of originary mourning, something that, it seems to me, neither Heidegger nor Freud nor Lévinas were able to do" (323; 339.). Although I have chosen to follow Derrida in his elaboration of what he is here calling *originary mourning*, I would note two reservations on this point: one concerns his interpretation of the relations between *Mitsein, Sein-zum-Tode* and *Jemeinigkeit* (see above), the other his remarks here on Freud, which strike me as being overly hasty.

63. *Aporias* 324; 39–40. Translation slightly modified.

64. In the course of his text, Derrida comments on three such accounts: *Essais sur l'histoire de la mort en Occident du Moyen Age à nos jours* and *L'Homme devant la mort* by Philippe Ariès and Louis-Vincent Thomas's *Anthropologie de la mort*. See *Aporias* 318ff; 24ff.

65. See *Aporias* 324; 41.

66. An attestation, it should be remembered, that is *existentiell*; the *existential* analytic cannot avoid a certain contamination by the existentiell.

67. See *Aporias* 328; 53. See also "The Ends of Man" (*Margins* 147ff; 123ff). Derrida's evident unease as regards the theme of the proximity and necessity of beginning with the being we always *are*, in the face of a certain anthropologism and humanism, seems to become more clear—and more important, at least in our times—if one reads it in relation to the question of what Derrida calls *survival*. The concern is no longer only to distance French Existentialism, but to describe another relation to finitude.

68. *Being and Time* 248; 292, cited in *Aporias* 328–9; 53. Heidegger's emphasis.

69. [It should be noted that, in Martinau's French translation, followed here by both Derrida and Marrati, Heidegger's candid admission, "bleibe hier unentschieden," gains a decisive or imperative sense, "doit rester ici undécidé," wholly absent from the original but central to the arguments being made as regards his text.—Trans.]

70. What Derrida wants to call into question is not the necessity of a decision or a testimony that do not belong to the order of the theoretical, but *the phenomenological mode* of this testimony or this decision.

71. See *Aporias* 329; 54–5. See also—or at least, since the theme is a recurrent one—*Of Spirit* 176ff; 107ff and *The Gift of Death* 29; 23.

72. *Aporias* 329; 55.

73. *Aporias* 329; 55. Here, as elsewhere, Derrida points out that Heidegger is resolutely on the side of Kant, on the side of finitude, and not on the side of Hegel. For Derrida, as we have already underlined, the question of finitude is wholly inescapable, albeit problematic; the simple opposition between finite and infinite is ultimately unsatisfactory. And we should recall that this stance is one taken by Derrida from the very start; recall, once again, that in *Voice and Phenomena* infinite différance is *finite*.

74. [In the context of Heidegger's decision to begin from hither side of death, it should be borne in mind that whilst the French *décider de* translates as "to decide" or "to decide on," it also carries the literal sense of "to decide from."—Trans.]

75. *Aporias* 329–30; 56. The undecidable here is not the method of a non-method but that through which a decision can, eventually, be taken. See Conclusions, below.

76. *Aporias* 333; 61. This comes back to the fundamental theme of the relation between the constituted and the constitutive, empirical and transcendental, ontic and ontological, etc.

77. If narcissism exists, Derrida thinks that its structure is already so complex that the other, dead or living, is not reduced to the same. The other already marked the self of the relation to the self, the first arrival being that of the other. See *Mémoires pour Paul de Man* (Paris: Galilée, 1988), 43ff; translated by Cecile Lindsay as *Mémoires for Paul de Man* (New York: Columbia University Press, 1986), 21ff.

78. *Mémoires* 53; 33–4. In the passage immediately following this, Derrida adds that possible mourning is precisely impossible mourning. Upon the death of the other, there remains for us only the memory, and so the interiorization, since the other, who is outside of us, is no more. Yet it is precisely through the nothing of this irrevocable absence that the other appears as *other*, as other for us, and resists all interiorization. If, for Freud, the "successful" work of mourning consists in this gesture of interiorization, mourning, at least as Derrida wants to think it, takes on the form of an aporia: "the possible remains impossible. Where *success fails*. And where faithful interiorization bears the other and constitutes him or her in me (in us), at once living and dead. It makes the other a *part* of us, between us—and then the other no longer quite seems to be the other, because we grieve for him or her and bear him or her *in us*, like an unborn child, like a future. And inversely, *the failure succeeds*: the aborted interiorization is at the same time a respect for the other as other, a sort of tender rejection, a movement of renunciation which leaves the other alone, outside, over there, in his death, outside of us. Can we accept this schema? I do not think so, even though it is *in part* a hard and undeniable necessity, the very one that makes *true mourning* impossible." (*Mémoires* 54; 35). See also "Fors," preface to *Le Verbier de l'homme aux loups* (Paris: Aubier-Flammarion, 1975), by Nicholas Abraham and Maria Torok.

79. See *Mémoires* 49–50.

80. *Mémoires* 57; 39.

81. *Aporias* 331; 62. ["Impendence" here translates *imminence*, itself a translation—another translation, as Marrati shows—of *bevorstehen*. See *Being and Time* 250: "The end is impending for Dasein [*Das Ende steht dem Dasein bevor*]."—Trans.]

82. *Being and Time* 250; 294, cited in *Aporias* 332; 64. [In *Aporias*, whose subtitle—"Dying—Awaiting [*s'attendre*] at the 'limits of truth'—should be borne in mind here, Derrida translates as follows: "Avec la mort, le Dasein s'at-tend lui-même dans son pouvoir être *le plus propre.*" Maquarrie and Robinson's translation of *bevorstehen* as "to stand before itself" has thus been modified, following Dutoit's translation of *Aporias*. See also the previous Translator's note—Trans.]

83. On the question of possible/impossible translation and the effects of idiom, see, among many others, "Tours de Babel" (*Psyché* 203–235); English translation in *Difference in Translation*, ed. Joseph Graham (Ithaca: Cornell University Press, 1985), 165–207.

84. *Aporias* 333 (118); 65. The Greek word *ama* refers us back to "*Ousia* and *grammè*," as Derrida himself notes at the outset of *Aporias*: "The simple question from which I was trying to draw the consequences (and from which one may never finish drawing them) would be this: What if there was no other concept of time than the one Heidegger calls "vulgar"? What if, consequently, opposing another concept to this one were itself impracticable, nonviable, and impossible? What if it was the same for death, for a vulgar concept of death? What if the exoteric aporia therefore remained in a certain way irreducible, calling for an endurance, or shall we rather say an *experience* other than that consisting in opposing, from both sides of an indivisible line, an other concept, a nonvulgar concept, to the so-called vulgar concept?" (*Aporias* 314; 14). This seems to me to confirm our earlier interpretation of "*Ousia* and *grammè*" (see Ch. 2.2, above). And it seems to me also that it would be important here to stress what Derrida terms an experience *other* than what is usually thought under this name, rather than to stress the apparent formalism of a "logic" of deconstruction (or of metaphysics, which would amount to the same, given that the one rests on the other).

85. See *Aporias* 333; 67.

86. *Aporias* 333–4; 68, citing *Being and Time* 250; 294.

87. *Aporias* 334; 69, citing *Being and Time* 250; 294.

88. Derrida is obviously not Carnap, and scarcely reproaches Heidegger for not having held to the logical form of judgment. Derrida's own thought of the impossible, of the persistence of a contradiction or of an aporia, is not the same as Heidegger's, however, nor is his attitude as regards logic, technology and science. So far as Derrida is concerned, deconstruction has always maintained relations with a thinking of technology and of science (see *The Gift of Death* 35ff; 21ff and *Mémoires* 108ff; 106ff).

89. *Aporias* 334; 70, citing *Being and Time* 262.

90. See *Aporias* 335; 71.
91. See *Aporias* 335; 75.
92. *Aporias* 335; 76.
93. *Aporias* 335; 76.
94. *Aporias* 335; 76.

95. "These distinctions are threatened in their very principle, and, in truth, they remain impracticable as soon as one admits that an ultimate possibility is nothing other than the possibility of an impossibility and that the *Enteignis* always inhabited or, in truth in its untruth, haunted *Eigentlichkeit* even before being named there—indeed, this will happen later" (*Aporias* 337; 77, translation slightly modified).

96. If Heidegger attempts to elaborate an ontology of life without ever really managing to do so, it is for one extremely straightforward reason: what place is there for the animal within the categories of *Being and Time* once the animal is declared to be neither *vorhanden* nor *zuhanden* nor Dasein, once it can be thought in neither *existential* nor in *categorial* terms? See *On Spirit* 89; 57 and "Geschlect *II: Heidegger's Hand*" (429 note 1; trans. John P. Leavey, Jr., in *Deconstruction and Philosophy*, edited by John Sallis [Chicago: University of Chicago Press, 1987], 161–196, 174 note 20).

97. See *Aporias* 338; 79. Derrida points out that one could say the much same thing about Lévinas or Freud.

98. In *Of Grammatology*, raising the question of the relation of linguistics to Heidegger's ontology, Derrida writes: "Not only is its field no longer simply ontic, but the limits of ontology that correspond to it no longer have anything regional about them. And can what I say here of linguistics, or at least of a certain work that may be undertaken within it and thanks to it, not also be said of all research *in as much as and to the strict extent that* it would finally deconstitute the founding concept-words of ontology, of being in its privilege? Outside of linguistics, it is in psychoanalytic research that this breakthrough seems at present to have the greatest likelihood of being expanded. Within the strictly limited space of this breakthrough, these 'sciences' are no longer *dominated* by the questions of a transcendental phenomenology or a fundamental ontology" (35; 21). See also "Tympan" (*Margins* xiiiff; xff.).

99. See *Aporias* 338; 80.

CONCLUSIONS

1. The new, like the future, always relates to a passivity of time, how could it be understood. See *Specters of Marx* 111ff; 65ff.
2. *PGH* 14; xxvi.
3. See *PGH* 112; 56.
4. See *Speech* 93ff; 83ff.
5. Heidegger's interpretation of Kant is doubtless highly significant here: orig-

inary finitude is bound to temporality as pure self-affection. "The finitude of knowledge rests on the finitude of intuitions, that is, on taking-on-board [*Hinnehmen*]. Pure knowledge, that is, the knowing of objects in general [*Gegenstehendem überhaupt*], the pure concept, is grounded thereby in an intuition that takesthings-on-board. *Pure* taking-on-board, however, means: to be affected without experience, i.e., to be affected by oneself" (*Kant and the Problem of Metaphysics* 190. Emphasis added.).

6. *Grammatology* 69; 47.

7. From this point of view, the increasing number of declarations on Derrida's part denying deconstruction the status of method by bringing it under the sign of the impossible begin to sound a little like a form of denial. The denial in question, however, always assuming it is one, is a denial oriented toward the temptation, not always a happy one, to formalize the unformalizable. The temptation is even less felicitous because the thought of the undecidable and the impossible is placed under the sign of an ethical urgency that is ill suited to any formalism whatsoever.

8. Everything that Derrida has written against the possibility of a metalanguage, as well as his remarks on what always unites form and force, his critique of structuralism, should counsel against any metastructural interpretation of his thinking. See, for example, "Force and Signification" and "Structure, Sign and Play in the Discourse of the Human Sciences" in *Writing and Difference*.

9. This is one of the points on which Derrida is closest to Lévinas.

10. Would there be here a secret complicity between phenomenology and positivism? See Lévinas, "Enigme et phénomène" in *Discovering Existence with Husserl* 203–217.

11. See *Circumfession* 48ff; 48ff and Ch. 1.3, above.

12. Joyce, *Ulysses* 571. See also Ch. 1.3, above.

13. *Politics of Friendship* 35; 18. Translation slightly modified.

14. *Politics of Friendship* 35; 17.

15. This theme is still very much in evidence in Derrida's more recent works: "It takes time to reach a stability or a certainty which wrenches itself from time. It takes time to do without time"(*Politics of Friendship* 34; 17).

16. The thought of *Ereignis* would probably give rise to other questions. Such, at least, is what Derrida suggests in *Given Time*, where he refers to a second (unpublished) part of this essay that will deal with precisely such questions (*Given Time* 45; 20 note 10).

17. "Tympan" in *Margins* viii; xvi.

18. See "Tympan" xiii; xix.

19. See *Zollikon Seminars* 266.

20. "One of the reasons why I am keeping my distance from all these horizons, from the Kantian regulative idea or from the messianic advent, for example, or at least from their conventional interpretation, is that they are precisely *horizons*. An horizon, as its Greek name indicates, is both the opening and the limit that defines either an infinite progress or an awaiting. *But justice, however unpresentable it may*

be, does not wait. It is what must not be kept waiting" (*Force de loi* [Paris: Galilée, 1994] 57; trans. Mary Quaintance as "Force of Law" in *Deconstruction and the Possibility of Justice* [London: Routledge, 1992], 26). Emphasis added.

21. "A trace is a way of being excluded from the body, of leaving the body. The trace remains, although not permanently, but by separating itself from the body. It is part of the body, it is a body; it is part of the body, but the part that detaches itself from the body." *Moscou aller-retour* (La Tour d'Aigues: Editions de l'Aube, 1995), 148.

22. See *Shibboleth, passim.*

23. *Shibboleth* 65; 38. Emphasis added.

24. *Shibboleth* 66; 39.

25. *Shibboleth* 67; 39.

26. *Shibboleth* 30; 15.

27. *Shibboleth* 96; 58.

28. See *Given Time* 17ff; 7ff.

29. *Given Time* 25; 13.

30. *Given Time* 42; 27.

31. See *Given Time* 27; 14.

32. *Given Time* 42; 27.

33. *Politics of Friendship* 59; 38–39.

34. *Politics of Friendship* 46; 29.

35. *Given Time* 45; 29.

36. *Given Time* 130; 100.

37. *Given Time* 132; 102.

Works Cited

English translations immediately follow the reference to the original text. When abbreviated titles have been used in the notes, they are indicated in brackets following the reference.

WORKS BY DERRIDA

Apories. Paris: Galilée, 1996. Originally published as "Apories. Mourir—s'attendre aux 'limites de la vérité.'" In *Le passage des frontières. Autour du travail de Jacques Derrida*, Cérisy-la-salle, 1994 July 11–21, 1992.

Aporias. Translated by Thomas Dutoit. Stanford: Stanford University Press, 1993.

"Circonfession." In *Jacques Derrida*. By Jacques Derrida and Geoffrey Bennington. Paris: Seuil, 1991.

"Circumfession." In *Jacques Derrida*. By Jacques Derrida and Geoffrey Bennington. Translated by Geoffrey Bennington. Chicago: The University of Chicago Press, 1993.

"Conversazione con J. Derrida." In *Ritorno da Mosca. Omaggio a J. Derrida.* Milan: Guerini, 1993.

De l'esprit. Heidegger et la question. Paris: Galilée, 1987.

Of Spirit: Heidegger and the Question. Translated by Geoffrey Bennington and Rachael Bowlby. Chicago: The University of Chicago Press, 1989.

De la grammatologie. Paris: Minuit, 1967.

Of Grammatology. Translated by Gayatri Spivak. Baltimore: Johns Hopkins University Press, 1978.

"Donner La Mort." In *L'éthique du don. Jacques Derrida et la pensée du don.* Colloque de Royaumont: Métaillé, 1992.

The Gift of Death. Translated by David Wills. Chicago: The University of Chicago Press, 1995.

Donner le temps. I. La fausse monnaie. Paris: Galilée, 1991.

Given Time: 1. Counterfeit Money. Translated by Peggy Kamuf. Chicago: The University of Chicago Press, 1992.

D'un ton apocalyptique adopté naguère en philosophie. Paris: Galilée, 1983.

Éperons. Les styles de Nietzsche. Paris: Champs-Flammarion, 1978.

Spurs: Of Nietzsche's Styles. Translated by Barbara Harlow. Chicago: The University of Chicago Press, 1979.

Force de loi. Paris: Galilée, 1994.

"Force of Law: The 'Mystical Foundation of Authority.'" Translated by Mary Quaintance. *Deconstruction and the Possibility of Justice.* Edited by Drucilla Cornell, Michel Rosenfeld, and David Gray Carlson. New York and London: Routledge, 1992.

"Fors." Preface to *Le Verbier de l'homme aux loups.* Nicholas Abraham and Maria Torok. Paris: Aubier-Flammarion, 1976.

"Introduction" and translation of Edmund Husserl's *L'origine de la géometrie.* Paris: PUF, 1962.

Edmund Husserl's Origin of Geometry: An Introduction. Translated by Jr. John P. Leavey, Jr. Lincoln: University of Nebraska Press, 1989. [*IOG*]

L'écriture et la différence. Paris: Seuil, 1967.

Writing and Difference. Translated by Alan Bass. London: Routledge, 1978.

La carte postale. De Socrate à Freud et au-delà. Paris: Flammarion, 1980.

The Post Card: From Socrates to Freud and Beyond. Translated by Alan Bass. Chicago: The University of Chicago Press, 1987.

La dissémination. Paris: Seuil, 1972.

Dissemination. Translated by Barbara Johnson. Chicago: The University of Chicago Press, 1982.

La voix et le phénomène. Introduction au problème du signe dans la phénoménologie de Husserl. Paris: PUF, 1967.

Speech and Phenomena. Translated by David Allison. Evanston: Northwestern University Press, 1973. [*Speech*]

Le problème de la genèse dans la philosophie de Husserl. Paris: PUF, 1990.

The Problem of Genesis in Husserl's Philosophy. Translated by Marian Hobson. Chicago and London: The University of Chicago Press, 2003. [*PGH*]

Limited Inc. Paris: Galilée, 1990.

Limited Inc. Translated by Samuel Weber. Evanston: Northwestern University Press, 1988.

Marges de la philosophie. Paris: Minuit, 1972.

Margins of Philosophy. Translated by Alan Bass. Chicago: The University of Chicago Press, 1982.

Mémoires pour Paul de Man. Paris: Galilée, 1988.

Mémoires for Paul de Man. Translated by Jonathan Culler, Cecile Lindsay and Eduardo Cadaver. New York: Columbia University Press, 1986.

Moscou aller-retour. La tour d'Aigues: Editions de l'Aube, 1995.

Parages. Paris: Galilée, 1986.

"Living On: Borderlines." Translated by James Hulbert. In *Deconstruction and Criticism.* New York: Seabury, 1979. 75–175.

Politiques de l'amitié. Paris: Galilée, 1994.

Politics of Friendship. Translated by George Collins. London and New York: Verso, 1997.

"Philopolemologies: Heidegger's Ear." In *Reading Heidegger: Commemorations.* Edited by John Sallis. Bloomington: Indiana University Press, 1993.

"Geschlect *II: Heidegger's Hand"* Translated by John P. Leavey, Jr. In *Deconstruction and Philosophy.* Edited by John Sallis. Chicago: The University of Chicago Press, 1987. 161–196.

Positions. Paris: Minuit, 1972.

Positions. Translated by Alan Bass. Chicago: The University of Chicago Press, 1984.

Psyché. Inventions de l'autre. Paris: Galilée, 1987.

"Retreat of Metaphor." Translated by Frieda Gasdner, Biodun Ignlia, Richard Madden and William West. *Enclitic* 2, no. 2 (1978): 5–33.

"Sending: On Representation." In *Transforming the Hermeneutic Context: From Nietzsche to Nancy.* Edited by Gayle L. Ormiston and Alan D. Schrift. Albany: State University of New York Press, 1990. 107–137.

"Tours de Babel" In *Difference in Translation.* Edited by Joseph Graham. Ithaca: Cornell University Press, 1985. 165–207.

Schibboleth. Pour Paul Celan. Paris: Galilée, 1986.

"Shibboleth: For Paul Celan." In *Word Traces: Readings of Paul Celan,* edited by Aris Fioretos. Baltimore: The Johns Hopkins University Press, 1994.

Spectres de Marx. Paris: Galilée, 1993.

Specters of Marx. Translated by Peggy Kamuf. London: Routledge, 1996.

Ulysse grammophone. Deux Mots Pour Joyce. Paris: Galilée, 1987.

OTHER WORKS

Agamben, Giorgio. *The Idea of Prose.* Translated by Michael Sullivan and Sam Whitsitt. Albany: SUNY Press, 1995.

———. *Language and Death.* Translated by Karen Pinkus and Michael Hardt. Minneapolis: Minnesota University Press, 1994.

Althusser, Louis. *Écrits sur la psychanalyse. Freud et Lacan.* Paris: Stock-Imec, 1993.

———. *Writings on Psychoanalysis.* Translated by Jeffrey Mehlman. New York: Columbia University Press, 1996.

Badiou, Alain. *Ethics: An Essay on the Understanding of Evil.* Translated by Peter Hallward. New York and London: Verso, 2001.

———. *L'éthique. Essai sur la conscience du mal.* Paris: Hatier, 1993.

Bernet, Rudolf. "Einlutung" to Edmund Husserl's *Texte Zur Phänomenologie Des Inneren Zeitbewusstsein (1893–1917).* Hamburg: Felix Meiner, 1985.

————. *La vie du sujet. Recherches sur l'interpretation de Husserl dans la phénoménologie.* Paris: PUF, 1994.

Bernhard, Thomas. *Old Masters.* Translated by Ewald Osers. Chicago: The University of Chicago Press, 1992.

Binswanger, Ludwig. *Délire.* Translated by J.-M. Azorin and Y. Tatossian. Grenoble: Millon, 1993.

Brague, Rémi. *Europe, la Voie Romaine.* Paris: Critérion, 1992.

Brand, Gerd. *Welt, Ich, Zeit. Nach Unveröffentlichten Manuscripten Edmund Husserls.* The Hague: M. Nijhoff, 1955.

Brentano, Franz. *Grundzüge Der Aesthetik.* Bern: Francke, 1959.

————. *Philosophische Untersuchungen zu Raum, Zeit und Kontinuum.* Hamburg: Meiner, 1976.

Cacciari, Massimo. *Geofilosofia dell'europa.* Milan: Adelphi, 1994.

Celan, Paul. *Der Meridian und Andere Prosa.* Frankfurt am Main: Suhrkamp, 1983.

Courtine, Jean-François. *Heidegger et la phénoménologie.* Paris: Vrin, 1990.

Dastur, Françoise. *Heidegger et la question du temps.* Paris: PUF, 1990.

————. *La Mort. Essai sur la finitude.* Paris: Hatier, 1994.

Deleuze, Gilles. *Critique et clinique.* Paris: Minuit, 1993.

————. *Essays Critical and Clinical.* Translated by Daniel W. Smith and Michael A. Greco. Minneapolis: University of Minnesota Press, 1997.

Fink, Eugen. *De la Phénoménologie.* Paris: Minuit, 1974.

Foucault, Michel. *Dits et Ecrits.* Vol. III. Paris: Gallimard, 1994.

————. "My Body, This Paper, This Fire," *Oxford Literary Review* 4: 1 (1979), 5–28.

Franck, Didier. *Chair et corps. Sur la phenomenology de Husserl.* Paris: Minuit, 1974.

Frege, Gottlob. *The Frege Reader.* Edited by Michael Beaney. Oxford: Blackwell, 1997.

Freud, Sigmund. "On Transience." In *The Standard Edition of the Complete Psychological Works of Sigmund Freud.* London: Hogarth, 1953–74.

Gargani, Aldo G. *Il testo del tempo.* Bari: Laterza, 1992.

————. *Lo stupore e il caso.* Bari: Laterza, 1986.

Gasché, Rodolphe. *The Tain of the Mirror.* Cambridge: Harvard University Press, 1986.

Gennart, Michèlle and Raphaël Célis. "Amour et Souci: Les deux formes fondamentales de la nostrité humaine dans l'analytique existentiale de L. Binswanger." In *Figures de la subjectivité.* Edited by Jean-François Courtine. Paris: Editions du CNRS, 1992.

Granel, Gérard. *Le sens du temps et de la perception chez E. Husserl.* Paris: Gallimard, 1968.

————. *Traditionis Traditio.* Paris: Gallimard, 1972.

Greisch, Jean. *Ontologie et temporalité. Esquisse d'une interprétation intégrale de* Sein und Zeit. Paris: PUF, 1994.

Guénoun, Denis. "Qu'est-ce qu'une tragédie contemporaine?" *Théâtre et démocratie, Du théâtre* 3, no. March (1995).

————. *Transferts d'un corps enlevé. Hypothèses sur l'europe.* Paris: Circé, 2000.

Heidegger, Martin. *Basic Writings.* Edited by David Farrell Krell. New York: Harper and Row, 1977.

————. *Early Greek Thinking.* Translated by David Farrell Krell and Frank A. Capuzzi. New York: Harper and Row, 1975.

————. *Einführung in Die Metaphysik.* Frankfurt am Main: Klostermann, 1983.

————. *Introduction to Metaphysics.* Translated by Gegory Fried and Richard Polt. New Haven and London: Yale University Press, 2000.

————. *Die Grundbegriffe der Metaphysik. Welt-Endlichkeit-Einsamkeit.* Frankfurt am Main: Klostermann, 1992.

————. *The Fundamental Concepts of Metaphysics: World, Finitude, Solitude.* Translated by William McNeill and Nicholas Walker. Bloomington: Indiana University Press, 2001.

————. *Hölderlins Hymnen "Germanien" und "Der Rhein."* Frankfurt am Main: Klostermann, 1980.

————. *Holzwege.* Frankfurt am Main: Klostermann, 1980.

————. *Identity and Difference.* Translated by Joan Stambaugh. New York: Harper and Row, 1969.

————. *Kant und das Problem der Metaphysik.* Frankfurt am Main: Klostermann, 1965.

————. *Kant and the Problem of Metaphysics.* Translated by Richard Taft. Bloomington: Indiana University Press, 1994.

————. *Nietzsche* I and II. Pfullingen: Neske, 1961.

————. *Nietzsche* I and II. Translated by David Farrell Krell. San Francisco: Harper Collins, 1991.

————. *On the Way to Language.* Translated by Peter Hertz. New York: Harper Collins, 1979.

————. *On Time and Being.* Translated by Joan Stambaugh. New York: Harper Collins, 1977.

————. *Sein und Zeit.* Tübingen: Niemeyer, 1986.

————. *Being and Time.* Translated by John Macquarrie and Edward Robinson. New York: Harper Collins, 1962.

————. *Questions Ouvertes, Cahiers Du Collège International de Philosophie.* Paris: Osiris, 1988.

————. *Unterwegs zur Sprache.* Frankfurt am Main: Klostermann, 1985.

————. *Vorträge und Aufsätze.* Pfullingen: Neske, 1985.

————. *Was Heisst Denken?* 3rd ed. Tübingen: Niemeyer, 1971.

————. *What is Called Thinking?* Translated by J. Glenn Gray. New York: Harper and Row, 1968.

————. *Wegmarken.* 2nd ed. Frankfurt am Main: Klostermann, 1978.

————. *Pathmarks.* Translated by Thomas Sheehan. Edited by William McNeill. Cambridge: Cambridge University Press, 1998.

————. *Zollikoner Seminare.* Edited by Medard Boss. Frankfurt am Main: Klostermann, 1987.

————. *Zollikon Seminars.* Translated by Franz Mayr and Richard Askay. Edited by Medard Boss. Evanston: Northwestern University Press, 2001.

————. *Zur Sache Des Denkens.* 3rd ed. Tübingen: Niemeyer, 1988.

Husserl, Edmund. *Cartesian Meditations: An Introduction to Phenomenology.* Translated by Dorion Cairns. The Hague: Martinus Nijhoff, 1960.

————. *The Crisis of European Sciences and Transcendental Phenomenology.* Translated by David Carr. Evanston: Northwestern University Press, 1970. [*Crisis*]

————. *Experience and Judgment.* Translated by James Churchill and Karl Ameriks. Evanston: Northwestern University Press, 1973.

————. *Ideas: General Introduction to Pure Phenomenology.* Translated by W. R. Boyce Gibson. London: Collier Books, 1962. [*Ideas*]

————. *Logical Investigations.* Translated by J. N. Findlay. New York: Humanities Press, 1977. [*LI*]

————. "The Origin of Geometry." In *The Crisis of European Sciences and Transcendental Phenomenology,* 353–78. Evanston: Northwestern University Press, 1970.

————. *The Phenomenology of Internal Time-Consciousness.* Translated by James S. Churchill. Bloomington: Indiana University Press, 1964. [*Lectures*]

Joyce, James. *Ulysses.* Harmondsworth: Penguin, 1986.

Kojève, Alexandre. *Introduction à la lecture de Hegel.* Paris: Gallimard, 1947; Tel 1992.

Lacoue-Labarthe, Philippe. "Poetry's Courage" in *The Solid Letter: Readings of Friedrich Hölderlin.* Edited by Aris Fioretos. Stanford: Stanford University Press, 1999. 74–93.

————. "De l'éthique: à propos d'Antigone." In *Lacan avec les philosophes.* Paris: Albin Michel, 1991.

————. *La fiction du politique. Heidegger, l'art et la politique.* Paris: Bourgois, 1987.

————. *Heidegger Art and Politics.* Translated by Chris Turner. Oxford: Blackwell, 1992.

————. *L'imitation des modernes. Typographies II.* Paris: Galilée, 1986.

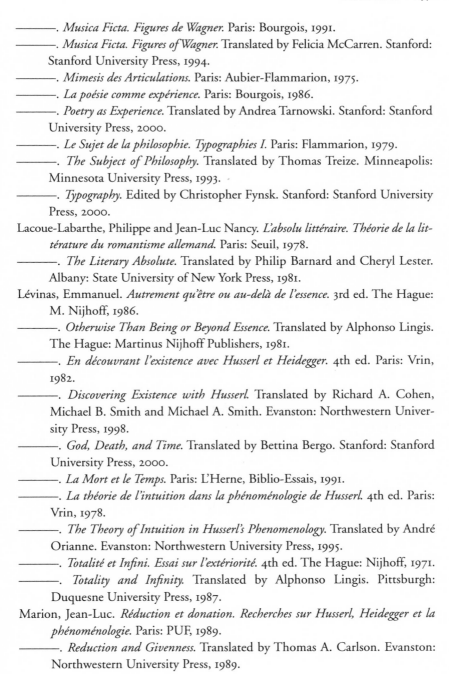

————. *Musica Ficta. Figures de Wagner*. Paris: Bourgois, 1991.

————. *Musica Ficta. Figures of Wagner*. Translated by Felicia McCarren. Stanford: Stanford University Press, 1994.

————. *Mimesis des Articulations*. Paris: Aubier-Flammarion, 1975.

————. *La poésie comme expérience*. Paris: Bourgois, 1986.

————. *Poetry as Experience*. Translated by Andrea Tarnowski. Stanford: Stanford University Press, 2000.

————. *Le Sujet de la philosophie. Typographies I*. Paris: Flammarion, 1979.

————. *The Subject of Philosophy*. Translated by Thomas Treize. Minneapolis: Minnesota University Press, 1993.

————. *Typography*. Edited by Christopher Fynsk. Stanford: Stanford University Press, 2000.

Lacoue-Labarthe, Philippe and Jean-Luc Nancy. *L'absolu littéraire. Théorie de la littérature du romantisme allemand*. Paris: Seuil, 1978.

————. *The Literary Absolute*. Translated by Philip Barnard and Cheryl Lester. Albany: State University of New York Press, 1981.

Lévinas, Emmanuel. *Autrement qu'être ou au-delà de l'essence*. 3rd ed. The Hague: M. Nijhoff, 1986.

————. *Otherwise Than Being or Beyond Essence*. Translated by Alphonso Lingis. The Hague: Martinus Nijhoff Publishers, 1981.

————. *En découvrant l'existence avec Husserl et Heidegger*. 4th ed. Paris: Vrin, 1982.

————. *Discovering Existence with Husserl*. Translated by Richard A. Cohen, Michael B. Smith and Michael A. Smith. Evanston: Northwestern University Press, 1998.

————. *God, Death, and Time*. Translated by Bettina Bergo. Stanford: Stanford University Press, 2000.

————. *La Mort et le Temps*. Paris: L'Herne, Biblio-Essais, 1991.

————. *La théorie de l'intuition dans la phénoménologie de Husserl*. 4th ed. Paris: Vrin, 1978.

————. *The Theory of Intuition in Husserl's Phenomenology*. Translated by André Orianne. Evanston: Northwestern University Press, 1995.

————. *Totalité et Infini. Essai sur l'extériorité*. 4th ed. The Hague: Nijhoff, 1971.

————. *Totality and Infinity*. Translated by Alphonso Lingis. Pittsburgh: Duquesne University Press, 1987.

Marion, Jean-Luc. *Réduction et donation. Recherches sur Husserl, Heidegger et la phénoménologie*. Paris: PUF, 1989.

————. *Reduction and Givenness*. Translated by Thomas A. Carlson. Evanston: Northwestern University Press, 1989.

Marrati, Paola. "Derrida et Lévinas: Ethique, écriture et historicité." In *Les Cahiers Philosophiques de Strasbourg*, 1997.

———. "Pensée de l'être et la maladie psychique: Les séminaires de Heidegger à Zollikon." In *Les Cahiers Philosophiques de Strasbourg*, 1996.

———. "Le Rêve et le danger." in *L'éthique du don. Jacques Derrida et la pensée du don*.

Nancy, Jean-Luc. *The Birth to Presence*. Translated by Brian Holmes. Stanford: Stanford University Press, 1993.

———. *Homme et sujet. La subjectivité en question dans les sciences*. Paris: L'Harmattan, 1992.

———. *Une Pensée Finie*. Paris: Galilée, 1990.

Petrosino, Silvano. *J. Derrida e la legge del possibile*. Naples: Guida, 1983.

Pöggeler, Otto. *La pensée de Heidegger*. Paris: Aubier-Montaigne, 1967.

Rancière, Jacques. *Les noms de l'histoire. Essai de poétique du savoir*. Paris: Seuil, 1992.

Ricoeur, Paul. *Temps et Récit III*. Paris: Seuil, 1985.

———. *Time and Narrative*. Translated by Katherine Blamey and David Pellauer. Chicago: The University of Chicago Press, 1987.

Rorty, Richard. *Contingency, Irony, and Solidarity*. Cambridge: Cambridge University Press, 1989.

Staten, Henry. *Wittgenstein and Derrida*. Oxford: Blackwell, 1985.

Taminiaux, Jacques. *La fille de Thrace e le penseur professionel*. Paris: Payot, 1992.

———. *Lectures de l'ontologie fondamentale*. Grenoble: Millon, 1989.

Vattimo, Gianni. *The Adventure of Difference*. Translated by Cyprian Blamires. Baltimore: Johns Hopkins University Press, 1993.

———. *Essere, storia et linguaggio in Heidegger*. Turin: Edizioni di Filosofia, 1963.

———. *Le avventure della differenza*. Milan: Garzanti, 1980.

Wittgenstein, Ludwig. *The Blue and Brown Books*. New York: Harper Collins, 1986.

———. *Philosophical Investigations*. Translated by G. E. M. Anscombe. Oxford: Blackwell, 1958.

Zarader, Marlène. *Heidegger et les paroles de l'origine*. Paris: Vrin, 1986.

Zima, Pierre V. *La déconstruction. Une critique*. Paris: PUF, 1994.

Cultural Memory | *in the Present*

Jean-Luc Nancy, *A Finite Thinking*, edited by Simon Sparks

Theodor W. Adorno, *Can One Live after Auschwitz? A Philosophical Reader*, edited by Rolf Tiedemann

Patricia Pisters, *The Matrix of Visual Culture: Working with Deleuze in Film Theory*

Andreas Huyssen, *Present Pasts: Urban Palimpsests and the Politics of Memory*

Talal Asad, *Formations of the Secular: Christianity, Islam, Modernity*

Dorothea von Mücke, *The Rise of the Fantastic Tale*

Marc Redfield, *The Politics of Aesthetics: Nationalism, Gender, Romanticism*

Emmanuel Levinas, *On Escape*

Dan Zahavi, *Husserl's Phenomenology*

Rodolphe Gasché, *The Idea of Form: Rethinking Kant's Aesthetics*

Michael Naas, *Taking on the Tradition: Jacques Derrida and the Legacies of Deconstruction*

Herlinde Pauer-Studer, ed., *Constructions of Practical Reason: Interviews on Moral and Political Philosophy*

Jean-Luc Marion, *Being Given: Toward a Phenomenology of Givenness*

Theodor W. Adorno and Max Horkheimer, *Dialectic of Enlightenment*

Ian Balfour, *The Rhetoric of Romantic Prophecy*

Martin Stokhof, *World and Life as One: Ethics and Ontology in Wittgenstein's Early Thought*

Gianni Vattimo, *Nietzsche: An Introduction*

Jacques Derrida, *Negotiations: Interventions and Interviews, 1971–1998*, ed. Elizabeth Rottenberg

Brett Levinson, *The Ends of Literature: Post-transition and Neoliberalism in the Wake of the "Boom"*

Timothy J. Reiss, *Against Autonomy: Global Dialectics of Cultural Exchange*

Hent de Vries and Samuel Weber, eds., *Religion and Media*

Niklas Luhmann, *Theories of Distinction: Redescribing the Descriptions of Modernity*, ed. and introd. William Rasch

Johannes Fabian, *Anthropology with an Attitude: Critical Essays*

Michel Henry, *I Am the Truth: Toward a Philosophy of Christianity*

Gil Anidjar, *"Our Place in Al-Andalus": Kabbalah, Philosophy, Literature in Arab-Jewish Letters*

Hélène Cixous and Jacques Derrida, *Veils*

F. R. Ankersmit, *Historical Representation*

F. R. Ankersmit, *Political Representation*

Elissa Marder, *Dead Time: Temporal Disorders in the Wake of Modernity (Baudelaire and Flaubert)*

Reinhart Koselleck, *The Practice of Conceptual History: Timing History, Spacing Concepts*

Niklas Luhmann, *The Reality of the Mass Media*

Hubert Damisch, *A Childhood Memory by Piero della Francesca*

Hubert Damisch, *A Theory of /Cloud/: Toward a History of Painting*

Jean-Luc Nancy, *The Speculative Remark (One of Hegel's Bons Mots)*

Jean-François Lyotard, *Soundproof Room: Malraux's Anti-Aesthetics*

Jan Patočka, *Plato and Europe*

Hubert Damisch, *Skyline: The Narcissistic City*

Isabel Hoving, *In Praise of New Travelers: Reading Caribbean Migrant Women Writers*

Richard Rand, ed., *Futures: Of Derrida*

William Rasch, *Niklas Luhmann's Modernity: The Paradox of System Differentiation*

Jacques Derrida and Anne Dufourmantelle, *Of Hospitality*

Jean-François Lyotard, *The Confession of Augustine*

Kaja Silverman, *World Spectators*

Samuel Weber, *Institution and Interpretation: Expanded Edition*

Jeffrey S. Librett, *The Rhetoric of Cultural Dialogue: Jews and Germans in the Epoch of Emancipation*

Ulrich Baer, *Remnants of Song: Trauma and the Experience of Modernity in Charles Baudelaire and Paul Celan*

Samuel C. Wheeler III, *Deconstruction as Analytic Philosophy*

David S. Ferris, *Silent Urns: Romanticism, Hellenism, Modernity*

Rodolphe Gasché, *Of Minimal Things: Studies on the Notion of Relation*

Sarah Winter, *Freud and the Institution of Psychoanalytic Knowledge*

Samuel Weber, *The Legend of Freud: Expanded Edition*

Aris Fioretos, ed., *The Solid Letter: Readings of Friedrich Hölderlin*

J. Hillis Miller / Manuel Asensi, *Black Holes / J. Hillis Miller; or, Boustrophedonic Reading*

Miryam Sas, *Fault Lines: Cultural Memory and Japanese Surrealism*

Peter Schwenger, *Fantasm and Fiction: On Textual Envisioning*

Didier Maleuvre, *Museum Memories: History, Technology, Art*

Jacques Derrida, *Monolingualism of the Other; or, The Prosthesis of Origin*

Andrew Baruch Wachtel, *Making a Nation, Breaking a Nation: Literature and Cultural Politics in Yugoslavia*

Niklas Luhmann, *Love as Passion: The Codification of Intimacy*

Mieke Bal, ed., *The Practice of Cultural Analysis: Exposing Interdisciplinary Interpretation*

Jacques Derrida and Gianni Vattimo, eds., *Religion*